soGreat aCause!

A SURPRISING NEW LOOK AT THE
LATTER DAY SAINTS

*Selected from Sacred Scriptures
including those of the Latter-day Saints*
by Kenneth D. Stephens

Copyright © 1973 Kenneth D. Stephens
All Rights Reserved

Paper Edition ISBN 0-87961-006-9
Cloth Edition ISBN 0-87961-007-7

Library of Congress Catalog Card Number: 72-13406
Naturegraph Publishers, Healdsburg, California 95448

Bob Rosenkranz

ACKNOWLEDGEMENTS

I wish to offer my grateful acknowledgement to each of the authors and publishers whose words are quoted in this book. A full listing of these sources is contained in the Bibliography. I acknowledge the great assistance of my son Dean Stephens, now pioneering in Porto Rico, in the West Indies, for reading earlier copies of the manuscript and in offering many helpful suggestions which have been incorporated in the present volume. I extend sincere thanks to my son, Ronald Stephens, of Reno, Nevada, for the Title Page design, the design of the section pages for Section I and II, and for the *"Tree of Life"* chart in chapter 22. To Dianne Carter of Salt Lake City, Utah, to Julie West of Winnemucca, Nevada, and to my daughter Judy Barnes of Sparks, Nevada, I wish to extend my appreciation for their long hours of painful reading of my handwritten manuscript, for their suggestions and transforming of much of this into legible typewritten copy for the publisher. To the latter I also offer sincere thanks for his patience with my many mistakes and the extra help of David Moore and David Duncan in final printing stages.

I am further indebted to many friends who read previous copies of earlier manuscripts, and whose suggestions and encouragement led to the writing of the present edition. I wish especially to mention Mrs. Lamira Day of Vernal, Utah. Finally, my thanks are due to numerous other friends in both the Utah and Reorganized Latter-day Saint churches, as well as those in the Bahá'í Faith, who have encouraged me to produce something which would be of use to the former in understanding their own scripture and in coming to realize that all of the prophecies contained therein have been or are now being fulfilled. The Lord has come! and His word is now rolling forth from Mount Carmel in the Holy Land, as a *"little stone"* which shall become a *"great mountain"* and fill the whole earth, or, as the prophet Daniel explains, this is the Kingdom of God which shall *"break in pieces and consume"* all other kingdoms and peoples! Certainly ours is a *"day of judgement"* but even more, the *"dawn of the New Day of God"*![1]

> *"How beautiful upon the mountains are the feet of those that bring glad tidings of good things, and that say unto Zion: Behold, thy God reigneth! As the dews of Carmel, so shall the knowledge of God descend upon them!"*[2]

1. See Daniel 2:27-45, 10:13-14, 12:1-4.
2. *D. & C.* 128:19b; *Reorganized D. & C.* 110:19b.

Dedicated to those sincere seekers after truth who follow the admonitions revealed through their beloved prophet—Joseph Smith—.

> "We believe all that God has revealed, all that He does now reveal, and we believe that He will yet reveal many great and important things pertaining to the Kingdom of God. . . . If there is anything virtuous,, lovely, or of good report or praiseworthy, we seek after these things."

> "Remember this, which I tell you before, that you may lay it to heart, and receive that which is to follow. Behold, verily I say unto you, for this cause have I sent you—that you might be obedient, and that your hearts might be prepared to bear testimony of the things which are to come."

> "Behold, thou wast sent forth, even as John, to prepare the way before me, and before Elijah which should come, and thou knewest it not."

> "And as all have not faith, seek ye diligently and teach one another words of wisdom; yea, seek ye out of the best books words of wisdom; seek learning even by study and also by faith. . . . Pray always, that ye may not faint until I come. Behold, and lo, I will come quickly, and receive you unto myself. Amen."

From the following Latter-day Saint Scriptures, in this order: Articles of Faith, numbers 9 and 13; *Doctrine and Covenants* (Utah Edition) 58:5-6; 35:4; 88:118, 126; (Reorganized Edition) 58:3a-b; 34:2b; 85:36a, 38c.

CONTENTS

Acknowledgements	3
Dedication	4
Illustrations listed	11
Foreword—"*The Challenge*"	12

SECTION I: "BEHOLD, THY GOD REIGNETH!"

Introduction to Section I

All Things Which are Good Cometh From God	20
The Oneness of God's Revelation	21
The Testimony of Two Nations to Come Together in One	24
The Origin and Dispersion of High Civilization in America	31
The Fulness of the Gospel to Go to the House of Israel	35
The Important Role of the Land of Persia	36
One Mighty and Strong	40
Seek Ye First the Kingdom of God, and His Righteousness	41

CHAPTER ONE

God's Revelation is Universal and Progressive

The Revelation of God is to All Mankind	42
God Reveals His Attributes and His Will for Each Age Through a Series of High Prophets	44
The Lesser Prophets or Forerunners of Each New Dispensation	46
What is Meant by the "Return" of a Previous Messenger of God?	46
The Two Great Prophets of the Day of God	48

CHAPTER TWO

The Purpose of the Restoration of the Gospel of Jesus Christ

Joseph Smith Came to Prepare the Way for These Two Prophets	53
To Make a Clear Distinction Between the Station of Joseph Smith and That of the Two Great Prophets to Come After Him	56

6 ... So Great A Cause

A "Choice Seer" to be Raised Up to the Gentiles	57
The Kingdom of God is at Hand	58
A Comparison Between the Missions of John the Baptist and of Joseph Smith	60

CHAPTER THREE
Why Do Ye Speak Unto Them in Parables?

By Their Fruits Ye Shall Know Them	63
An Explanation of the "Return" of Elijah and of Jesus Christ	64
Seek Ye Diligently	68
The Lord Will Be Called by a New Name	69

CHAPTER FOUR
The Expected Return of the Lord in 1844

"One Mighty and Strong" to Arise in the Year of Joseph Smith's Martyrdom, 1844	70
The Great Adventist Movement of 1843 to 1845	73
I Will Come on Thee as a Thief in the Night	76

CHAPTER FIVE
Signs of the Times

The Necessity of Earnest Search	81
Some True Signs to Look for to Discern the Second Coming	82
The Light of the Morning Cometh Out of the East	83
The Lord Sent a Word Unto Jacob and It Hath Lighted Upon Israel	85
The Children of Israel to Return to the Holy Land With Their Prophets	85
Elam and Assyria (Modern Persia) to First See the New Day of God.	86

CHAPTER SIX
The Gate to the Kingdom

I Will Set My Throne in Elam	89
One Mighty and Strong, Holding the Scepter of Power	90
Whose Mouth Shall Utter Words, Eternal Words; While His Bowels Shall Be a Fountain of Truth, to Set in Order the House of God	91
The Ministries of the Báb and of Joseph Smith Compared	94

CHAPTER SEVEN
The Glory of the Father

Thou Wast Sent Forth to Prepare the Way Before Me and Before Elijah	96
A Great Prince Among the Persians	100

He Will Come to Thee From Assyria	101
Imprisonment in Akka	105
Restrictions Relaxed	108

CHAPTER EIGHT
The Glories Which were to be Revealed

A Great and Marvelous Work	110
Thou Shalt See the Face of the Son of Man	113
World Unity the Goal	114
That Men Might be Made Partakers of the Glories Which Were to be Revealed	119

SECTION II: "SEEK YE DILIGENTLY OUT OF THE BEST BOOKS WORDS OF WISDOM"

Introduction to Section II

The Truth Shall be Distinguished From Error and the Wisdom of Every Command Shall be Tested	123
The Blind Men and the Elephant	124
Progressive Revelation Through a Series of Dispensations	126
The Great or Ancient Covenant of God	129
A Marvelous Work and a Wonder	132
Seek Learning Even by Study and Also by Faith	132

PART A
GOD HAS A PLAN

CHAPTER NINE
How Do We Know God and His Will?

A.	The Great Prophets and Messengers of God Each Revealed His Oneness	135
B.	The Meaning of the Word "Gods" and "Sons of God"	135
C.	Ways of Knowing God and His Will	136
D.	The Dispensations of Divine Truth	138

CHAPTER TEN
Progressive Revelation and the Independant Investigation of Truth

A.	The Eternal Creative Word of God	139
B.	Divine Revelation is Continuous and Progressive	139
C.	Man Possesses the Free Agency to Investigate Truth for Himself	140
D.	The Greatest Goals of Life	141

CHAPTER ELEVEN
The Creative Plan of God

A.	God's Promises to Mankind if They Obey Him	144

B. The Renewal of the Religion of God Through a Series of
     Great Prophets   145
  C. The Universality of God's Revelation   145

PART B
THE SPECIAL ROLES OF ISRAEL AND AMERICA

CHAPTER TWELVE
God's Plan Unfolds—The Special Mission of Joseph Smith
  A. A New Covenant Promised for the Age of Maturity   149
  B. Prepare Ye the Way of the Lord   149
  C. Joseph Smith Was a Forerunner to the Coming of the
     Two Great Prophets of the New Day of God, Similar to
     John the Baptist and Samuel the Lamanite in the Dispensation of Christ.   152

CHAPTER THIRTEEN
What Happened to Zionism and United Order
  A. Keys to the Kingdom   153
  B. God Said That the Saints Were Not Yet Ready to Receive
     the Kingdom   154
  C. The Ancient Priesthood Was Restored in Order to Prepare the Saints for the Administrative Order of the Lord
     of the Kingdom   156

CHAPTER FOURTEEN
The Fulness of the Gospel to go to the House of Israel
  A. Israel to Be Redeemed—The Glory of the Lord to Come
     to the Land of Jerusalem   157
  B. Judgements of the Lord Upon the Saints—The Fulness of
     the Gospel to Be Taken From Them and to Go to the
     Seed of Abraham   157
  C. The Work of God in Human History   159
  D. The Day of Judgement; to Be Followed by the Kingdom
     of God on Earth   162

CHAPTER FIFTEEN
The Destiny of America: Latter-day Saints and American Indians
  A. The Latter-day Saints to Be Redeemed if They Return
     Unto the Lord   163
  B. Indian Peoples of America Are Promised Great Blessings   163
  C. The Gentiles and Indians May Together Build a New
     Divine Civilization in America   164
  D. The Sacred Scriptures of the Church of Jesus Christ of
     Latter-day Saints Have Many Valuable Guidelines to Assist
     the Sincere Seeker After Truth   165

So Great A Cause ... 9

PART C
THE PROMISED DAY HAS COME

CHAPTER SIXTEEN
The Time of the Lord's Advent Foretold
- A. The "Lord" or "One Mighty and Strong" to Come in the Year 1844 — 167
- B. The Year 1844 Was Also Given in Both the Old and New Testaments as the Year of the Coming of the Lord and the Beginning of the New Age. — 168
- C. Rend the Veil of Unbelief — 170
- D. Two Messengers of God to Usher in the Kingdom — 171

CHAPTER SEVENTEEN
I am in your Midst and Ye Cannot See Me
- A. Why the Jews Failed to Recognize Christ — 172
- B. The Meaning of the "Return" of a Great Prophet (and of His Forerunner), Who Had Lived in a Previous Dispensation — 173
- C. Elijah and Jesus Will Not Return Again in a Literal Sense to Usher in the Kingdom — 174
- D. The "Return" of Michael or Adam — 175

CHAPTER EIGHTEEN
Study it out in your Mind—Seek and Ye Shall Find
- A. The Language of Prophecy — 177
- B. Veils of Darkness — 178
- C. The Lord Will Not Come With Visible Signs and Wonders — 179
- D. The True Signs of the Coming of the Son of Man — 179

CHAPTER NINETEEN
Persia and Babylon to see His Glory
- A. The Prophets Foretold That the Twin Manifestations of the New Day of God Would First Arise in the East — 181
- B. The First of the Two Holy Prophets Was to Come to Elam (now southern Persia) — 182
- C. A Chief Prince Among the Persians — 182
- D. Israel to Be Redeemed in Babylon (Modern Iraq) — 183
- E. The Significance of Elam, Assyria and Babylonia in the History of Israel — 184
- F. A Remnant of Israel and of Judah to Be Gathered From the Lands of Their Dispersion, to Be Reunited in the Land of Jerusalem in the Last Days, or at the End of the Age — 186

PART D
THE WORD OF THE LORD FROM JERUSALEM

CHAPTER TWENTY
Israel—A Light to The Nations
- A. Two Great Prophets to Be Raised Up to the Children of Israel in the Last Days 189
- B. Watch, That Ye May Be Ready 190
- C. The Land of Israel is to Be Established as a World Capital and as the Center of Worship for All Mankind 191
- D. The Valley of Sharon, the Fortified City of Akka, and Mount Carmel are All to Behold the Glory of God, the Great Prophet of the Millennial Dispensation 192

CHAPTER TWENTY-ONE
The Gate To The Kingdom and The Glory of God
- A. The Distinction Between the Lesser and the Great Prophets or Manifestations of God 194
- B. There Will Be Forerunners to the New Day of God Both In The East and In the West 195
- C. The New Messengers of God Will Be Called by New Names Indicative of Their Missions 196
- D. The Children of Light or Glory 197

CHAPTER TWENTY-TWO
By Their Fruits Ye Shall Know Them
- A. How Shall We Know the Two Prophets of the New Day of God 199
- B. The Fruits of the Tree of Life 202

CHAPTER TWENTY-THREE
Thy Kingdom Come, Thy Will Be Done On Earth
- A. He Will Guide You Unto All Truth...And Show You Things to Come 207
- B. The Books of God Are Opened 208
- C. Some Answered Questions 209
- D. Seek the Guidance of the Holy Spirit in Order to Find the Kingdom of God 210
- E. How Do We Test a Writing Which Claims to Be From God 211

Bibliography 212

ILLUSTRATIONS

Mount Carmel showing the Bahá'í Archives Building	18
Mount Carmel in 1900	19
Map I — Testimony of Two Nations: The Revelation of God in Former Dispensations through the Seed of Abraham	28,29
Metal Plates of Gold and Silver	30
Lehi Stone	34
Map II — The Dispersion of Israel and Judah about 722 and 600 B.C.	38
Salt Lake Temple	54
Wilmette Bahá'í Temple	55
Map III — Travels of Abraham, the Báb and Bahá'u'lláh	106,107
Map IV — The Return of a Remnant of Israel from Assyria and of Judah from all nations	112
The Twelve Principles	117
Out of the Best Books	122
Proofs of Prophethood	128
'Abdu'l-Baha — Center of the Covenant	130
The Perfect Mirror	137
Geneology of Abraham	143
Map V — Testimony of Two Nations: The Revelations of God In the Latter-days or in the Dispensation of the Fulness of Times	160,161
The Cheif with the Twelve Feathers	201
The Tree of Life	203

FOREWORD

"The Challenge"

"I am in your midst and ye cannot see me; but the day **soon** *cometh that ye shall see me, and know that I am; for the veil of darkness shall* **soon** *be rent, and he that is not purified shall not abide the day. Wherefore, gird up your loins and be prepared."*[1]

These words, were revealed through Joseph Smith, the Mormon prophet, at Fayette, New York, January 2, 1831, at a conference of the Church of Jesus Christ of Latter-day Saints. What can be their meaning? Notice the emphasis on the word **soon**, yet this warning was given over a hundred and forty years ago! Either Joseph Smith was mistaken in his prophecy or something happened that was unseen or unrecognized by most men. Remember, Jesus lived among the Jews for over thirty years before announcing that He was their Messiah, long-promised in the prophecies of the Old Testament, or Jewish Torah. Even then He was still not recognized and it took nearly 200 years before any large number of people believed in him.

Why is it so difficult for people to admit or understand that history could repeat itself, that, again, even as in the time of Jesus, men would be tested and found wanting because of their blindness? Recall also that the time of Joseph Smith was a time of religious ferment. All over America, in fact, all over the world, millions of people were looking for the *"return of Christ"*. Wolff in Asia, Edward Irving in England, Davis in South Carolina, William Miller in Pennsylvania, Leonard H. Keller in Germany, and many other religious leaders and scholars in each of the continents of the globe believed that this was the *"time of the end "*.

But what desolation is worse than to have watched for the coming of the Lord and then not to have perceived it? William Miller had set the date of His coming as March 21, 1844. When this date came and went with no visible sign of the coming of the Lord **"in the heavens, seated upon a cloud"** as they expected, his followers were grief stricken and many did commit suicide, just as were the Saints grief stricken and bewildered when their prophet was taken so suddenly in 1844, with no evidence that they could perceive that the Lord, for whom he had given his life, had come. Yet think carefully of the meaning of the words, set down by

---

1. *Doctrine and Covenants* 38:7-9; Reorganized *D. & C.* 38:2b.

Joseph Smith, "a light shall break forth among them who sit in darkness...but they receive it not".[2] Was this not exactly what happened in the days of Jesus? How few indeed recognized the Messiah in those days!

Is it possible, my brothers and sisters, that Christ "delayeth his coming until the end of the earth", or have we failed to perceive the "Light" which has already dawned in the East. Have the two Prophets whom Joseph Smith foretold as the "two witnesses" already come to Israel? Why not pay heed to Peter's warning in the New Testament which says: *"But the day of the Lord will come as a thief in the night; in the which the heavens shall pass away with a great noise, and the elements shall melt with fervent heat, the earth also and the works that are therein shall be burnt up"?*[3]

Are we like the Jews in the time of Jesus of Nazareth, "looking beyond the mark" to the literal fulfillment of every word of scripture, rather than perceiving the inner spiritual meaning thereof?[4] Have we overlooked altogether some of the prophecies concerning His coming, and of the "Elijah" or Forerunner who would prepare the way before Him? For instance in Jeremiah we are told that in the latter days the Lord would first set His throne in Elam.[5] Elam was an ancient kingdom occupying what is now southern Persia or Iran, around the city of Shiraz. Have we forgotten the prophecy in Micah which says that the Lord would come to Israel from Assyria, "and from the fortified cities, and from the fortress even to the river, and from sea to sea, and from mountain to mountain"?[6] The ancient land of Assyria is now also a part of Persia. In fact the capital city of all Persia, Teheran, is in that part of northern Iran which was anciently the kingdom of Assyria. Daniel had foretold that the Lord, or deliverer of Israel, would be a "Great Prince" among the Persians, and that His kingdom would be like a stone that "was cut out of the mountain without hands" to roll forth and gain momemtum until "it shall break in pieces and consume all these kingdoms, and it shall stand forever".[7]

What of Israel of which there is so much prophecy concerning the latter days, of Mount Carmel, of the prison city of Acca (anciently spelled Achor), and the Valley of Sharon, all of which were promised that

2. *D. & C.* 45:28-29; Reorganized *D. & C.* 45:4b-c.
3. II Peter 3:10.
4. Jacob 4:14; Reorganized Edition, Jacob 3:22-25; see also Jeremiah 5:20-31.
5. Jeremiah 49:38-39.
6. Micah 7:12-16; see also verse 7.
7. Daniel 2:44-45; 7:13-14, 27; 10:13-13; 12:1-4.

14 ... *So Great A Cause*

they would see the Lord, whose ministry would last as long as **"the days of thy coming out of the land of Egypt"**?[8] (This means 40 years; the same 40 years of the wandering of the Jews in the deserts of Sinai!)

Are we still looking for the literal return of Jesus Christ, and of Elijah to prepare the way before Him? Remember that when the Jews accused Jesus of being a false Messiah because Elijah had not yet come He replied that Elijah had come already, **"then the disciples understood that he spake unto them of John the Baptist."**[9] In his gospel Luke explains that John would go before the Christ **"in the spirit and power of Elias,** to turn the hearts of the fathers to the children, and the disobedient to the wisdom of the just; to make ready a people prepared for the Lord".**[10] So could it also be with the new Manifestation who would prepare the way before the Lord of the Kingdom, the Son of Man who would come in the full power and Glory of God.

I believe the same Spirit that was in Jesus Christ has returned. He appeared once in the first vision to Joseph Smith. He appeared a second time, to Joseph Smith and Oliver Cowdery, in the temple at Kirtland, Ohio, April 3, 1836, [11] just as He had promised He would.[12] However, this same Jesus told His Nephite and Lamanite followers on this continent that in the last days He would be raised up first to bring to the Gentiles the fulness of His Gospel, after which it would be carried by the Gentiles unto them. He then went on to say: *"Then will the Father gather them together again (i.e. the children of Israel), and give unto them Jerusalem for the land of their inheritance".*[13] To the Jews He had said:

"I have yet many things to say unto you, but ye cannot bear them now. Howbeit when He, the **Spirit of Truth,** *is come, He will guide you into all truth: for He shall not speak of Himself; but whatsoever He shall hear, that shall He speak: and He will show you things to come. He shall glorify Me: for He shall receive of Mine, and shall show it unto you. All things that the Father hath are mine: therefore said I, that He shall take of Mine, and shall shew it unto you."*[14]

8. See also Chapter 20, *"Israel—A Light to the Nations".*
9. Matthew 17:10-13; also Mark 9:11-13.
10. Luke 1:13-17.
11. *D. & C.* 110:1-10, Utah Edition.
12. John 16:22; Acts 1:9-11.
13. See 3 Nephi 20:26-35; 21:5-10; Reorganized Edition 9:64-71, 91-97.
14. John 16:12-15.

"For the Son of Man shall come in the glory of His Father with His angels; and He shall reward every man according to his works."[15]

These last two prophecies refer to the same Holy Messenger, a Great Prophet of God who will bear the same Spirit of Truth which Jesus bore. Nevertheless, He will glorify Christ because He will lead mankind into all truth. He is spoken of as the "**Glory of the Father**" or the "**Glory of God**" because He will come to the earth in an age when mankind is mature and can then bear the full glory of God's revelation. Jesus had said that He spoke unto His disciples in parables because they were not yet able to understand all of the things of God. However, when the Spirit of Truth returns, through a new Holy Tabernacle, He will no longer speak unto them in parables but will show them plainly of the Father.

My friends, this is that Day spoken of in all of the prophecies of the past as the dispensation of the fulness of times, the new heaven and the new earth, the new Jerusalem spoken of by John the Revelator, the kingdom of God on earth, and the millennial dispensation. According to the overwhelming record of prophecy the light of this New Day has already dawned in the East. It is now time that we search for this light until we find it, for Joseph Smith warned that many would fail to see it for failure to search.

This book is written not just to the Latter-day Saints, nor to the Seventh-day Adventists alone, but to all Christians, to the Jews, to the Moslems, to the American Indians, and to all people of all religions or no religion at all. This glorious Day was foretold not only by prophets but by poets, by philosophers, by great medicine men, and by learned scholars. In the pages that follow I explore these prophecies and promises in greater depth and detail. I pray that my search might help bring you glorious fruit. Let us now open our minds and hearts to the same Holy Spirit which inspired these noble men with thoughts such as these:

"*And the Lord shall be king over all the earth: in that day shall there be one Lord, and his name one.*"[16]

"*And when it is said to them, 'Believe in what God hath sent down,' they say, 'In that which hath been sent down to us we believe': but what hath since been sent down they disbelieve, although it be the truth and confirmatory of their scriptures. SAY: Why then have ye of old slain God's prophets, if ye are indeed believers?*"[17]

15. Matthew 16:27.
16. Zechariah 14:8-9.
17. *Koran* 2:86.

"*I look for the hour when that supreme Beauty which ravished the souls of those Eastern men, and chiefly those Hebrews, and through their lips spoke oracles to all time, shall speak in the West also. . . . I look for the new Teacher that shall follow so far those shining laws that he shall see them come full circle; shall see their rounding complete grace; shall see the world as the mirror of the soul; shall see the identity of the law of gravitation with purity of heart; and shall show that the Ought, that Duty, is one thing with Beauty, and with Joy.*" [18]

"*This year. . . . O glorious year! the trump of jubilee will be blown, the exiled children will return, the pilgrims reach their home, from earth and heaven the scattered remnants come and meet in middle air . . . fathers before the flood, Noah and his sons—Abraham and his, Jew and the Gentile,—This year! the long looked-for year of years! the best! it has come!*" [19]

"*The New Faith comes also to the Indians like the sun at dawn. As the sun rises it touches the peaks and buttes first with its light; then slowly moves down into the canyons. The light is at first visible only to a few who are awake, high up and watching. Some of the Navajo and other Indian peoples are like people down in a deep canyon. They are listening for the voice of the Great Creator, but they do not know where to look for it yet because the dark shadows blind them. But there are some Indians who are as if they are on the mountain tops and they begin very early to dance and sing with joy when they see the Glory coming.*" [20]

"*Brethren, shall we not go on in so great a cause? Go forward and not backward. Courage, brethren; and on, on to the victory!.. Behold, the great day of the Lord is at hand; and who can abide the day of his coming, and who can stand when he appeareth?*" [21]

---

18. *"Divinity School Address"* — Ralph Waldo Emerson.
19. William Miller, regarding the year 1844.
20. *"Four Remarkable Indian Prophecies"* — Annie Kahn.
21. *D. & C.* 128:22a; Reorganized *D. & C.* 110:22a, 24a.

Section I

"BEHOLD, THY GOD REIGNETH!"

18 ... *So Great A Cause*

The photograph above shows Mount Carmel as it appears today. This picture was taken during the world conference of the Faith in 1963 at which time the National Spiritual Assemblies of all nations elected the first Universal House of Justice, that supreme Bahá'í administrative body which was promised by Bahá'u'lláh to have infallibility.

The delegates are seated on the steps of the Bahá'í Archives Building in which is housed all of the original Writings of the Twin Prophets of the New Day of God. The dome shaped building shown in the background is the Shrine of the Báb, the Prophet forerunner to Bahá'u'lláh, the Glory of God, Who ushered in the Millennial Dispensation—the Kingdom of God on earth, and Whose coming is foretold in all of the Holy Scriptures of each of the world's great religions.

The photograph above shows Mount Carmel as it appeared in 1900, before the Bahá'í World Faith had begun transforming this *"mountain of God"* to its present state of beauty. This desert mountain has indeed begun to *"blossom as the rose"* as the Holy Bible foretold, and the Word of God is indeed flowing down *"as the dews of Carmel"* from this World Center of the Faith of God.

"As the dews of Carmel, so shall the knowledge of God descend upon them!"
D. & C. 128:19b; Reorganized D. & C. 110:19b

INTRODUCTION TO SECTION I

All Things Which Are Good Cometh From God

    This first section, comprising chapters one through six, contains selected references from the sacred writings. The references which I have used are all from the scriptures of the seed of Abraham, that chosen seed promised by God to be the one through whom *"all the families of the earth shall be blessed"*. These are: The *Bible* (containing both the Jewish *Torah* and the Christian *Gospels),* the *Koran* (also spelled *Quran),* the *Book of Mormon,* the *Doctrine and Covenants,* and *Pearl of Great Price.* I recognize that many of you will not accept some of these books as being inspired of God. For this reason I have tried to include sufficient quotations from each of these volumes of scripture to fully answer each reader's questions from their own holy books.

    Christian students will find that I have used the familiar wording of the King James translation of the *Holy Bible.* The *Book of Mormon* is accepted as scripture by all sects of the Latter-day Saint religion, with the same wording in each. However there is much variation in the way each separate edition is divided inasmuch as the chapters and verses of each of the books is concerned. I selected the editions used by the two largest denominations, the Church of Jesus Christ of Latter-day Saints, with headquarters in Salt Lake City, Utah, and the Reorganized Church of Jesus Christ of Latter-day Saints, with headquarters in Independence, Missouri. Throughout this book I have first footnoted the reference to chapter and verse as given in the Utah Edition of the *Book of Mormon,* followed immediately by the comparative chapter and verse as it is found in the Reorganized Church Edition.

    The two volumes, known as the *Doctrine and Covenants* and the *Pearl of Great Price,* presented a somewhat different kind of problem. While both the Church of Jesus Christ of Latter-day Saints and the Reorganized Church of Jesus Christ of Latter-day Saints, accept fundamentally the same inspired writings of their prophet, Joseph Smith, the order of these writings in their scriptures is somewhat different. I have used the same method as that used in giving reference to the *Book of Mormon,* in referring to material in the *Doctrine and Covenants.* Members of the Reorganized Latter-day Saint church will find some quoted passages to be missing from their own *Doctrine and Covenants.* The reason for this is that, while both churches originally used the 1843 edition of this book as published during the lifetime of Joseph Smith, the Utah church added some twenty-six sections at a later date, including other writings of the prophet Joseph, gleaned from old letters and other early church documents.

The inclusion of quotations from the *Pearl of Great Price* may likewise be found puzzling to members of the Reorganized Church of Jesus Christ of Latter-day Saints. However, I discovered that most of the writings quoted can be found in other volumes of scripture published by that church. For example, chapters one and seventeen in the *Book of Moses* correspond to sections twenty-two and thirty-six of the Reorganized Edition of the *Doctrine and Covenants*, while chapters two through six correspond with the early portion of the Book of Genesis as found in the *Inspired Revision of the Holy Bible*. Joseph Smith 1 is the same as Matthew 23:39 through chapter 24 in the *Inspired Revision*. Joseph Smith 2 contains material from *"Joseph Smith's Own Story"*, published separately as a pamphlet and also to be found in the *History of the Church*.

In the back of this book the reader will find a full bibliography of the holy writings, and other writings quoted in the text, with a listing of the books contained in each book of scripture, and an additional explanation of the differences between the sacred scriptures of the Utah and Missouri branches of the Chruch of Jesus Christ of Latter-day Saints.

Some of the charts and diagrams used throughout this treatise were taken from the book, *Aids to Teaching*, compiled and presented by Margery McCormick, with illustrations by William Musler, distributed by the Baha'i Distribution and Service Department, Wilmette, Illinois, 1963. All of the maps, some of the diagrams, the entire text of Part I, together with all of the mistakes contained therein, are my own doing, and I can blame no one else.

The Oneness of God's Revelation

This book is the result of my own earnest search for the Kingdom of God.

I read my first book of holy scripture, the *Book of Mormon*, when I was eleven years old. I can still recall how fascinated I was with its story. What impressed me most was the universality of God's love shown in this marvelous volume. I found this entire book to be a testimony of the love of God for all mankind. I learned that He invites all men everywhere to partake of His goodness without any reservations whatsoever.

I found this theme running through every chapter. If God loves all mankind then of course He had not denied any of His children of His Word. The prophet Alma tells us this in these words:

> "For behold, the Lord doth grant unto all nations, of their own nation and tongue to teach his word, yea, in wisdom, all that he seeth fit that they should have; therefore we see that the Lord doth counsel in wisdom, according to that which is just and true."[1]

According to the prophet Moroni, "All things which are good cometh from God. Everything which inviteth and enticeth to do good, and to serve him, is inspired of God."[2] What a glorious thought! Such a principle, if applied to the world of contending religions, philosophies, ideologies and creeds, would quickly resolve all difficulties. This principle then means that all truth is one, whether it is discovered by the scientist working in his laboratory, by the mystic meditating on the greatness and majesty of God's creation, or by the prophet who seeks a direct answer through prayer from the Source of all enlightenment.

I found this universal revelation to be filled with purpose, as the prophet Nephi expressed with these thoughts of divine inspiration:

> "I shall speak unto the Jews and they shall write it; and I shall speak unto the Nephites and they shall write it; and I shall also speak unto the other tribes of the house of Israel, which I have led away, and they shall write it; and I shall also speak unto all nations of the earth and they shall write it."

He then concludes with this prophecy concerning the last days, or the dispensation of time in which we are now living:

> "And it shall come to pass that my people, which are of the house of Israel, shall be gathered home unto the lands of their possessions; and my word also shall be gathered in one."[3]

How wonderful, I thought, the house of Israel will at last be gathered home to the ancient land of their inheritance, variously known in history as Canaan, Palestine, and Israel. The second part of this divine promise was even more exciting: God's word, which He had revealed to all nations was at last to be gathered together in one. Did this mean that there would then be only one religion, the universal Religion of God, and that all men everywhere would come to recognize one another's

---

1. Alma 29:8; Reorganized Edition, Alma 15:59.
2. Moroni 7:12-13; Reorganized Edition, Moroni 7:10-11.
3. 2 Nephi 29:12-14; Reorganized Edition, 2 Nephi 12:67-73.

prophets and holy messengers? Would I be able to recognize this religion, and to accept God's revelation from other nations and peoples? I knew that God had revealed His word through the Hebrews and, before them, through the ancient Sumerians, as recorded in the Jewish *Torah* and in the Christian *Gospels*. I also knew that He had revealed His word to the Nephites and Lamanites on this continent, and before them to the Jaredites, as recorded in the pages of the *Book of Mormon*. And finally, in this day, He had given His revelation to the Gentiles through Joseph Smith, as recorded in the pages of the *Doctrine and Covenants*. This revelation, to the Jews, to the Nephites and to the Gentiles, I realized was being gathered into one as God had promised. But where was I to find His revelation to the "**other tribes of the house of Israel**" which He had led away, and where were His words to "**all nations of the earth**"?

I knew that it was imperative that I find and recognize this revelation. Not only was it important to know every word which is revealed from God but I knew our very salvation depends upon it. And I found divine words of warning, revealed through Nephi, clearly addressing a people who have become *"at ease in Zion"*, to warn *"them that turn aside the just for a thing of naught and revile against that which is good, and say that it is of no worth!"*[4]

Did the Lord really mean these words, and many more? Did he really mean that we, the Latter-day Saints, might say: *"We have received the word of God, and we need no more of the word of God, for we have enough!"* Did He really mean that those of us who have established the new Zion in the latter days would become complacent, so much so that we would reject the further revelation from God for which Joseph Smith came to prepare the way? He had told us that *"in that day when the Lord shall come, he shall reveal all things"*.[5] Will we be able to accept this revelation when it comes to us? The next verse from the prophet Nephi caused me to quiver in alarm as it foretold that which was to come:

> *"Wo be unto the Gentiles, saith the Lord God of Hosts! For notwithstanding I shall lengthen out mine arm unto them, from day to day,* **they will deny me;** *nevertheless, I will be merciful unto them, saith the Lord God, if they will repent and come unto me; for mine arm is lengthened out all the day long, saith the Lord God of Hosts."*[6]

4. 2 Nephi 28:16, 24-31; Reorganized Edition, 2 Nephi 12:19, 30-39.
5. *D. & C.* 101:32; Reorganized *D. & C.* 98:5g.
6. 2 Nephi 28:32; Reorganized Edition, 2 Nephi 12:40-41.

I knew that I was of those people referred to as Gentiles, and that this revelation had special reference to those Gentiles who had heard and accepted the revelation of God which had come forth through Joseph Smith in the last days of the Christian dispensation.[7] Would I be one of those Gentiles who would reject the further revelation of God when it would come to us from the Lord who was to come after Joseph Smith? Would I fail to recognize the Lord of the Millennial Dispensation just as the Jews failed to recognize the Lord of the Christian Dispensation? The very thought caused me deepest consternation.

The Testimony of Two Nations to Come Together in One

But how was I to know whence this further revelation would come, to what land or lands would the Great Prophet who was to usher in the Kingdom of God on earth come to minister? The prophet Nephi had written:

"Wherefore murmur ye, because that ye shall receive more of my word? Know ye not that the testimony of two nations is a witness unto you that I am God, that I remember one nation like unto another? Wherefore, I speak the same words unto one nation like unto another. And when the two nations shall run together the testimony of the two nations shall run together also."[8]

I knew that in ancient times God had chosen two special groups of people in each age to be the nucleus of His revelation in each of the two hemispheres of the globe. In the Dispensation of Noah these two groups of people had been the ancient Sumerians in Mesopotamia in the Old World and the Jaredites in Middle America in the New World. In the Dispensations of Moses and of Jesus Christ these two groups of people had been the children of Israel in Palestine and the Nephite-Lamanite people in Middle America.

When the Lord directed Abraham to flee from Ur in the land of the Chaldeas (Mesopotamia), to the land of Canaan, and later chose Moses to lead the children of Israel to this same **"promised land"**, He was in fact not only choosing a special seed to be the nucleus of His revelation to the world from that time hence but He was also choosing a special land in the Eastern Hemisphere to be the nucleus or heartland of this revelation. The ancient land called Canaan is today the same land which we know as Israel. This land occupies a very strategic geographical

---

7. *D. & C.* 109:60; Utah Edition.
8. 2 Nephi 29:8; Reorganized Edition, 2 Nephi 12:58-61.

location in relation to the three continents which make up the Old World or Eastern Hemisphere. Israel lies astride all of the ancient trade routes from Asia to Africa, and in turn from Africa and Asia to Europe in the north. Both by land and by sea this region has from time immemorial been the important connecting link binding together the three great continents of the Eastern Hemisphere.

At no time in human history has this small country ever lacked this strategic importance. Anciently Canaan, as this region was then called, was the connecting bridge between the Sumerian and Egyptian cultures, the two most ancient civilizations known to archaeologists. Later Israel served as the channel of communication between the Egyptian and Ethiopian civilizations to the west and the Babylonian, Assyrian and, later, the great Persian empires to the east. In still more recent times she bound together the highly advanced Graecian and Egyptian cultures. Then came the Romans, and still later the Arabic Moslems, both of whom used Israel as the connecting link between the African and the Asian parts of their great empires.

I recalled also the Christian Crusades and the important role which Israel, then under the Islamic Turks, bore in revealing the high civilization of the Muhammedans to the then barbarious feudal states of Western Europe. Indeed, it is difficult to conceive of a single nation which has had greater importance throughout the millenia, from earliest times down to the present, than the nation of Israel. Again in the first and second world wars, and even today, Israel lies at the heart of communication and hence of conflict between the East and the West. No wonder God named Israel as a promised land, and chose her people to be His "light to the nations"!

If we turn our attention to a world globe we see that just as the continents of the Eastern Hemisphere are connected at the point where Israel and Egypt come together across the Sinai Peninsula, so also are the two continents of the Western Hemisphere connected where Columbia and the smaller nations of Central America unite across the Isthmus of Panama. Further to the north these same Central American republics are brought together with Mexico and the United States by way of the Isthmus of Tehuantepec.

Here again we see the wisdom of the Lord in providing a bridge by means of which both high civilization and the Religion of God could be dispersed from a central heartland, southward to the ancient peoples of South America and northward to the lands of North America. For as I had read the pages of the *Book of Mormon* I learned that, just as He had led Abraham from Ur of the Chaldeas to the land of Jerusalem, and later led Moses and the children of Israel from Egypt to this same land, God similarly directed at least three separate colonies of people from the Old to the New World. To this region of America God led the colonies of Jared, Mulek and Lehi, these last two being the ancestors of the Nephites and Lamanites. The Lord referred to this land, again as in the Old Testament, as a new **"promised land, choice above all other lands"**.[9] Nor are these countries of less significance today as we build a Pan American Highway through this narrow neck of land to join the nations of North and South America, and as we construct canals across the Isthmus of Panama to connect the Atlantic and Pacific Oceans, thus providing a water route between the nations of the West and those of the Far East.

I was later to learn, through my studies in anthropology and history, that the highly cultured peoples of the high Andes region in South America, of the eastern and the southwestern regions of what is now the United States, and even those of the Polynesian Islands of the Pacific, not only derived their original cultural impetus from Middle America, but that the physical characteristics of the populations in these areas bear a stronger resemblance to the Caucasian than to the Mongolian

9. The references in the *Book of Mormon* to the geographical features of the lands in which the Jaredite and later Nephite civilizations developed are found in Alma 22:27-34; 50:31-34; 52:9-13; 63:4-10; Helaman 4:5-8; Mormon 2:29; 3:5; and Ether 10:19-21. Reorganized Editon, Alma 13:68-80; 22:32-35; 24:10-15; 30:5-14; Helaman 2:38-40; Mormon 1:61-62; 69; Ether 4:66-70.

Latter-day Saint authors who have co-ordinated these references with the actual geography of the American continents, and with the high civilizations occurring during Book of Mormon times in America, are: Paul M. Hanson, *Jesus Christ Among the Ancient Americans,* Independence, Missouri, 1947, Appendix—Note XX; T. S. Ferguson, *Cumorah—Where?,* Independence, Missouri, 1947; Lynn C. Layton, "An Ideal Book of Mormon Geography" *The Improvement Era,* July, 1938; Joel Ricks, *Geography of Book of Mormon Lands,* 1940; J. A. and J. N. Washburn, *An Approach to the Study of Book of Mormon Geography,* Provo, Utah, 1939; Dr. John A. Widttoe, *"Is Book of Mormon Geography Known?",* The Improvement Era, July, 1950; Orvin G. Wilde, *Landmarks of Ancient American People,* 1947.

(Editor's Note): *To non-Mormons, these accounts of ancient America from the standpoint of the Book of Mormon may seem fantasies or, at best, highly improbable. However we non-Mormons should have the wisdom to admit that we do not have the evidence yet to disprove them, so we should keep our minds open. Actually the major thesis of this book which is that Joseph Smith foresaw for a specific time a major spiritual event which has actually happened but been ignored by a dogmatic and doctrine-blinded mankind is entirely separate from and does not depend upon the truth or fiction of these Mormon accounts of ancient America.*

race. Both the peoples concerned and their cultures bear a marked similarity to the peoples and civilizations of ancient Sumeria, Egypt, Israel and Assyria.

It seems likely to me then, that the nations of Israel in the Old World, and Middle America in the New, are the "two nations" referred to in Nephi's prophecy, when he said, *"Know ye not that the testimony of two nations is a witness unto you that I am God, that I remember one nation like unto another and when the two nations shall run together the testimony of the two nations shall run together also"?* [10] But this can also apply to all nations in general.

I knew that the *Bible* was God's *"testimony"* in ancient times, first through the Sumerians and then through the children of Israel, in the Eastern Hemisphere. I knew also that the *Book of Mormon* was similarly His "testimony through branches" of these same two peoples, who had been led to the Western Hemisphere by the hand of God. What puzzled me were the additional words of the Lord through the prophet Nephi, as follows:

"For behold, I shall speak unto the Jews and they shall write it; and I shall also speak unto the Nephites and they shall write it; and **I shall also speak unto the other tribes of the house of Israel, which I have led away, and they shall write it; and I shall also speak unto all nations of the earth and they shall write it.**

"And it shall come to pass that the Jews shall have the words of the Nephites, and the Nephites shall have the words of the Jews; **and the Nephites and the Jews shall have the words of the lost tribes of Israel; and the lost tribes of Israel shall have the words of the Nephites and the Jews."** [11]

This portion of the prophecy seemed to me to be only partially fulfilled. Again, the same question arose: if the *Bible* were indeed the word of God to the Jews, and the *Book of Mormon* His word to the Nephites, where then was His further word to the "lost tribes of Israel" and "unto all nations"?

I had also been struck with the promise that *"it shall come to pass that my people, which are of the house of Israel, shall be gathered home unto the lands of their possessions; and my word also shall be gathered in one".*

10. 2 Nephi 29:8; Reorganized Edition 2 Nephi 12:59-61.
11. 2 Nephi 29:12-13; Reorganized Edition, 2 Nephi 12:65-74.

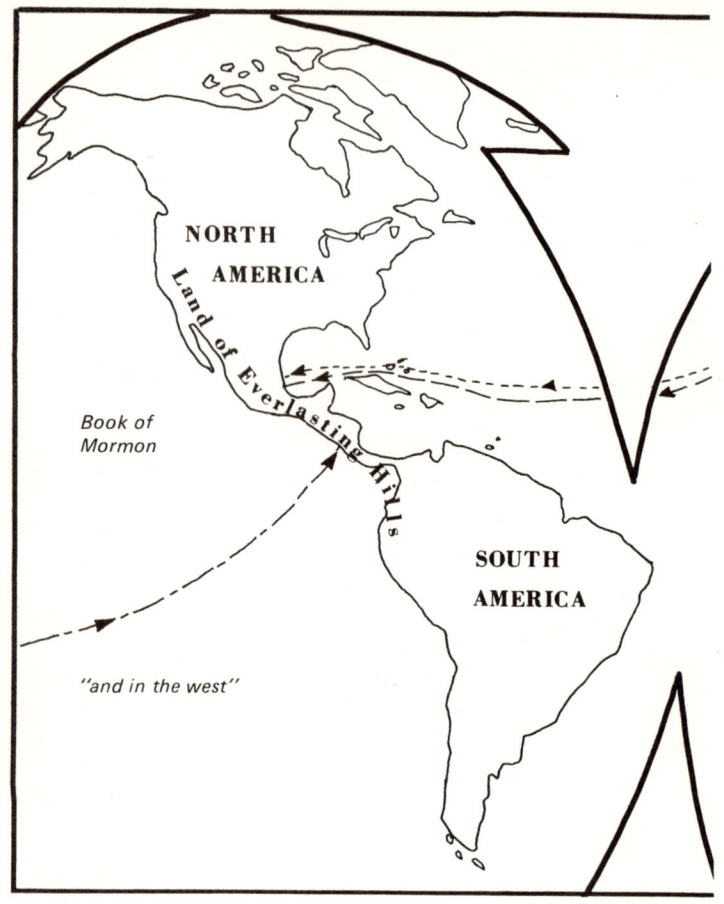

Map I: Testimony of Two Nations—The Revelation of God in Former Dispensations Through the Seed of Abraham.

◄----- Journey of the Jaredites from ancient Sumer to America.
◄ ── Route of the colony of Mulek from Jerusalem to America.
──►── Approximate route of colony of Lehi from Israel to America.

"In Thee and in Thy seed after Thee shall all the families of the earth be blessed, even with the blessings of the Gospel, which are the blessings of salvation, even life eternal."

—Abraham 2:11 (Compare Genesis 17:5-7)

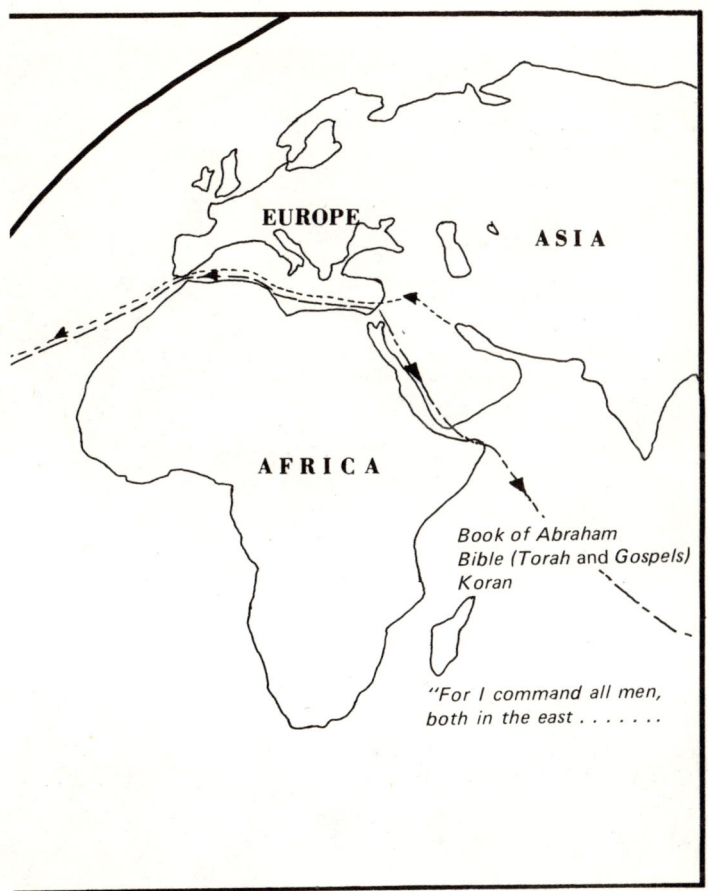

"I command all men, both in the east and in the west, and in the north, and in the south, and in the islands of the sea that they shall write the words which I speak unto them: for out of the books which shall be written I will judge the world, every man according to their works, according to that which is written... And it shall come to pass that my people, which are of the house of Israel, shall be gathered home unto the lands of their possessions; and my word also shall be gathered in one."

2 Nephi 29:11, 14a; Reorganized Edition, 2 Nephi 12:65-66, 73

"And other sheep I have, which are not of this fold: them also must I bring, and they shall hear my voice; and there shall be one fold, and one shepherd." John 10:16.

—John 10:16 (See also 3 Nephi 15:15-24; 16:1-5; Reorganized Edition, 3 Nephi 7:15-29

30 . . . *So Great A Cause*

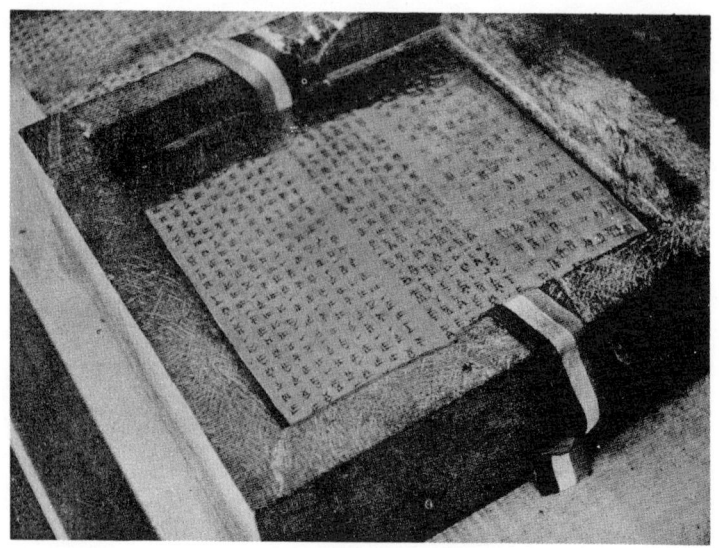

The above photographs are of metal plates of gold and silver, similar to those from which the *Book of Mormon* was translated by Joseph Smith. Gold and silver plates were common in ancient times both in the Old and New Worlds. The first set of gold and silver plates which are shown in a stone box, in which they were sealed, was inscribed during the reign of Darius I of Persia (518 to 515 B.C.), carrying a text in three ancient languages. The second set of gold plates was found in prehistoric tombs near Tuquerres, Columbia, on the border of Equador. Such plates have also been found in southern Mexico, clearly establishing their use in ancient times.

At that time, in my young childhood, Palestine was a colony of the British Empire. When she wrested this ancient Holy Land from the Turks, Britain had issued the Balfour Declaration, in which that government declared that it viewed with favor *"the establishment in Palestine of a national home for the Jewish people"*. This hope had only begun to be realized as a few Jews began to drift back to the lands of their ancient heritage, amidst a predominance of Arabs.

Nephi's further words now came to me with thundering impact:

"O ye Gentiles, have ye remembered the Jews, mine ancient covenant people? Nay, but ye have cursed them, and have hated them, and have not sought to recover them. But behold, I will return all these things upon your own heads; for I the Lord have not forgotten my people."

It was then that Nephi went on to the promise, proclaiming more of God's word to come, of the running together of the two nations and their testimonies. *"And I do this that I may prove unto many that I am the same yesterday, today, and forever; and that I speak forth my words according to mine own pleasure."* 12

This then is the context in which the Lord's word's concerning the "two nations" is embedded. In ancient times God had revealed His word through the children of Israel in the Old World in the writings collectively known as the *Bible*. During essentially the same period He had revealed His will in the New World through a branch of the children of Israel, the Nephites and Lamanites (descended from the original colonies of Lehi and Mulek), written on Gold Plates, later translated by Joseph Smith in what is called the *Book of Mormon*. These two separate branches of the house of Israel had each carried the word of God to other surrounding peoples, spoken of by them as "the nations of the Gentiles". I began to look towards Israel for the testimony "to all nations" of the gathering of the word in "one".

The Origin and Dispersion of High Civilization in America

For a short time the Religion of God on both hemispheres remained essentially pure. But, in the Old World, as the apostles of Christ were each martyred and many of the loyal disciples passed away, changes began to creep into the Christian religion. The word of God itself was written down by hand, copied and recopied again and again. As the

---

12. 2 Nephi 29:5, 9a; Reorganized Edition, 2 Nephi 12:50-52, 55-62.

language of the believers changed so also was it necessary to translate the holy text from one language into another. Inevitably changes slipped into the text until the *Bible* which we use today is not the same as the original writings of the ancient prophets and apostles.

The situation in the New World was somewhat different. Here the word of God was written down and preserved by chosen prophets of God for a period of approximately one thousand years, until finally abridged and copied onto the Gold Plates by the prophets Mormon and Moroni. Moroni witnessed the destruction of his own people, the Nephites, and himself fled before the conquering armies of the Lamanites. After years of travel he finally arrived in the eastern part of what is now New York where he buried the Gold Plates in a small hill, now called Cumorah by Latter-day Saints, named after the mountain in Middle America where the original records of the Nephite nation were buried. As a consequence of earnest prayer Joseph Smith was called of God to be His instrument to bring forth and to translate these plates and thus restore the original pure teachings of Christ and the Nephite prophets recorded therein. While some scholars have contended that even this translation shows some influence from the mind and the words of Joseph Smith, it nevertheless should have validity as great as the *Bible*, having been translated only once from the original plates of Mormon.

I was later to learn, from my studies in anthropology, that the founders of the Mound Builder culture in the eastern portion of what is now the United States, came into that region from Middle America, beginning in about 400 A. D. I could not help but wonder if the bearers of this culture, so similar to that of Middle America, were not some of the armed Lamanite bands which Moroni describes as pursuing him as he fled northward with the precious gold tablets.

The Lamanite faction of the original Israelite people in America does not appear to have possessed a pure written account of their religious history and teachings. (This is perhaps why they were so zealous in their pursuit of Moroni, the last of the Nephite prophets, because he had such a record in his possession.) Nevertheless, they did preserve a knowledge of some of the most important events in their history, as well as some of the high moral teachings of Christ and the Nephite prophets. These were written down by some of the Maya and Aztec scholars who learned to write in Spanish, as well as by some of the Catholic priests and missionaries who lived among them, and bear a remarkable resemblance to historical accounts given in the pages of the *Book of Mormon.* [13]

Such accounts as the Lamanites did possess of their earlier history and of the high culture and religion which they shared with their brethren the Nephites, were carried by their descendants through the lands they occupied after the destruction of the Nephites and, by those adventurous bands who spread out from the higher cultural centers of Middle America, into other regions of North and South America. There they mingled with the peoples already occupying these lands. [14] Widespread among the Indians of the eastern and southwestern parts of the

13. The Spanish conquerors of Mexico and Central America destroyed all of the historical writings of the Indian peoples of this region written in the native languages, with the exception of a few more recently discovered manuscripts which have not yet been translated. To make doubly sure that the Indians would forget their own religious beliefs and historical past, the Spaniards ruthlessly executed all of the priestly class who were alone able to read and write the native languages. They did a very thorough job. Not one literate native remained.

Later the Spaniards regretted their mistake. The records we now have concerning the history and religious beliefs of the peoples of this region prior to the coming of the Spaniards, are of two kinds—those written by the Indians themselves, educated to read and write in the Spanish language, and who wrote the history of their people as they remembered it from their priests and told in the original histories, and those written by the Catholic padres and missionaries in Mexico and Central America during the sixteenth century.

Among the native Indian writings are the Historical Works of Don Fernando de Alva Ixlilxochitl, an Aztec prince and historian, written between 1590 and 1600, using earlier historical sources; the Popul Vuh, the sacred book of the ancient Mayas, written in the sixteenth century by learned natives; Historical Recollections of Gaspar Antonio Chi, written by members of the royal Xihil family and descendants of Oxlahul Tzii, king of the Cakchiquel branch of the Mayas; Chilam Balam de Mani, a sixteenth century book from Yucatan; Tilulo de los Senores de Tolonicapan, a record from the Queche Mayas of Guatemala written in 1554.

There are three highly valid writings of the early Catholic fathers, reliable because of the objectivity of their writers and their long acquaintance with the native peoples. These are the writings of Diago de Landa, the first Catholic bishop of Yucatan, 1524-1579; Bernardino de Sahagun, a Catholic padre who lived in Mexico from 1529 to 1590, and Juan de Torquemada, who lived in sixteenth century Mexico for many years.

The first translation of any of these writings into English appeared in Antiquities of Mexico, written by Lord Edward King Kingsborough, in nine volumes, between 1831 and 1848, the ninth volume, containing the writings of Ixlilxochitl, appearing in the latter year. This nine volume set was published by Henry G. Bohn in London, England and is available in most university libraries. The first edition of the *Book of Mormon* was in 1830. It is thus easily provable that Joseph Smith had no access to any of these earlier accounts concerning the history and religious teachings of the early Indian civilizations in Middle America at the time of the translation of the gold plates into what is now known as the *Book of Mormon.*

14. I found Dr. Paul Radin's book, *The Story of the American Indian,* published

THE LEHI STONE—Stela 5, Teapa, Chiapas, Mexico

The author's rough drawing shows a stone monument or stela found at Teapa, Chiapas, in southeastern Mexico in 1941. Designated as *"Stela 5"* by archaeologists, this monument is believed by Dr. M. Wells Jakeman of the Brigham Young University Archaeology Department to be a representation of the vision of the prophet Lehi, described in 1 Nephi 8:10-35 and 11:21, 22, 25, 35, 36. Note the lettered figures in the drawing. Reorganized Edition 1 Nephi 2:49-85; 3:63, 64, 68, 69, 89-95.

The old bearded man shown in an attitude of worship (A) is believed to represent Lehi, as indicated by the name-glyph (B) above his head containing a jawbone. (The Hębrew place name *"Lehi"* is defined as *"jaw"* or *"jawbone"*.) Behind the old man is a female figure (C) wearing an elaborate headdress corresponding to those worn in the Near East by royalty. (The wife of Lehi was Sariah which means *"princess of Jehovah"*.)

The figure (D) with a light beard signifying youth, wears a headdress closely resembling that of the Egyptian grain god, Nepi. This may indicate that this person is Nephi, the young son of Lehi, author of the books of 1 and 2 Nephi in the *Book of Mormon*. He appears to be assisted by another person (E), who might well have been Sam, his trusted brother and supporter.

Figures (F) and (G) are thought by Dr. Jakeman to correspond with Laman and Lemuel, the two older brothers of Nephi who rebelled against him and turned their backs upon the *"tree of life"* shown in figure (H). Nephi describes the tree of life as representing the love of God *"which sheddeth itself abroad in the hearts of the children of men, wherefore it is the most desirable above all things"*.

Another feature in the stela (I) is a straight deep groove. Lehi describes a *"straight and narrow path, extending along the bank of a river"* which led up to the *"tree of life"*. Next to the path was a *"rod of iron"* described as the *"word of God"* which leads mankind to the tree of life or love of God. Lehi also saw a *"great and spacious building"* representing the *"pride of the world"*. Although quite indistinguishable in this drawing, the features shown to the extreme right and at the top of the stela may represent such a building.

United States, as well as among the highly civilized Chibcas and Incas of South America, I found the legends of a bearded *"white God"* who once lived among the people, teaching them high spiritual and moral principles, and who disappeared quite suddenly but promised to *"return"* again at the end of the age to usher in a New Era of love and unity. In Mexico and Central America these accounts are even clearer and in greater detail, testifying to a time when Christ's Spirit did walk among these ancient Americans. [15]

The Fulness of the Gospel to Go to the House of Israel

Joseph Smith was not a Jew. He belonged to that group of people referred to in the *Book of Mormon* as "Gentiles". Both the prophet Nephi and Jesus Christ promised the Nephite-Lamanite peoples on this continent that in the latter days their religious history would come forth to them from the Gentiles, after which the work of "the Father" would commence among all the dispersed children of Israel, in whatever parts of the world they have gone. Nephi wrote thusly:

"For, behold, saith the Lamb: I will manifest myself unto thy seed, that they shall write many things which I shall minister unto them, which shall be plain and precious; and after thy seed shall be destroyed, and dwindle in unbelief, and also the seed of thy brethren, behold, these things shall be hid up, to come forth unto the Gentiles, by the gift and power of the Lamb. And in them shall be written my gospel, saith the Lamb, and my rock and my salvation. And blessed are they who seek to bring forth my Zion at that day...

By Liverright Publishing Corp., New York, 1944, to be one of the best short summaries of the process of cultural diffusion throughout the Americas. Perhaps the best presentation of the theory of the diffusion of Old World Civilization to America, written by a non-Mormon, is Harold Sterling Gladwin's, *Men Out of Asia,* published by Whittlesey House, New York 18, New York, 1947. The *Book of Mormon* itself gives accounts of both of these processes. See for example Alma 63:4-10; Reorganized Edition Alma 30:5-14.

15. See for example Wissler, Clark, *The American Indian,* Oxford University Press, New York, New York, 1938, esp. pp. 213-214. Among the references by Latter-day Saint archaeologists presenting the evidences for the diffusion of culture from the Near East to America, and of the actual appearance of Jesus Christ on this hemisphere, are the following: Ferguson, Thomas Stuart, *One Fold and One Shepherd,* Olympus Publishing Co., Salt Lake City, Utah, Revised Edition, 1962, Hanson, Paul M., *Jesus Christ Among the Ancient Americans,* Herald Publishing Trust, Independence, Missouri, 1947; Milton R. Hunter, *Archaeology and the Book of Mormon,* and *Christ in Ancient America,* Deseret Book Co., Salt Lake City, Utah; and Milton R. Hunter and Thomas S. Ferguson, *Ancient America and the Book of Mormon,* Kolob Book Co., Oakland, California, Seventh Printing, 1964.

"*And it came to pass that I beheld the remnant of the seed of my brethren, and also the book of the Lamb of God, which had proceeded forth from the mouth of the Jew, that it came forth from the Gentiles unto the remnant of the seed of my brethren. . . . And the angel spake unto me, saying: These last records, which thou hast seen among the Gentiles, shall establish the truth of the first, which are of the twelve apostles of the Lamb, and shall make known the plain and precious things which have been taken away from them. . .therefore they* **both shall be established in one; for there is one God and one Shepherd over all the earth.**"

Nephi then went on to foretell the new revelation which would come first to the Jews after the restoration of the Gospel of Jesus Christ in America:

"*And the time cometh that He (God) shall manifest himself unto all nations; both unto the Jews and also unto the Gentiles; and* **after he has manifested himself unto the Jews and also unto the Gentiles, then he shall manifest himself unto the Gentiles and also unto the Jews, and the last shall be first and the first shall be last.**" [16]

I knew that I had entered upon a great quest. I knew that my church, the restored Church of Jesus Christ of Latter-day Saints, was but a forerunner to the revelation of God which must come again to the house of Israel, and that this ancient covenant people would have **"the knowledge of the fulness of my gospel"**. I also knew that except my own people, the Gentiles, should repent and "return" unto God, to a recognition of His revelation in the latter days through Israel, they would be forever cut off:

"*But if they will not turn unto me, and hearken unto my voice, I will suffer them, yea, I will suffer my people, O house of Israel, that they shall go through among them, and shall tread them down, and they shall be as salt that hath lost its savor, which is thenceforth good for nothing, but to be cast out, and to be trodden under foot of my people, O house of Israel.*" [17]

The Important Role of the Land of Persia

As I continued to read I learned many other promises concerning God's revelation in this Day, first through the Gentiles, and afterward

---

16. See the full context in which these verses are found in 1 Nephi 13:35-42; Reorganized Edition, 3:184-200.
17. 3 Nephi 16:15; Reorganized Edition, 7:40-41.

to the children of Israel. Through additional years of study, in theology, history and anthropology, I learned a great deal more concerning the seed of Israel. I learned that the Hebrews, after entering the Holy Land from Egypt had divided into two nations, the one to the north known thereafter as Israel or Sameria, and the one to the south known as Judah. I learned that after many more years of history the ten tribes of Israel residing in the northern kingdom were conquered and taken away captive into Assyria and Media, by the then great Assyrian Empire. This event occurred in 721 B.C. There is no historical evidence that these *"lost tribes of Israel"* ever went anywhere else than this region which now constitutes the northern portion of Persia or Iran.

I also learned that in 600 B. C. the kingdom of Judah was beseiged by the armies of the Babylonian Empire and, after several years was likewise defeated and its people taken into captivity, that is those who had not already fled to Egypt and the two colonies we have stated came to America. These captive Israelites, thereafter known as Jews, were taken to the province of Elam in what is now southern Persia or Iran.

After another seventy years, with the conquest of Babylonia by the god-fearing Persians, some of these Jewish exiles, but not all, returned to the land of Judah to restore the temple and to rebuild the *"waste places of Jerusalem"*. These were the Jews among whom Jesus Christ was born, and who were the first to receive His message. These same Jewish people were dispersed a second time, as the result of their rebellion against the Roman Empire and their rejection of their Messiah. They were scattered widely throughout Roman lands and have since been dispersed throughout the world.

But what of the original colonies of Israel which remained in the land of Persia, the ten tribes in the north and the other two tribes, Judah and Benjamin, in the south of that land? I wondered. Surely God had not forgotten them. As I learned more concerning world history, and especially through my studies in world religion, I found that God had indeed sent another Great Prophet to this land. Zoroaster reaffirmed the Religion of God as it had been revealed successively through Adam, Noah, Abraham and Moses, and in turn foretold the birth of both Jesus Christ in Bethlehem of Judea, and of another Chosen Messenger who would come at the end of the age, to unite all nations and religions, and to usher in a golden age of universal peace.

I discovered that the word *"magi"* was the name of the hereditary priestly class among the Persians, and that the three magi or *"wise*

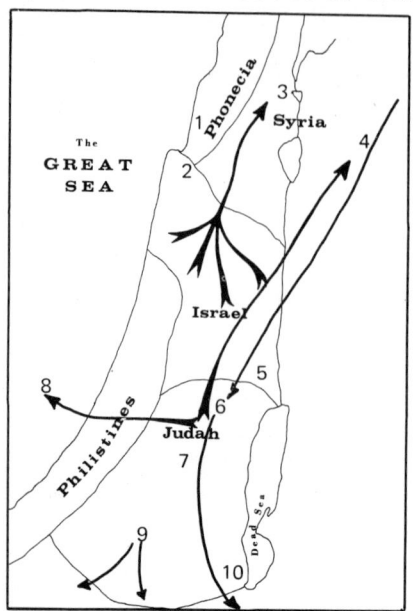

1. Achor
2. Mount Carmel
3. Ten tribes were deported north to Assyria 734 B.C.
4. Many Jews were deported to Babylonia and Elam 587 B.C.
5. Some Jews return after 538 B.C.
6. Jerusalem (All Jews were dispersed a second time after 70 A.D.)
7. Israelite and Jewish peasants left behind intermarry with Assyrian and Babylonian colonists to become Samaritans.
8. Colony of Mulek leave for America about 587 B.C.
9. Some Jews fled to Egypt.
10. Colony of Lehi leave for America 600 B.C.

Map II: The Dispersion of Israel and Judah, about 722 and 600 B.C. and a second time after 70 A.D..

"I will make of thee a multitude of people, and I will give this land to thy seed after thee for an everlasting possession."
—Genesis 48:4

"Joseph is a fruitful bough, even a fruitful bough by a well; whose branches run over the walls...unto the utmost bounds of the everlasting hills; ... The blessing of thy fathers...shall be on the head of Joseph."
—Genesis 49:22,26

"And I will also give thee for a light to the Gentiles, that thou mayest be my salvation unto the end of the earth."
—Isaiah 49:6

"And other sheep I have which are not of this fold: them also I must bring, and they shall hear my voice; and there shall be one fold, and one shepherd."
—John 10:16

"And this I have told you concerning Jerusalem; and when that day shall come, shall a remnant be scattered among all nations; but they shall be gathered again; but they shall remain until the times of the Gentiles be fulfilled."
—D. & C. 45:24-25; Reorganized D. & C. 45:3f

men" from the East who came to pay homage to the infant Jesus were Zoroastrian priests, following the instructions of their Prophet as left to them in His sacred Writings. Had not the message of this Great Figure impressed me that He was indeed a Prophet of God, on the same order as Moses, Abraham and even Jesus Christ, this precise prophecy concerning the birth of Jesus would have done so.

In succeeding centuries, about 600 years after the time of Christ, the Prophet Muhammad was born in Arabia of the lineage of Abraham through Ishmael. Muhammad proclaimed that He was a successor to Abraham, and to Moses and to Jesus Christ. He did not deny that which these High Prophets had revealed. In fact He declared the oneness of God and of religion. He called upon all mankind to give up their manmade differences and submit to the will of the one true Creator. I learned that the Islamic or Muslim Faith spread across north Africa to the west of Arabia, and across southern Asia to the east, thus coming to embrace the people of Persia among its adherents.

It was thus with great interest that I read these prophecies (some set forth in the *"Challenge"*) concerning the destiny of Persia (including the ancient lands of Elam and Assyria) in the last days:

"The word of the Lord that came to Jeremiah the prophet against Elam in the beginning of the reign of Zedekiah king of Judah, saying, thus saith the Lord of hosts; Behold, I will break the bow of Elam, the chief of their might. . . And I will set my throne in Elam, and will destroy from thence the king and the princes, saith the Lord. But it shall come to pass in the latter days, that I will bring again the captivity of Elam, saith the Lord." [18]

"Therefore I will look unto the Lord; I will wait for the God of my salvation: my God will hear me. . . . In that day also he shall come even to thee from Assyria, and from the fortified cities, and from the fortress even to the river, and from sea to sea, and from mountain to mountain." [19]

I learned that the prophet Daniel was in the land of Elam when he had his visions of the Kingdom of God to be set up in the last days, one such prophecy reading as follows:

"I saw in the night visions, and behold, one like the Son of man came with the clouds of heaven, and came to the Ancient of days, and they

18. Jeremiah 49:34, 35, 38, 39.
19. Micah 7:7, 12.

brought him near before him. *And there was given him dominion, and glory, and a kingdom, that all people, nations, and languages, should serve him: his dominion is an everlasting dominion, which shall not pass away, and his kingdom that which shall not be destroyed.*" [20]

I found that in other prophecies Daniel spoke of this One who would redeem Israel and establish unity as Michael, which I learned is a title meaning: *"One who looks like God"*, i.e. a divine Messenger. He also spoke of Him as a Great Prince, or Chief Prince among the Persians:

"Then said he unto me, Fear not, Daniel: for from the first day that thou didst set thine heart to understand, and to chasten thyself before thy God, thy words were heard, and I am come for thy words. But the prince of the kingdom of Persia withstood me one and twenty days: but, lo, **Michael, one of the chief princes, came to help me;** *and I remained there with the kings of Persia. Now I am come to make thee understand what shall befall thy people in the latter days: for yet the vision is for many days. . . .*

"At that time shall Michael stand up, the great prince which standeth for the children of thy people: and there shall be a time of trouble, such as never was since there was a nation even to that same time: and at that time thy people shall be delivered, every one that shall be found written in the book." [21]

One Mighty and Strong

Daniel even told the year (2300 days) when this redemption would begin to take place. [22] To my amazement this year was the exact year to which Joseph Smith had alluded, with the termination of his ministry, as the year of the coming of the Lord who would usher in the Millennial Dispensation.[23] (See Chapter 4.)

Joseph Smith was martyred on June 27, **1844**. He was shot and fell immediately, *"by the shaft of death, like as a tree that is smitten by the vivid shaft of lightning"*. What about still other prophecies and allusions? Had the Great Prophet who was to usher in the Kingdom of God also appeared in that same year? I learned from American history that this was the very same year which William Miller, and countless other adventist scholars, had picked as the year of the *"second coming"* of

---

20. Daniel 7:13-14.
21. Daniel 10:12-14; 12:1.
22. For a full explanation of this prophecy see Chapter 16, entitled: The Time of the Lord's Advent Foretold.
23. *D. & C.* 35:18; 112:15, 34; 85:7-8; Reorganized *D. & C.* 34:4e-f; 105:6a,13b

Christ. I also knew that Jesus had repeatedly warned His apostles that in the latter days the Son of Man would come as a *"thief in the night"* and would *"take men unawares"*. He told us that we must *"watch closely"* and study the *"signs of the times"* in order to recognize the coming of the Lord. What were these signs? Would I be able to find them by studying the holy scriptures? Some of them already seemed clear to me—the time and the place of the Lord's advent. Were I to look to the lands of Persia and Israel to those events transpiring around the time of the year 1844 would I be rewarded with finding the Object of my life search?

Seek Ye First the Kingdom of God, and His Righteousness

Such thoughts as these spurred on my quest. May I say that my search has been fully rewarded, as will yours if you truly seek the Kingdom of God, as Jesus commanded us to do. In Section 1 of this book I have attempted to tell you, my readers, in as few words as possible, how I made use of the scriptures as *"road signs"* to guide me along the *"straight and narrow way"* leading to the knowledge of the twin Manifestations of the New Day of God. Jesus commanded us to seek the Kingdom of God before all else, and, when we have found it, to sell all that we have to purchase this *"pearl of great price"*.[24] Here are some of His additional words on the importance of searching the scriptures for a knowledge of the coming Kingdom:

"Seek ye first the kingdom of God, and his righteousness; and all these things shall be added unto you."[25]

"And as all have not faith, seek ye diligently and teach one another words of wisdom; yea, seek ye out of the best books words of wisdom; seek learning even by study and also by faith." [26]

"And now, behold, I say unto you, that ye ought to search these things. Yea, a commandment I give unto you that ye search these things diligently; for great are the words of Isaiah. For surely he spake as touching all things concerning my people which are of the house of Israel; therefore it must needs be that he must speak also to the Gentiles. . . . Search the prophets, for many there be that testify of these things." [27]

---

24. See Matthew 6:24-34; 13:44-46.
25. Matthew 6:33.
26. *D. & C.* 88:118; 109:7; Reorganized *D. & C.* 85:36a.
27. 3 Nephi 23:1-2, 5; Reorganized Edition, 3 Nephi 10:26-28, 32.

Chapter 1

GOD'S REVELATION IS UNIVERSAL AND PROGRESSIVE

The Revelation of God is to All Mankind

The story of the life and teachings of Jesus Christ has aptly been called *"the greatest story ever told"*. Even so this story was not one of great conquests nor of other marvelous human achievements. It was rather the story of a humble carpenter's son who grew up in an obscure village in a remote province of the ancient Roman Empire. This same child was born of a nation of people who have probably been hated and persecuted more intensely than any other people on the whole earth. In his own time he was hardly recognized as important even by his own people. He was able to claim only a small band of followers, and even these deserted him when he was brought to trial for alleged misdeeds. He was condemned and nailed to a cross to die ignominiously between two thieves. Still, nineteen centuries have gone by and this man remains the focal point of worship for over seven hundred million people in every continent of the globe.

Certainly it was not the humanity of Jesus of Nazareth which made him the object of devotion for nearly one fourth of the human race. Nor is Christ the only person who occupies or has occupied such an important place in the lives of millions of followers. If we examine carefully the life and original teachings of Guatama Buddha we find a very close parallel to the story of Jesus Christ, and for just as many sincere followers he remains the *"blessed Lord Buddha"*.

Other millions of devoted followers turn to Krishna, Moses, Zoroaster, Muhammad or Baha'u'llah as the Manifestations of the attributes and will of God among His earthly children. Each of these Divine Messengers, or spiritual Sons of God, was, for the people of his day, the Word of God, the Light of Truth, the Sun of Reality. The essence of each one of these Founders of the world's great religions was the Holy Spirit or Holy Ghost. This Spirit of the Lord caused each one of them to walk the earth as the reflection of the Divine Reality. The differences in their messages were not due to the difference in the Messengers themselves but rather to the needs and conditions of the people in whose time they came. This fact is clearly attested to by two of the greatest writers of the *Book of Mormon.*

In a burst of enthusiasm for the message of salvation which had come down to him through the holy Prophets of God, Alma exclaimed:

"O, that I were an angel, and could have the wish of mine heart, that I might go forth and speak with the trump of God, with a voice to shake the earth, and cry repentance unto every people! Yea, I would declare unto every soul, as with the voice of thunder, repentance and the plan of redemption, that they should repent and come unto our God, that there might not be more sorrow upon all the face of the earth."

And then, as if by further reflection, Alma went on to teach us this great lesson concerning the universal love of God for all of His children:

"But behold, I am a man, and do sin in my wish; for I ought to be content with the things which the Lord hath allotted unto me. I ought not to harrow up in my desire the firm decree of a just God, for I know that he granteth unto men according to their desire, whether it be unto death or unto life; yea, I know that he allotteth unto men according to their wills, whether they be unto salvation or unto destruction. Yea, and I know that good and evil have come before all men..." [1] It was here that Alma made the wonderful pronouncement that **"The Lord doth grant unto all nations, of their own nation and tongue, to teach his word..."**

A similar thought was expressed by Nephi in these words of divine inspiration:

"Know ye not that there are more nations than one? Know ye not that I, the Lord your God, have created all men, and that I remember those who are upon the isles of the sea; and that I rule in the heavens above and in the earth beneath; and I bring forth my word unto the children of men, yea, even upon all the nations of the earth?

"Wherefore murmur ye, because that ye shall receive more of my word? Know ye not that the testimony of two nations is a witness unto you that I am God, that I remember one nation like unto another. And when the two nations shall run together the testimony of the two nations shall run together also...."

---

1. Alma 29:1-8; Reorganized Edition, Alma 15:52-59.

"*For I command all men, both in the east and in the west, and in the north, and in the south, and in the islands of the sea, that they shall write the words which I speak unto them; for out of the books which shall be written I will judge the world, every man according to their works, according to that which is written.*" 2

God Reveals His Attributes and His Will for Each Age Through a Series of High Prophets

Just as plants do not spring to new life from the heat of yesterday's sun, human souls do not re-awaken to the call of the Messenger of God of a previous dispensation. Each morning the world awakens to the warmth of a new day. Each year life leaps into being from the waters of a fresh springtime. In like manner, the world of humankind re-awakens spiritually at regular intervals to the invigorating breezes of a "*New Day of God*", a "**New Divine Springtime**".

These periods of spiritual re-enlightenment are well understood by Latter-day Saints, who speak of them as the "*dispensations of the gospel*". What is not so generally understood is that these times of spiritual quickening were not confined alone to the children of Israel, nor to their spiritual heirs—the peoples of the Christian Dispensation. All over the earth, wherever and whenever the spiritual darkness becomes most intense, God sends a new Prophet, a new Heavenly Messenger, bringing the gospel of salvation and of eternal life to the people of that day and in that portion of the earth. This is what both Alma and Nephi have taught us. In another of my favorite references from the prophet Nephi we read:

"*For behold, my beloved brethren, I say unto you that the Lord God worketh not in darkness. He doeth not anything save it be for the benefit of the world; for he loveth the world, even that he layeth down his own life that he may draw all men unto him. Wherefore, he commandeth none that they shall not partake of his salvation.*

"*Behold, doth he cry unto any, saying: Depart from me? Behold, I say unto you, Nay; but he saith: Come unto me all ye ends of the earth, buy milk and honey, without money and without price. Behold, hath he commanded any that they should depart out of the synagogues, or out of the houses of worship? Behold, I say unto you, Nay. Hath he commanded any that they should not partake of his salvation: Behold I say unto you, Nay; but he hath given it free for all men; and he hath*

2. 2 Nephi 29:7-11; Reorganized Edition, 2 Nephi 12:55-66.

commanded his people that they should persuade all men to repentance. Behold, hath the Lord commanded any that they should not partake of his goodness? Behold I say unto you, Nay; but all men are privileged, the one like unto the other, and none are forbidden.

"He commanded that there should be no priestcrafts; for, behold, priestcrafts are that men preach and set themselves up for a light unto the world, that they may get gain and praise of the world; but they seek not the welfare of Zion. Behold, the Lord hath forbidden this thing; wherefore, the Lord God hath given a commandment that all men should have charity, which charity is love. And except they should have charity they were nothing. Wherefore, if they have charity they would not suffer the laborer in Zion to perish. But the laborer in Zion shall labor for Zion; for if they labor for money they shall perish.

"And again, the Lord God hath commanded that men should not murder; that they should not lie; that they should not steal; that they should not take the name of the Lord their God in vain; that they should not envy; that they should not have malice; that they should not contend one with another; that they should not commit whoredoms; and that they should do none of these things; for whoso doeth them shall perish. For none of these iniquities come of **the Lord;** for he **doeth that which is good among the children of men;** and he doeth nothing save it be plain unto the children of men; **and he inviteth them all to come unto him, and partake of his goodness; and he denieth none that come unto him, black and white, bond and free, male and female; and he remembereth the heathen; and all are alike unto God, both Jew and Gentile."** [3]

These teachings are the foundation of all of the great religions, and all of the Holy Prophets have taught them. Nevertheless, after a season, their followers have drifted from these pure teachings and it is then necessary for God to send a new Messenger to renew the Divine Religion. These Manifestations of Holiness were chosen in the Great Plan of God before men came even to exist as mortal beings on the earth. This fact is clearly shown by this revelation to one of such Holy Prophets:

"Now the Lord had shown unto me, Abraham, the intelligences that were organized before the world was; and among all these were many noble and great ones; and God saw these souls that they were good, and he stood in the midst of them, and he said: These I will make my

---

3. 2 Nephi 26:23-33; Reorganized Edition, 2 Nephi 11:95-115.

rulers; for he stood among those that were spirits, and he saw that they were good; and he said unto me: Abraham, thou art one of them; thou wast chosen before thou was born."[4]

The Lesser Prophets or Forerunners of Each New Dispensation

Prior to the appearance of each of the Founders of a new religion or dispensation, there must be a preparation. Since each of these Great Prophets appears after a long night of spiritual darkness, or spiritual apostasy from the teachings of the previous Manifestation, there must be someone sent before that Messenger comes. Mankind is called to repentance, to an awareness of the true teachings of the previous Ambassador of God, and to warn them of the judgment to come through the teachings of the new Prophet. The essence of the teachings of the new Prophet would be the same as those taught by the previous Messenger but they would be couched in more up-to-date language and in new laws and ordinances adapted to the needs of a new and advanced civilization. We thus read that in the Dispensation of Moses, Aaron and Miriam were chosen to prepare the way for the Founder of the religion of Judaism. In a later dispensation, John the Baptist among the Jews, and Samuel the Lamanite, among the Nephite-Lamanite peoples on this hemisphere, came to prepare the way for Jesus Christ and the ushering in of the Christian Dispensation.

These *"forerunners"* or *"heralds"* of a new era of Divine civilization did two things: first, they restored the purity of the ordinances and teachings of the dispensation in which they came, and second, they announced the glad tidings of the imminent return of the Spirit of God, or Holy Spirit, through another Divine Messenger.

What is Meant by the "Return" of a Previous Messenger of God?

The Head of each new dispensation likewise foretold the coming of His Successor. In order to make this coming of the New Prophet a judgment or selection process whereby each person would have to carefully analyze the Message of the next Manifestation, the statements concerning this return of the Spirit of God were given in spiritual language. The majority of followers of each of the Divine Messengers have tended to worship the Messenger rather than the Message of God which He brings to mankind. They also see their Prophet as the greatest, the *"only"* Son of God, the *"seal of the Prophets"* and usually the last to

---

4. Abraham 3:22-23.

bring God's revelation to man. They have misinterpreted their Prophet's promise of the return of the Holy Spirit through another Holy Messenger as a promise of His own literal return in the body.

Man has always made the mistake of worshipping the *"Lamp"* rather than the *"Light of God"* which comes through this Lamp. Surely today we need the new Light of God, the Spirit of Truth promised by Jesus, and the Servant of God referred to by Him, who will come in the name of the Father:

"Behold, my servant shall deal prudently; he shall be exalted and extolled and be very high. As many were astonished at thee—his visage was so marred, more than any man, and his form more than the sons of men—so shall he sprinkle many nations: the kings shall shut their mouths at him, for that which had not been told them shall they see; and that which they had not heard shall they consider. . . . For in that day, for my sake shall the Father work a work, which shall be a great and a marvelous work among them; and there shall be among them those who will not believe it, although a man shall declare it unto them. But behold, the life of my servant shall be in my hand; therefore they shall not hurt him, although he shall be marred because of them. Yet I will heal him, for I will show unto them that my wisdom is greater than the cunning of the devil. . .

"And then shall the work of the Father commence at that day, even when this gospel shall be preached among the remnant of this people. Verily I say unto you, at that day shall the work of the Father commence among all the dispersed of my people, yea, even the tribes which have been lost, which the Father hath led out of Jerusalem. . . . Yea, and then shall the work commence, with the Father, among all nations, in preparing the way whereby his people may be gathered home to the land of their inheritance."[5]

That man misinterprets the promise of his Prophets is especially true of the great dispensation which each of the Manifestations foretold would come at the end of the Adamic Cycle, sometimes referred to as the *"time of the end"*. Two Great Messengers were promised to usher in that Day of Days or Kingdom of God on Earth. Malachi and Joseph Smith spoke of these two Prophets as Elijah and the Lord.[6] Jesus spoke of the coming of the Spirit of Truth, or His own glorification through

---

5. 3 Nephi 20:43-45; 21:9-10, 26 and 28, Reorganized Edition, 3 Nephi 9:81-83; 95-97; 10:4-5, 7.
6. See Malachi 3:1-3; 4:5-6 and *D. & C.* 35:4; 77:14-15. Reorganized *D. & C.* 34:2

the coming of the Father.⁷ Gautama Buddha referred to the coming of the *"fifth"* Buddha who would unite all religions and be the Lord of all mankind. In the Old Testament there are many references to the coming of the Lord or the *"Glory of God"* through the *"Gate"* that *"looketh toward"* or *"cometh from the East"*.

The Two Great Prophets of the Day of God

When the angel Moroni appeared to Joseph Smith in 1823, as related in *Joseph Smith's Own Story*, he commenced quoting the prophecies of the Old Testament: *"He first quoted part of the third chapter of Malachi; and he quoted also the fourth or last chapter of the same prophecy. . . . In addition to these, he quoted the eleventh chapter of Isaiah, saying that it was about to be fulfilled. . . . He also quoted the second chapter of Joel, from the twenty-eighth verse to the last. He said that this was not yet fulfilled but was soon to be. And he further stated that the fulness of the Gentiles was soon to come in."*⁸

If we examine these prophecies separately we see that each relates to the *"time of the end"* or the *"latter days"* when two Holy Messengers of God would come in rapid succession, to establish justice and righteousness throughout the earth. Turning first to Malachi we read as follows:

"Behold, I will send my messenger, and he shall prepare the way before me: and the Lord, whom ye seek, shall suddenly come to his temple, even the messenger of the covenant, whom ye delight in: behold, he shall come, saith the Lord of hosts. But who may abide the day of his coming? and who shall stand when he appeareth? for he is like a refiner's fire, and like fullers' soap: And he shall sit as a refiner and purifier of silver: and he shall purify the sons of Levi, and purge them as gold and silver, that they may offer unto the Lord an offering in righteousness. Then shall the offering of Judah and Jerusalem be pleasant unto the Lord, as in days of old, and as in former years. . .

*"Behold, I will send you Elijah the prophet before the coming of the great and dreadful day of the Lord. And he shall turn the heart of the fathers to the children, and the heart of the children to their fathers, lest I come and smite the earth with a curse."*⁹

---

7. See John 16:12-15; 3 Nephi 16:7-20; 20:26-46; 21:3-10. Reorganized Edition 3 Nephi , 7:31-45; 9:64-85; 89-97.
8. Joseph Smith 2:36, 40, 41.
9. Malachi 3:1-4; 4:5-6.

Note that this prophecy, stated in two different ways by Malachi, speaks of the coming of the Lord and also of a Messenger to prepare the way before Him. The reference to the return of Elijah is not to be taken literally.[10] Malachi is here speaking of a Messenger who will come in the station of Elijah, that is as a forerunner to the *"great and dreadful day of the Lord"*, the day of judgment when men will be called upon to recognize the Lord by His life and works. This prophecy applied both to the day as confirmed by Christ, of the coming of Jesus and His forerunner, John the Baptist, and also to the coming of the Lord and Herald of the Millennial Dispensation, as confirmed by both Christ and Joseph Smith.[11]

The eleventh chapter of Isaiah likewise speaks of the coming of two Prophets in the last days, and reads in part as follows:

"And there shall come forth a rod out of the stem of Jesse, and a Branch shall grow out of his roots: And the spirit of the Lord shall rest upon him, the spirit of wisdom and understanding, the spirit of counsel and might, the spirit of knowledge and of the fear of the Lord; and he shall make him of quick understanding in the fear of the Lord: and he shall not judge after the sight of his eyes, neither reprove after the hearing of his ears: but with righteousness shall he judge the poor, and reprove with equity for the meek of the earth and he shall smite the earth with the rod of his mouth, and with the breath of his lips shall he slay the wicked. And righteousness shall be the girdle of his loins, and faithfulness the girdle of his reins.[12]

"The wolf also shall dwell with the lamb, and the leopard shall lie down with the kid; and the calf and the young lion and the fatling together; and a little child shall lead them. And the cow and the bear shall feed; their young ones shall lie down together; and the lion shall eat straw like the ox. And the suckling child shall play on the hole of the asp, and the weaned child shall put his hand on the cockatrices' den."[13]

Of course, this prophecy also is given in spiritual or figurative language. The prophet is not concerned to show that in the dispensation of these two Prophets the members of the animal kingdom will no longer

10. See Chapters 3, 16, 17, 18, and 21.
11. Matthew 17:10-13; 3 Nephi 25; Reorganized Edition 3 Nephi 11:22-27 D. & C. 35:3-4; Reorganized D. & C. 34:2a-b.
12. Doesn't this sound like a reference to the same Messenger spoken of by Jesus in John 16:7-15?
13. Isaiah 11:1-8.

prey upon one another. Rather the meaning is that the various nations, great and small, and the various races and peoples of the earth will all come to dwell in peace and harmony together. Isaiah concluded with this verse:

"*They shall not hurt nor destroy in all my holy mountain for the earth shall be full of the knowledge of the Lord, as the waters cover the sea.*"

The next three verses, plus verse 16, clearly show that the time when this prophecy shall be fulfilled is after the latter days of the Christian Dispensation, when the Lord shall gather His people, Israel, from among the nations of the earth:

"*And in that day there shall be a root of Jesse, which shall stand for an ensign of the people; to it shall the Gentiles seek: and his rest shall be glorious. And it shall come to pass in that day, that the Lord shall set his hand the second time to recover the remnant of his people, which shall be left, from Assyria, and from Egypt, and from Pathros, and from Cush, and from Elam, and from Shinar, and from Hamoth, and from the islands of the sea. And he shall set up an ensign for the nations, and shall assemble the outcasts of Israel, and gather together the dispersed of Judah from the four quarters of the earth. The envy also of Ephraim shall depart, and the adversaries of Judah shall be cut off: Ephraim shall not envy Judah, and Judah shall not vex Ephraim. . . .*

"*And there shall be a highway for the remnant of his people, which shall be left from Assyria; like as it was to Israel in the day that he came up out of the land of Egypt.*" [14]

Later in Joseph Smith's writings he explained who was meant by these three Holy Ones, concluding that the "*rod*" and "*root*" of Jesse are symbolic references to two Servants of God who will come to gather Israel and to establish the Kingdom of God in the last days:

"*Who is the* **Stem** *of Jesse spoken of in the 1st, 2nd, 3rd, 4th, and 5th verses of the 11th chapter of Isaiah? Verily thus saith the Lord: It is Christ.*

"*What is the* **rod** *spoken of in the first verse of the 11th chapter of Isaiah, that shall come of the Stem of Jesse? Behold, thus saith the Lord: It is a servant in the hands of Christ, who is partly a descendant of Jesse as well as of Ephraim, or of the house of Joseph, on whom there is laid much power.*

14. Isaiah 11:9-12, 16.

"What is the root of Jesse spoken of in the 10th verse of the 11th chapter? Behold, thus saith the Lord, it is a descendant of Jesse, as well as of Joseph, unto whom rightly belongs the priesthood, and the keys of the kingdom, for an ensign, and for the gathering of my people in the last days."[15]

The quotations from the book of Joel, given by Moroni, also refer to the last days when the Spirit of the Lord would be poured out upon the nations and when all those who sincerely seek the Messenger of God shall find deliverance: *"For in mount Zion and in Jerusalem shall be deliverance, as the Lord hath said, and in the remnant whom the Lord shall call."*[16]

In the New Testament, John the Revelator had spoken much of the latter days, when judgment would be brought upon the nations after which **"a new heaven and a new earth"** would be established and the **"Glory of God"** would come down from heaven. While the interpretation of most of this prophecy was sealed until the *"Spirit of Truth"* should come to reveal all truths, nevertheless, Joseph Smith was inspired to understand, again, that John had prophesied that the new dispensation would be ushered in not by one Holy Manifestation of God alone but by two. When asked: *"What is to be understood by the two witnesses, in the eleventh chapter of revelation?"*, Joseph Smith replied: **"They are two prophets that are to be raised up to the Jewish nation in the last days, at the time of the restoration,** *and to prophesy to the Jews after they are gathered and have built the city of Jerusalem in the land of their fathers."*[17]

There are several other scriptural references which speak of these twin Prophets who shall usher in the Kingdom of God. There are two names by which these Messengers are most frequently referred to, they are the *"Gate"* or *"Door"* to the Kingdom, and the *"King of Glory"* or *"Glory of God".* Such a reference is found in the Psalms of David as follows:

"Lift up your heads, O ye gates; and be ye lift up, ye everlasting doors; and the King of glory shall come in. Who is this King of glory? The Lord strong and mighty, the Lord mighty in battle.

"Lift up your heads, O ye gates; even lift them up, ye everlasting

---

15. *D. & C.* 113:1-6, Utah Edition.
16. See Joel 2:28-32.
17. *D. & C.* 77:15; Utah Edition.

doors; and the King of glory shall come in. Who is this King of glory? The Lord of hosts, he is the King of glory."18

In the pages of the *Book of Mormon* we have also seen many prophecies concerning the coming Kingly Way of God which was to follow shortly after the restoration of the Church of Christ of Latter-day Saints. Nevertheless, it was in mount Zion and in Jerusalem that the world was to find deliverance from its woes, and in the remnant whom the Lord would call from Assyria, with their Prophet, to establish Zion, the new Jerusalem in the land of Israel. 19

I once had asked: *"But where was I to find His revelation to the 'other tribes of the house of Israel' which He had led away, and where were His words to 'all nations of the earth'?"*20

---

18. Psalm 24:7-10.
19. See Micah 4:1-7; 17, 18; 7:12-16; Revelation 21:1-7.
20. See Introduction, page 41.

Chapter 2

THE PURPOSE OF THE RESTORATION OF THE GOSPEL OF JESUS CHRIST

Joseph Smith Came to Prepare the Way for These Two Prophets

It had been in 1820 that young Joseph Smith, then only a youth of fifteen years, had gone into the woods to pray. In answer to his sincere supplication to God he had received his first heavenly vision, in which he saw two Personages. The first, pointing to the other, had addressed him with these words: *"This is My beloved Son. Hear Him!"*

Joseph had sought the Lord in prayer to know which of all the contending sects of Christianity might be the right one, and which he should join. The Personage who then addressed him answered that he should join none of them, for they were all wrong and that their creeds were an abomination in His sight.

Three years passed before Joseph again sought from the Lord further insight as to his special mission. He had suffered much persecution during those three years as the result of having told his minister of this first vision experience. Feeling that he might have found disfavor with God, he again went before Him in earnest prayer.

On this occasion Joseph had his second great vision. A figure appeared to him in dazzling white, saying that he was a messenger sent from the presence of God, and that his name was Moroni, and that God had work for Joseph Smith to do. He said that his name would be known for good and evil among all nations, kindreds, and tongues. He further said that there was a book deposited, written upon Gold Plates, giving an account of the former inhabitants of this continent and the source from which they sprang. He also said that the fulness of the everlasting Gospel was contained in it, as delivered by the Savior to these ancient American inhabitants. It was from these Gold Plates that Joseph later translated the *Book of Mormon*.

After telling Joseph Smith these things Moroni began quoting the prophecies of the Old Testament concerning the last days of the Christian

The Latter-day Saint temple in Salt Lake City, Utah. Note the bronze figure of an angel on top of the highest spire, trumpeting the coming of the *"day of judgement"* after which the Kingdom of God will be set up on the earth. (See Revelation 14:6-7, 21:1-5, 22:1-7).

So Great A Cause . . . 55

The Baha'i Temple in Wilmette, Illinois, shown above, is one of six similar present day edifices, one being situated in each of the continents of the globe. The services in these temples are open to people of every race, nationality and religion and serve to demonstrate the oneness of God and of His revelation to all peoples, throughout all ages. (See 2 Nephi 29:7-14; Reorganized Edition 2 Nephi 12:55-74)

dispensation, saying that this dispensation was about to be rolled up and a new dispensation spread out in its stead.

Many visions and revelations followed this early vision and instruction from the angel Moroni. In these further inspired thoughts and visions from the Lord Jesus, Joseph Smith was clearly told that he and his counselors had been chosen to restore the pure teachings and priesthood of the original Gospel of Jesus Christ, and to [prepare...] the way for the Two High Prophets of the Day of God: *"Thou art blessed, for thou shalt do great things. Behold thou wast sent forth, even as John, to prepare the way before me, and before Elijah which should come, and thou knewest it not."* [1]

If we will remember that Joseph Smith came to prepare the way for two Manifestations of God who would usher in the Millennial Dispensation, and who would come to the land of Jerusalem at the time of the restoration of the Gospel of Jesus Christ in the west, then many of the problems concerning different places and different dates as to where and when the *"Lord"* or *"Son of Man"* should appear will become clear.

To Make a Clear Distinction Between the Station of Joseph Smith and That of the Two Great Prophets to Come After Him

Sometimes there is confusion among the followers of a lesser prophet or forerunner to a new dispensation. It seems difficult to understand the difference between the station of their prophet leader and that of the Manifestations of God for whom he is preparing the way. Even at times the lesser prophet or prophets become uncertain of their own station. **We read in the Old Testament the extraordinary fact that Miriam and Aaron spoke out against Moses, the Prophet Founder of the Mosaic Dispensation, whose coming they had foretold!**

"And Miriam and Aaron spoke against Moses because of the Ethiopian woman whom he had married: for he had married an Ethiopian woman. And they said, Hath the Lord indeed spoken only by Moses? hath he not spoken also by us? And the Lord heard it. . . .

"And the Lord came down in the pillar of the cloud, and stood in the door of the tabernacle, and called Aaron and Miriam and they both came forth. And he said, Hear now my words: If there be a prophet among you, I the Lord will make myself known unto him in a vision, and will speak unto him in a dream. My servant Moses is not so, who is

---

1. *D. & C.* 35:4; Reorganized *D. & C.* 34:2b.

faithful in all mine house. With him will I speak mouth to mouth, even apparently, and not in dark speeches; and the similitude of the Lord shall he behold: wherefore then were ye not afraid to speak against my servant Moses? And the anger of the Lord was kindled against them; and he departed." [2]

Nephi, who foresaw the coming forth of the restored Church of Jesus Christ prior to the coming of the Lord of the Millennial Dispensation, warned the saints against priding themselves on having already received the word of God and turning away from the further word of God to be brought by the Lord when He comes, and thus failing to recognize the Messengers for whom Joseph Smith was the harbinger:

"Wo unto them that turn aside the just for a thing of naught and revile against that which is good, and say that it is of no worth! For the day shall come that the Lord God will speedily visit the inhabitants of the earth; and in that day that they are fully ripe in iniquity they shall perish. . . . For behold, at that day shall he (Satan) rage in the hearts of the children of men, and stir them up to anger against that which is good.

"And others will he pacify and lull them away into carnal security, that they will say: All is well in Zion; yea, Zion prospereth, all is well— and thus the devil cheateth their souls, and leadeth them away carefully down to hell. . . . Therefore, wo be unto him that is at ease in Zion! Wo be unto him that crieth: All is well! Yea, wo be unto him that hearkeneth unto the precepts of men, and denieth the power of God, and the gift of the Holy Ghost!"

A "Choice Seer" to be Raised Up to the Gentiles

Joseph Smith's station as a seer or lesser prophet is clearly foretold in this prophecy quoted by Lehi in the *Book of Mormon* but attributed to Joseph, one of the twelve sons of Jacob of Israel:

"For Joseph truly testified, saying: A seer shall the Lord my God raise up, who shall be a choice seer unto the fruit of my loins. Yea, Joseph truly said: Thus saith the Lord unto me: **A choice seer will I raise up out of the fruit of thy loins;** *and he shall be esteemed highly among the fruit of thy loins. And unto him will I give commandment that* **he shall do a work for the fruit of thy loins, his brethren, which shall be of great worth unto them, even to the bringing of them to the**

---

2. Numbers 12:1-2, 5-9.

knowledge of the covenants which I have made with thy fathers. *And I will give unto him a commandment that he shall do none other work, save the work which I shall command him. And I will make him great in mine eyes; for he shall do my work.* . . .

"*And thus prophesied Joseph, saying: Behold,* that seer will the Lord bless. . . And his name shall be called after me; *and it shall be after the name of his father. And he shall be like unto me; for the thing, which the Lord shall bring forth by his hand, by the power of the Lord shall bring my people unto salvation.* . . .

"*And there shall rise up one mighty among them, who shall do much good, both in word and in deed, being an instrument in the hands of God, with exceeding faith, to work mighty wonders, and do that which is great in the sight of God, unto the* **bringing to pass much restoration unto the house of Israel, and unto the seed of thy brethren.**"[3]

The Kingdom of God is at Hand

The very great significance of the mission of Joseph Smith can be seen when we understand that it was his great privilege to declare to the nations of Christendom, as well as to the American Indian, the glad tidings of the imminent coming of the two Great Manifestations of God who were to usher in the Kingdom of God on earth, a Kingdom looked forward to by Christ and all of the prophets and Manifestations of former dispensations. He was, in addition, called upon to restore the truths of former dispensations in order that the Dispensation of the Fulness of Times might come in or be revealed in its fulness. Here are the words of this commission to Joseph Smith:

"*I will give you a quotation from one of the prophets, who had his eye fixed on the restoration of the priesthood, the glories to be revealed in the last days, and in an especial manner this most glorious of all subjects belonging to the everlasting gospel, namely, the baptism for the dead; for Malachi says, last chapter, the 5th and 6th verse; Behold, I will send you Elijah the prophet before the coming of the great and dreadful day of the Lord: And he shall turn the heart of the fathers to the children, and the heart of the children to their fathers, lest I come and smite the earth with a curse.* . . .

"*For it is necessary in the ushering in of* **the dispensation of the fulness of times, which dispensation is now beginning to usher in,** *that a*

---

3. 2 Nephi 3:6-8, 14-15, 24. Reorganized Edition, 2 Nephi 2:10-14, 25-30, 46-47

whole and complete and perfect union, and welding together of dispensations, and keys, and powers, and glories should take place, and be revealed from the days of Adam even to the present time. And not only this, but **those things which never have been revealed from the foundation of the world, but have been kept hid from the wise and prudent, shall be revealed** *unto babes and sucklings in this, the dispensation of the fulness of times."* [4]

Joseph Smith here appears to be referring partially to the Gospel of Jesus Christ which was restored through him, including the ancient order of priesthood and those principles and ordinances which had been revealed through the Holy Prophets from the days of Adam even down to his own time. Nevertheless, the first and last sentences of this quotation are the key ones! Remember, this revelation was given through the prophet's pen on September 6, 1842, eight years after the saints had been driven out of Missouri in consequence of their failure to live up to the principles of United Order, upon which Zion was to have been built, and just twenty-one months prior to Joseph Smith's martyrdom. It is the last revelation in point of time to appear in the 1843 edition of the *Doctrine and Covenants*, the last edition published during the lifetime of the prophet and the last to be approved by him. Certainly this **"choice seer"** was herein referring to a far greater revelation than his own which was soon to come to mankind and for which his own mission was but a precursor. In the next verse we get a clearer intimation as to the nature of this great event and whence this new revelation was to come:

"How beautiful upon the mountain are the feet of those that bring glad tidings of good things, and that say unto Zion: **Behold, thy God reigneth! As the dews of Carmel, so shall the knowledge of God descend upon them!"** [5] Is this not a clear indication that the famous holy Mount Carmel would hear the Messenger of God?

After going on to recount the glorious visions and revelations which had been received since the beginning of the coming forth of the restored Gospel of Jesus Christ, Joseph Smith then went on to urge the saints not to turn back, and not to glory in that which had already been received while denying the greater revelation of God which was soon to come:

"Brethren, shall we not go on in so great a cause? **Go forward and not backward.** *Courage, brethren; and on, on to the victory! Let your*

4. *D. & C.* 128:17, 18b; Reorganized *D. & C.* 110:17, 18d-e.
5. *Ibid.* Verse 19b.

hearts rejoice, and be exceedingly glad. Let the earth break forth into singing. Let the mountains shout for joy, and all ye valleys cry aloud; and all ye seas and dry lands tell the wonders of your eternal King!...*

"Behold, the great day of the Lord is at hand; *and who can abide the day of his coming, and who can stand when he appeareth?*[6]

At long last Malachi's prophecy concerning the coming of two Great Messengers of God to usher in God's Kingdom was about to be fulfilled. Joseph Smith had fulfilled his own great mission. He had prepared a people to be ready to receive the Lord and His Kingdom. Would they do so? The prophet concluded with these words of admonition:

"Let us, therefore, as a church and a people, and as Latter-day Saints, offer unto the Lord an offering in righteousness; and let us present in his holy temple, when it is finished, a book containing the records of our dead, which shall be worthy of all acceptation." [7]

A Comparison Between the Missions of John the Baptist and of Joseph Smith

This was the message of our beloved leader to us. It was not a call for us to remain fixed and immovable in the Gospel which had been revealed. It was rather a call to action, a call to **"go forward"** to even greater revelation. And for this cause was the fulness of the Gospel of Jesus Christ, sent forth unto the children of men; *"that they might have life and be made partakers of the glories which are to be revealed in the last days, as it was written by the prophets and apostles in days of old"*; and that they might be ready to receive the Kingdom of the Father.[8]

John the Baptist is not remembered because he restored the original purity of the teachings of Moses to the people of his day. Instead he is remembered as the divine harbinger of a new day of God. How remarkably similar were the missions of John the Baptist and of Joseph Smith! A few quotations telling of the lives and teachings of these two forerunners of a new dispensation will suffice to illustrate this point. Can you tell which quotations apply to John and which to Joseph Smith?

"Repent ye: for the kingdom of heaven is at hand. For this is he that was spoken of by the prophet Esaias, saying, The voice of one crying in the wilderness, Prepare ye the way of the Lord, make his paths straight."

---

6. Ibid. Verses 22a-b, 23a, 24a-b.
7. Ibid. Verse 24c.
8. See *D. & C.* 66:2; Reorganized *D. & C.* 66:1b. 3 Nephi 16; Reorganized Edition, 3 Nephi 7:24-45.

"Wherefore the voice of the Lord is unto the ends of the earth, that all that will hear may hear: Prepare ye, prepare ye for that which is to come, for the Lord is nigh; and the anger of the Lord is kindled, and his sword is bathed in heaven, and it shall fall upon the inhabitants of the earth."

"But when he saw many of the Pharisees and Saducees come to his baptism, he said unto them, O generation of vipers, who hath warned you to flee from the wrath to come? Bring forth therefore fruits meet for repentance: And think not to say within yourselves, We have Abraham for our father: for I say unto you, that God is able of these stones to raise up children unto Abraham. And now also the ax is laid unto the root of the trees; therefore every tree which bringeth not forth good fruit is hewn down, and cast into the fire."

"A great and marvelous work is about to come forth unto the children of men. Behold, I am God; give heed unto my word, which is quick and powerful, sharper than a two-edged sword, to the dividing asunder of both joints and marrow; therefore give heed unto my word. Behold, the field is white already to harvest; therefore, whoso desireth to reap, let him thrust in his sickle with his might, and reap while the day lasts, that he may treasure up for his soul everlasting salvation in the kingdom of God".

"Say nothing but repentance unto this generation; keep my commandments, and assist to bring forth my work, according to my commandments, and you shall be blessed."

"And I have sent forth the fulness of my gospel by the hand of my servant Joseph; and in weakness have I blessed him; and I have given unto him the keys of the mystery of those things which have been sealed, even things which were from the foundation of the world, and the things which shall come from this time until the time of my coming, If he abide in me, and if not, another will I plant in his stead."

"There cometh one mightier than I after me, the latchet of whose shoes I am not worthy to stoop down and unloose. I indeed have baptized you with water: but he shall baptize you with the Holy Ghost."

"Now, I say unto you, and what I say unto you, I say unto all the Twelve: Arise and gird up your loins, take up your cross, follow me, and feed my sheep. Exalt not yourselves; rebel not against my servant Joseph; for verily I say unto you, I am with him, and my hand shall be over him; and **the keys which I have given unto him,** and also to you-

ward, **shall not be taken from him till I come. Be faithful until I come, for I come quickly;** *and my reward is with me to recompense every man according as his work shall be.* **I am Alpha and Omega. Amen."** 12

Think! If the one was a forerunner of something that came very soon, why not the other? And was not the First who was foretold (Jesus) ignored and denied; indeed was not the power of His Cause hidden for many years from the eyes of men? And, again, cannot history repeat itself today, and men once more be tested as in the tragic time of Jesus, and be found wanting?

---

12. These quotations in order are from the following scriptures: Matthew 3:2-3; *D. & C.* 1:11-13; Reorganized *D. & C.* 1:3a-b; Matthew 3:7-10; *D. & C.* 6:1-3, 9; Reorganized *D. & C.* 6:1-2a, 4b; *D. & C.* 35: 17-18; Reorganized *D. & C.* 34:4e-f; Mark 1:7-8; *D. & C.* 112:14-15, 34; Reorganized *D. & C.* 105:6a-b, 13b.

Chapter 3

WHY DO YE SPEAK UNTO THEM IN PARABLES?

By Their Fruits Ye Shall Know Them

John the Baptist held the keys of the Mosaic Dispensation, and of revelation, until the declaration of the Voice of God at the river Jordan that Jesus was the Christ, the long expected Messiah for whom John had prepared the way. However, neither John nor any of the disciples of Jesus were told exactly who was to be this Messiah. The glorious gospel principle of free agency makes it mandatory that we each investigate truth for ourself, and search out the new Prophet of God for our dispensation or time unaided by direct knowledge or miraculous signs. So it was in Jesus' day, and so it is in ours, as attested to by Christ:

"The Pharisees and also the Saducees came, and tempting desired him that he would show them a sign from heaven. He answered and said unto them, When it is evening, ye say, It will be fair weather: for the sky is red. And in the morning, It will be foul weather today; for the sky is red and lowering. O ye hypocrites, ye can discern the face of the sky; but can ye not discern the signs of the times?

"A wicked and adulterous generation seeketh after a sign; and there shall no sign be given unto it, but the sign of the prophet Jonas. And he left them and departed."[1]

If we turn to the story of Jonah (spelled Jonas in Greek) we see that the sign Jesus referred to was the repentance of the Ninevites as a consequence of the teachings of Jonah. What a striking contrast there is between this attitude and the stubborn obstinacy and blindness of spirit of His own generation! The significance of the answer of Jesus to His contemporaries is that His prophetic words of wisdom are the real proof and guarantee of His divine mission. If men fail to appreciate and respond to that great message, no other sign will be given.

This same warning was given through a revelation to Joseph Smith for the saints of the latter days of the Christian Dispensation:

---

1. Matthew 16:1-4.

"Hearken, O ye people, and open your hearts and give ear from afar; and listen, you that call yourselves the people of the Lord, and hear the word of the Lord and his will concerning you. . . . Behold, I, the Lord, utter my voice, and it shall be obeyed.....

"And he that seeketh signs shall see signs, but not unto salvation. Verily, I say unto you, there are those among you who seek signs, and there have been such even from the beginning; but, **behold, faith cometh not by signs, but signs follow those that believe. Yea, signs come by faith, not by the will of men, nor as they please, but by the will of God.** Yea, signs come by faith unto mighty works. . . . .²

Even as in the days of Jesus we must judge the truths of the claims of a Manifestation of God by the fruits of His life and teachings:

"Now when John had heard in the prison the works of Christ, he sent two of his disciples, and said unto him, Art thou he that should come, or do we look for another?

"Jesus answered and said unto them, Go and show John again those things which you do hear and see: The blind receive their sight, and the lame walk, the lepers are cleansed, and the deaf hear, the dead are raised up, and the poor have the gospel preached to them. And blessed is he, whosoever shall not be offended in me."³

An Explanation of the "Return" of Elijah and of Jesus Christ

If John was not told directly the person of Him for whom he was preparing the way, should we expect that we should be told the person of the two Prophets of the Millennial Dispensation for whom Joseph Smith was preparing the way? Malachi made reference to the *"return"* of Elijah before the coming of the Lord, both in the dispensation of Jesus Christ and that of the Fulness of Times. The Jews in Christ's day accused him of being a false prophet and asked, if he were indeed the Messiah, then where was Elijah whom Malachi had said must first come:

"And his disciples asked him, saying, Why then say the scribes that Elias (Greek for Elijah) must first come? And Jesus answered and said unto them Elias truly shall first come, and restore all things. But I say unto you, That Elias is come already, and they knew him not, but have done unto him whatsoever they listed. Likewise shall also the Son of

2. *D. & C.* 63:1-12; Reorganized *D. & C.* 63: 1-4a.
3. Matthew 11:2-6.

man suffer of them. Then the disciples understood that he spake unto them of John the Baptist". [4]

Luke, another of the Gospel writers, understood this clearly and explained the *"return"* of Elijah (or Elias) as the coming of another person in a similar station or with a similar mission to that of Elijah:

"But the angel said unto him, Fear not, Zacharias: for thy prayer is heard; and thy wife Elizabeth shall bear thee a son, and thou shalt call his name John. And thou shalt have joy and gladness; and many shall rejoice at his birth. For he shall be great in the sight of the Lord, and shall drink neither wine nor strong drink; and he shall be filled with the Holy Ghost, even from the mother's womb. And many of the children of Israel shall he turn to the Lord their God.

"And **he shall go before him in the spirit and power of Elias,** *to turn the hearts of the fathers to the children, and the disobedient to the wisdom of the just; to make ready a people prepared for the Lord."* [5]

Not only did the Jews at the time of Christ's coming expect the literal return of Elijah but many of them expected that the Messiah Himself would be a return of the prophet-king David, as foretold symbolically in certain Old Testament prophecies.[6] This is the reason that the multitude sought to crown Jesus,[7] why even some of His disciples could not understand why He did not proclaim Himself king of the Jews,[8] and why, when He failed to do so at the last, most of His followers deserted Him.[9]

As we have found in Chapter 1, each of the Great Prophets has spoken of the coming of the next Manifestation of God after Him. These references are sometimes given in clear unmistakable language. More often, however, they are given in symbolic language. Frequently the Messenger of God speaks of His *"return".*

Just as Moses spoke of the time when God would raise up another Prophet *"like unto me"*, Jesus sometimes spoke of His *"return"* in the Glory of the Father. Many Christians have taken Jesus' statement to mean the literal return of Jesus of Nazareth, as others have taken just as literally His assertion that *"I and the Father are one"* and *"If you have seen me you have seen the Father",* this in spite of the fact

---

4. Matthew 17-10-13.
5. Luke 1:13-17.
6. See for example Ezekial 34:22-24; 37:24-25 and Zechariah 12:6-10.
7. As told in John 6:14-15.
8. In Matthew 20:20-21.
9. Matthew 21:8-9; 27:11-12, 20-22, 28-31, 36-39.

that Jesus foretold that *"many shall come in my name, saying, I am Christ; and shall deceive many"* and then warned His true disciples to judge the new Prophet by the *"fruits"* of His life and teachings.[10] Each of the Great Prophets was referred to as the Son of God, and yet God sent a series of these Prophets, each to usher in a separate dispensation of Divine Religion.[11]

Why then should He now send Jesus Christ a second time to usher in another dispensation? Is it not the Word of God or Holy Spirit that is important and not the human temple through which this Word is brought to mankind? God is the same yesterday, today and forever, if in the past He was not limited to one Holy Messenger neither is He today so limited. In Jesus' own words we read, *"Why callest thou me good? there is none good but one, that is God, but if thou wilt enter into life, Keep the commandments"* and, *"For I have not spoken of myself; but the Father which sent me, he gave me a commandment, what I should say, and what I should speak. And I know that his commandment is life everlasting: whatsoever I speak therefore, even as the Father said unto me, so I speak"*.[12]

Jesus' reference to the Holy Prophet who would come to usher in the Dispensation of the Fulness of times seems equally clear. Nevertheless, just as the Jews failed to understand that both Muhammad and Christ fulfilled the foregoing prophecy of Moses so also have the Christians failed to comprehend Jesus' prophecy:

"I have many things to say unto you, but ye cannot bear them now. Howbeit when he, the Spirit of truth, is come, he will guide you into all truth: for he shall not speak of himself; but whatsoever he shall hear, that shall he speak: and he will show you things to come.

"He shall glorify me: for he shall receive of mine, and shall show it unto you. All things that the Father hath are mine: therefore said I, that he shall take of Mine, and shall show it unto you."[13]

"For the Son of man shall come in the glory of his Father with his angels; and then he shall reward every man according to his works."[14]

The interpretation of these spiritual symbols in a strictly literal sense has always been a stumbling block to those who were not yet ready to

---

10. See Matthew 7:13-20; 24:4-5, 23-24; Also *D. & C.* 45:26-30. Reorganized *D. & C.* 45:4a-d and Joseph Smith 1:5-6, 21-27.
11. See Chapter 9.
12. Matthew 19:17 and John 12:49-50.
13. John 16:12-15.
14. Matthew 16:27.

receive new revelation from God. Literally hundreds of separate denominations have grown up, each claiming to have the correct interpretation of abstruse passages of holy scripture while denying the power of God to give the correct interpretation through a new Manifestation. Jesus' disciples once asked Him:

"*Why speakest thou unto them in parables? He answered and said unto them, because it is given unto you to know the mysteries of the kingdom of heaven, but to them it is not given. For whosoever hath, to him shall be given, and he shall have more abundance; but whosoever hath not, from him shall be taken away even that he hath. Therefore speak I to them in parables: because they seeing see not; and hearing they hear not, neither do they understand. . . . For this people's heart is waxed gross, and their ears are dull of hearing, and their eyes they have closed; lest at any time they should see with their eyes, and hear with their ears, and should understand with their heart, and should be converted, and I should heal them.*"[15] Is it not possible for eyes to be blind and ears deaf today in the same way after the Great Ones of God had come? Theirs must be a spiritual and not a spectacular return, as a test for men to grow in insight and love.

For those who would preceive the inner spiritual meaning of his teachings Jesus said: "**The kingdom of God cometh not with observation: neither shall they say, Lo here! or, lo there! for, behold, the kingdom of God is within you.**"[16] Even this prophecy has been misinterpreted by some of the literalists. Certainly one cannot read the twenty-fourth and twenty-fifth chapters of Saint Matthew and still believe that the Savior did not believe in an actual physical Kingdom of God on earth, or perhaps we should say, a Kingly way of God on earth, a time when His will would be done on earth as it is in heaven. Perhaps it is becuase some of the churches have overemphasized the concept that the new Manifestation of God would be a "*King*", in the grossly literal sense, with all of the material pomp and spendor of the greatest monarchs of old, that others have looked to the foregoing passage in a mistaken, literal way.

15. Matthew 13:10-13, 15. Jesus speaks here of healing those who are spiritually blind, those who are spiritually deaf and those who are spiritually dead. Doesn't it seem possible that many of the so-called *"healing miracles"* were actually accounts of Christ's healing of the spiritually sick, for is not the sickness of the soul of far greater significance than the infirmities of the physical body?
16. Luke 17:20-21.

But in the light of all of Jesus' teachings, we can see that Christ was telling His disciples, including those who today read His message, that those who truly seek the new Prophet of God and desire to enter His new world order must first search their own hearts. God is the same yesterday, today and forever. Even so the new Manifestation of God will in essence be one with Abraham, Moses and Christ. He will be a servant of mankind: a humble, pure and righteous being, whose very word and deed manifests the attributes and will of the Father.

Seek Ye Diligently

Jesus has told us clearly how to recognize the new Lord and His Kingdom:

"Ask, and it shall be given you; seek, and ye shall find; knock, and it shall be opened unto you: For every one that asketh receiveth; and he that seeketh findeth; and to him that knocketh it shall be opened....... Therefore all things whatsoever ye would that men should do to you, do ye even so to them: for this is the law and the prophets.

"Beware of false prophets, which come to you in sheep's clothing, but inwardly they are ravening wolves. Ye shall know them by their fruits. Do men gather grapes of thorns, or figs of thistles? Even so every good tree bringeth forth good fruit; but a corrupt tree bringeth forth evil fruit. A good tree cannot bring forth evil fruit, neither can a corrupt tree bring forth good fruit. . .Wherefore by their fruits ye shall know them."[17]

Why should Jesus have told us how to discern a true prophet from a false one unless both true and false prophets were coming after him? We have seen many figures arise with plans for a new world order, but always these *"demi-gods"* or false prophets have eventually taught the superiority of one race, nation or class over all others. Instead of bringing peace they have perpetuated the glory of revolution, tyranny and bloodshed. Surely when the true Prophet came He would teach the oneness of all mankind, justice and equality for every race, nation and people, the oneness of God and of His Prophets, and the oneness of truth.

Why should Christ have told us to "seek" the true Prophet of God?? If the same Jesus of Nazareth were going to appear suddenly in the sky with great glory, there would be no need to **"seek"** because everyone

---

17. Matthew 7:7-8,12,13-18,20.

would see him at the same time and no amount of seeking or preparation would do any good. It is obvious that Jesus' reference to the coming of the Lord in the clouds of heaven had a symbolic meaning. This meaning can be understood more fully if we look at the references in Daniel 7, verse 13 and in Revelation 1, verse 7, in which the Son of Man is said to come *"with clouds"*. We know that clouds are a visible mass of fog or haze suspended at a height in the air and which often obscures the light of the sun. Joseph Smith spoke frequently of the *"clouds"* or *"veils of darkness"* which must first be *"rent"* before the saints would *"see"* the Lord. [18]

The Lord Will Be Called by a New Name

One of the *"veils"* or *"clouds"* which has already intervened between the minds of men and the recognition of the two Prophets of the Day of God is the expectation of the return of Jesus Christ bearing His own name, Christ. Jesus warned us against making this mistake: *"Take heed that no man deceive you; for many shall come in my name, saying—I am Christ—and shall deceive many"*. [19] For he knew that the Promised One of the latter days would not bear that holy name. It would be the same Word of God which Jesus brought, the same Divine Reality, but another human temple and another name, just as Isaiah had foretold.

"The Spirit of the Lord God is upon me; because the Lord hath appointed me to preach good tidings unto the meek; he hath sent me to bind up the broken-hearted, to proclaim liberty to the captives, and the opening of the prison to them that are bound; to proclaim the acceptable year of the Lord. For Zion's sake will I not hold my peace, and for Jerusalem's sake I will not rest, until the righteousness, thereof go forth as brightness, and the salvation thereof as the lamp that burneth.

"And the Gentiles shall see thy righteousness, and all kings thy glory: and thou shalt be called by a new name, which the mouth of the Lord shall name." [20]

And in the last book of the New Testament: *"Behold, I come quickly: hold that fast which thou hast, that no man take thy crown. Him that overcometh will I make a pillar in the temple of my God; and he shall go no more out: and I will write upon him the name of my God, and the name of the city of my God, which is New Jerusalem, which cometh down out of heaven from my God: and I will write upon him my new name."* [21]

18. See *D. & C.* 34:7; 38:7-8; 45:7-10; 50:46; Reorganized *D. & C.* 33:1e; 38:2; 45:2a-e; 50:8g.
19. Joseph Smith 1:5-6; also Matthew 24:4-5, 23-24.
20. Isaiah 61:1-2; 62:1-2.
21. Revelation 3:11-12.

Chapter 4

THE EXPECTED RETURN OF THE LORD IN 1844

"One Mighty and Strong" to Arise in the Year of Joseph Smith's Martyrdom, 1844

When one reads the Gospels carefully it becomes apparent that neither John the Baptist and his disciples, nor any of the disciples of Jesus, ever really understood that He was the long-expected Messiah, at least until after His crucifixion. And yet there was a sense of awareness among all of the Jews at the time of Christ's ministry that the time of the Messiah's advent was near at hand. Everyone seemed to agree that the Lord, when he came, would appear in Israel, though there is no hint that anyone ever expected that He would come out of the insignificant village of Nazareth. The fact that even His disciples deserted Him at the end, one of them going so far as to betray Him to His enemies, serves to show how veiled were their minds to the station of this **"Prophet like unto Moses".**

Did Joseph Smith understand who the two Prophets were for whom he said he was preparing the way? Was he given any intimation of the time or the place of the appearance of either of these Holy Messengers of God?

Actually there are several revelations in all three of the modern scriptures revealed through Joseph Smith telling both the times and the places of the appearance of each of these Manifestations. Nevertheless, the history of what happened to the Church following the martyrdom of the prophet clearly shows that, like their early Jewish predecessors, the Latter-day Saints did not perceive the **"signs of the times".**

Generally, a forerunner to a new Great Prophet actually comes during the early life of the One for whom he is preparing the way. Observe for instance the cases of Miriam and Aaron, the lesser prophets who prepared the way for Moses; John the Baptist and Samuel the Lamanite, who announced to the east and to the west the glad tidings of the coming of Jesus Christ. Was the promised Successor to Joseph Smith actually living during the time of his ministry? Study this prophecy in your mind, a prophecy given through Joseph's pen on January 2, 1831:

"*But, behold verily, verily, I say unto you, that mine eyes are upon you.* I am in your midst and ye cannot see me; but the day soon cometh that ye shall see me, and know that I am; for the veil of darkness shall soon be rent, and he that is not purified shall not abide the day. Wherefore, gird up your lions and be prepared. . . .

"But, verily I say unto you that in time ye shall have no king nor ruler, for I will be your king and watch over you. Wherefore, hear my voice and follow me, and you shall be a free people, and ye shall have no laws but my laws when I come, for I am your lawgiver, and what can stay my hand?"[1]

In May of that same year the Saints were again told:

"Behold, ye are little children and ye cannot bear all things now; ye must grow in grace and in the knowledge of the truth. *Wherefore, I am in your midst, I am the good shepherd, and the stone of Israel. He that buildeth upon this rock shall never fall.* And the day cometh that you shall hear my voice and see me, and know that I am. *Watch, therefore, that ye may be ready. Even so. Amen.*"[2]

Remember that Jesus had lived among the Jews for thirty years before He declared to anyone that He was the Messiah. He did not even disclose His identity to John the Baptist but told him to judge by the things which he heard and saw: the fruit of His teachings.

The *Doctrine and Covenants* contains a series of revelations which tell us that Joseph Smith was given the *"keys"* of *"revelation and commandment"* or of the *"mysteries of the kingdom"* until the coming of the Lord.[3] Still other revelations were directed to the leaders and members of the Church, telling them not to rebel against Joseph since he alone would hold the *"keys"* to receive *"commandments and revelations"* in the Church until the coming of the Lord, if he remained faithful.[4] Perhaps the clearest prophecy of the martyrdom of Joseph Smith and the beginning of the ministry of his Successor is found in the eighty-fifth section of the *Doctrine and Covenants:*

"*Yea, thus saith the still small voice, which whispereth through and*

---

1. *D. & C.* 38:7-9, 21-22; Reorganized *D. & C.* 38:2a-b, 5a-b.
2. *D. & C.* 50:40, 44-46; Reorganized *D. & C.* 50:8d, f-g.
3. See *D. & C.* 28:7; 90:1-3; 112:14-15, 34; Reorganized *D. & C.* 27:2a; 87:1-2a; 105:6, 13b.
4. See *D. & C.* 28:2, 7; 35:3-4, 17-18; 43:1-3; 115:19; 132:7; Reorganized *D. & C.* 27:2d; 34:2a-b, 4e-f; 43:1.

pierceth all things, and often times it maketh my bones to quake while it maketh manifest, saying: And it shall come to pass that I, the Lord God, will send one mighty and strong, holding the scepter of power in his hand, clothed with light for a covering, whose mouth shall utter words, eternal words; while his bowels shall be a fountain of truth, to set in order the house of God, *and to arrange by lot the inheritances of the saints whose names are found, and the names of their fathers, and of their children, enrolled in the book of the law of God:*

"While that man, who was called of God and appointed, *that putteth forth his hand to steady the ark of God,* shall fall by the shaft of death, *like as a tree that is smitten* by the vivid shaft of lightning." [5]

Surely no dispensation was given clearer signs of the time of the coming of a Manifestation of God! Joseph Smith fell *"by the shaft of death"* on June 27, 1844. He had been imprisoned on false charges and, while the prison guards turned their backs an armed mob attacked the jail where he and other leaders of the Church were confined. Joseph Smith attempted to leap from the window, and was shot in the attempt.[6]

Why did the Saints not go out in search of the Promised One foretold in their beloved leader's prophecies? Why did they not search their scriptures diligently in order to know where the Lord was to be found? Instead, just as Christ's disciples had fled at the time of the crucifixion of their Lord, so did the followers of the prophet Joseph look to the protection of their own lives. Their enemies now swooped down upon them, pillaging their homes and driving them out into the wilderness. As they huddled together in their crude temporary shelters against the bitter cold of a Missouri winter, the inspired word of the Lord came to them through the president of the Quorum of Twelve Apostles, Brigham Young, as follows:

"Therefore, marvel not at these things, for **ye are not yet pure; ye can not yet bear my glory; but ye shall behold it if ye are faithful in keeping all my words that I have gvien you,** *from the days of Adam to Abraham, from Abraham to Moses, from Moses to Jesus and his apostles, and from Jesus and his apostles to Joseph Smith, whom I did call upon by mine angels, mine ministering servants, and by mine own voice out of the heavens, to bring forth my work; which foundation he did lay, and was faithful; and I took him to myself."*[7]

5. *D. & C.* 85:6-8, Utah Edition.
6. *D. & C.* 135:1; Reorganized *D. & C.* 113:1.
7. *D. & C.* 136:37-38; Utah Edition.

The Great Adventist Movement of 1843 to 1845

Not only was this a period of great trouble and extreme desolation for the Latter-day Saints but it was a time of spiritual darkness and commotion for hundreds of thousands of sincere Christians all over the world. During the same years that Joseph Smith was gathering his followers to Zion, another religious movement was sweeping over Europe and America, and even to other continents as well.

Alonzo L. Baker gives the following account of the origin of the religion now known as the Seventh-day Adventists:

"Seventh-day Adventists had their genesis in a time of great religious ferment and spiritual quickening. The third and fourth decades of the last century witnessed a mighty awakening among the evangelical churches on both sides of the Atlantic. Everywhere men and women turned to their Bibles as never before since the days of the Reformation of the sixteenth century. New Light sprang from the pages of Holy Scripture, and everywhere Christians seemed to get a fresh glimpse of God and the truths of the gospel. Spontaneous it seemed, but, of course, **owing to the influence of the Spirit of God, men went to their knees in renewed consecration to Heaven and in seeking after things divine.** The movement began in the Baptist, Methodist, Congregational, and Christian (Disciple) churches in New England; then it spread to other denominations all over the United States, and then across the sea to England and to Europe.

"The impulse for this renaissance in the world of religion was a profound belief in the imminent return of Jesus Christ in the clouds of heaven. Although the New Testament had for eighteen centuries prophesied that transcendent event and clearly foretold the signs that would presage the second advent, yet men had neglected a study of the prophetic portions of the Bible, and hence had overlooked this cardinal doctrine. But **early in the nineteenth century, Bible students in various parts of the world, unknown one to another, began to voice the conviction that Holy Writ predicted the (direct) coming of Christ. They declared that on the dial of God's great prophetic clock events of most extraordinary nature were due.**

"This mighty interest in the truth of the second coming of Christ was not confined to a corner, neither was it the fruitage of little-educated or fanatic minds. The movement held the center of the stage in the religious world, and men of the highest learning and most devout experience espoused the cause. In England, Edward Irving, a gifted London preacher, was the leading light in the exposition of prophecies relating to the second advent. By his side stood Henry Drummond, a member of Parliament; Rev. Hugh McNiel; Rev. James Haldane, Steward of the Established Church; Hatley Frere; George Muller, the great philanthropist and founder of the Bristol Orphanage; and others. In Scotland, Horatius Bonar and Alexander Keith, ministers of the Free Church, proclaimed in no uncertain tones that Christ was coming soon. In Holland, Hentzepeter, the curator of the Royal Museum at the Hague, published pamphlets on the prophecies and the second advent. In Bavaria, a devout Roman Catholic priest, Johann Georg Lutz, came to believe in the message of Christ's return. Three German scholars, Hengstenberg, Tholuck and Lange, all became able advocates of that doctrine. In South America, Lacunan, a Jesuit Priest of Chile, became one of the most forceful expounders of eschatological prophecies. The note was taken up in faraway Australia by Thomas Playford, a layman of Adelaide. In Europe, Joseph Wolff, son of a Jewish rabbi, and a famed traveler and orientalist, became a fervent believer in Christ's coming, and spread the message in many lands, especially to Moslems."[8]

In the Moslem world, a similar movement to that of the Adventists among the Christians, was led by two men whom their followers believed to be lesser prophets or seers. These two men, contemporaries of Joseph Smith in the West, were similarly preparing the way for two Messengers of God, foretold in the Koran and in later Moslem tradition. Shaykh Ahmad and his successor Siyyid Kázim each in turn proclaimed that when these twin Manifestations should arise this would mark the beginning of a new religious dispensation, one unrivaled by any of the dispensations of the past. While the second of these two prophets set the year of the announcement of this new era as 1844, this was unknown in the West among the Christian Adventists.[9]

Aside from Joseph Smith, Shaykh Ahmad and Siyyid Kázim, all of whom appear to have received direct divine guidance, none of the important figures proclaiming the imminent coming of the Lord, dared to set an exact date, although most of them said that the great event would take place sometime between the years 1843 and 1847, that is with one

8. Baker, *Belief and Work of Seventh-day Adventists,* Pacific Publishing Association, Mountain View, California 1942, pp. 8-11.
9. For a fascinating account of this great religious movement within the Moslem Faith see, *The Dawn Breakers,* written by Nabil-i-Azam, during the years 1887-1888, translated from the original Persian and edited by Shoghi Effendi, Baha'i Publishing Trust, New York, 1953.

So Great A Cause . . . 75

important exception. William Miller, an earnest New England farmer of Baptist background, did just that. Because of his precise dating of the time of the *"second advent"*, Miller became the recognized leader of the Adventist movement. Quoting again from Baker's account of this fascinating movement of the last century we read:

"*He (William Miller) was joined by Joshua V. Himes, a minister of the Christian (Disciple) church in Boston; Josiah Litch, Methodist minister of Philadelphia; Henry Dana Ward, a prominent minister of New York; Charles Fitch, pastor of the Marlboro Street chapel, Boston; Joseph Bates, a retired Massachusetts sea captain; and others. These men held conferences at which the advent doctrine was preached with conviction and power; they itinerated among the churches, drawing immense crowds and creating a profound impression: they published tracts, pamphlets, and periodicals, which were eagerly read by multiplied thousands.*

"*All these men the world around based their belief in Christ's coming on such prophecies as Matthew 24,25; Revelation 12, 13; Daniel 2, 7; 8:14. From this latter prophecy*—'**Unto two thousand and three hundred days; then shall the sanctuary be cleansed**'—*William Miller and his colleagues drew the unwarranted (sic) conclusion that the* '**sanctuary**' *to be cleansed was this earth, and that the text referred to its renovation at Christ's second advent. They established the time of this* '**cleansing**' *in the autumn of 1844. (1844, using Daniel's calendar and his same reference point for the* **first coming***, was 2300 years after an important Persian decree in 456 B.C.).*

"*That date came and went, but* **Christ did not appear as had been predicted.** *Tens of thousands who had believed in their preachings and who had stood on the heights of hope fell away into the slough of despond. Many became victims of spiritual discouragement and religious apathy.*"[10]

Dr. William W. Sweet, formerly of the University of Chicago, estimated that the number of Miller's followers may have been anywhere from fifty thousand to one million. Miller, he said, had first set the date of the *"second advent"* as March 21, 1843. His description of what followed this announcement is most interesting in the light of modern revelation:

"*Excitement grew as the time approached for the supposed end of the world. Great meetings were held in churches, tents, public buildings, and in the fields and groves, and finally when the year 1843*

10, Baker, op.cit, pp. 11-13.

dawned emotions of the believers were at white heat. In some instances insanity resulted, while under the stress of their emotions people fell to the floor and professed seeing visions and hearing heavenly voices. With the coming of the eventful year Miller thus addressed his followers: 'This year. . .O glorious year! the trump of jubilee will be blown, the exiled children will return, the pilgrims reach their home from earth and heaven the scattered remnants come and meet in the middle air, fathers before the flood, Noah and his sons—Abraham and his, the Jew and the Gentile,—This year! the long looked-for year of years! the best! it has come!'

"As March 21 dawned people in many places went out into the open fields or climbed to hilltops to await the coming of the Lord, but the day passed and nothing unusual occurred. Then Miller reminded his followers that he had never definitely fixed the exact day, but it might occur any time within the next year. The awful day was surely coming, and for another year the believers waited in nervous suspense. But the year passed and **March 21, 1844** came, but still things went along as usual. Miller was now almost prostrated with disappointment and dismay at the failure of his **careful calculations**. But some of his followers revised the figures and fixed another date, in the fall of the same year, for the coming of the Lord, and again there was excitement and preperation among the believers; stores were closed, homes were broken up, while the minds of the most credulous gave way, and even murders were committed under the excitement. Again the new day of prophecy dawned, October 22, 1844. Some people sought the graveyards as an appropriate place from which to ascend; others climbed to the housetops; some arrayed themselves in their best clothes, but it was all to no avail; **Christ did not appear in the clouds and the day passed**."[11]

I will Come on Thee as a Thief in the Night

Were all of these sincere Christians of the mid-nineteenth century wrong? Had they all entirely misinterpreted the prophecies of the Old and New Testaments concerning the time of the appearance of the Chosen Lord and the beginning of the Day of Judgement? This seems hardly possible, and even less so when we consider the agreement of these ancient prophecies with those of the three modern witnesses: Joseph Smith, Shayhk Ahmad and Siyyid Kazim. In Deuteronomy chapter 18, verse 22, Moses is reported as saying:

11. Sweet, *The Story of Religion in America,* Harper and Brothers, New York York and London, 1939, pp. 402-403.

"When a prophet speaketh in the name of the Lord, if the thing follow not, nor come to pass, that is the thing which the Lord hath not spoken, but the prophet hath spoken it presumptuously: thou shalt not be afraid of him."

There is still another possibility, these sincere Bible students, as well as the followers of Joseph Smith, had not sought widely enough nor studied the prophecies of their **scriptures deeply enough.** In the **Doctrine and Covenants** the Lord had revealed as follows:

"Draw near unto me and I will draw near unto you; seek me diligently and ye shall find me; ask, and ye shall receive; knock, and it shall be opened unto you. . . .Therefore, sanctify yourselves that your minds become single to God, and the days will come that you shall see him; for he will unveil his face unto you, and **it shall be in his own time, and in his own way, and according to his own will.** *. . . And as all have not faith, seek ye diligently and teach one another words of wisdom; yea,* **seek ye out of the best books words of wisdom;** *seek learning, even by study and also by faith."*[12]

Actually Joseph Smith had not only pointed out the self-same prophecies in Daniel and in the Gospel of Matthew as used by the adventist scholars (see Joseph Smith 1) but he also foretold the **"desolating sickness"** which would cover the earth as men failed to perceive the coming of the Lord **in the way that they had interpreted his coming.** This is Joseph Smith's revelation, also said by the Lord to have been originally given to Christ's disciples as He stood before them in the land of Jerusalem:

"And this I have told you concerning Jerusalem; and when that day shall come, shall a remnant be scattered among the nations; but they shall be gathered again; but they shall remain until the times of the Gentiles be fulfilled. And in that day shall be heard of wars and rumors of wars, and the whole earth shall be in commotion, and **men's hearts shall fail them, and they shall say that Christ delayeth his coming until the end of the earth. And the love of men shall wax cold, and iniquity shall abound.**

"And when the times of the Gentiles is come in, a light shall break forth among them that sit in darkness, and it shall be the fulness of my gospel; but they receive it not; for they perceive not the light, and they

---

12. *D. & C.* 88:63, 68, 118; Reorganized *D. & C.* 85:16b-e, 18b, 36a; see also 3 Nephi 23:1, 5; Reorganized Edition, 3 Nephi 10:26-27, 32.

turn their hearts from me because of the precepts of men. And in that generation shall the times of the Gentiles be fulfilled.

"And there shall be men standing in that generation, that shall not pass until they shall see an overflowing scourge; for a desolating sickness shall cover the land. But my disciples shall stand in holy places, and shall not be moved; but among the wicked, men shall lift up their voices and curse God and die."[14]

Has Christ indeed delayed His coming until the end of the earth? What is meant by the verse: "**And when the times of the Gentiles is come in, a light shall break forth among them that sit in darkness, and it shall be the fulness of the gospel; but they receive it not; for they perceive not the light**"?

Earlier in this section (Chapter 1, pages 48-49) we saw that when the angel Moroni appeared to Joseph Smith he told him that the prophecies of Malachi and of Isaiah, concerning the coming of the Lord and the Messenger who should prepare the way before him, were about to be fulfilled. He also said that the fulness of the Gentiles was soon to come in.[15] In numerous references from the *Doctrine and Covenants* and *Book of Mormon*, the Latter-day Saints are clearly referred to as Gentiles. One such reference is especially pertinent to gain a clearer understanding of the above prophecy from the *Doctrine and Covenants*. This passage, from the teachings of Jesus Christ to the ancient Americans, reads in part as follows:

"And blessed are the Gentiles, because of their belief in me, in and of the Holy Ghost, which witnesses unto them of me and of the Father. Behold, because of their belief in me, saith the Father, and because of the unbelief of you, O house of Israel, **in the latter day shall the truth come unto the Gentiles, that the fulness of these things shall be made known unto them.**

"And thus commandeth the Father that I should say unto you: At that day when **the Gentiles shall sin against my gospel, and shall be lifted up in the pride of their hearts above all nations, and above all the people of the whole earth,** *and shall be filled with all manner of lyings, and of deceits, and of mischiefs, and all manner of hypocrisy, and murders, and priestcrafts, and whoredoms, and of secret abominations; and*

---

14. *D. & C.* 45:24-32; Reorganized *D. & C.* 45:3f, 4a-e.
15. See Joseph Smith 2:36, 40, 41.

if they shall do all these things and shall reject the fulness of my gospel, behold, saith the Father, I will bring the fulness of my gospel from among them.

"*And then will I remember the covenant which I have made unto my people, O house of Israel, and I will bring my gospel unto them. And I will show unto thee, O house of Israel, that the Gentiles shall not have power over you; but* **I will remember my covenant unto you, O house of Israel, and ye shall come unto the knowledge of the fulness of my gospel.** *But if the Gentiles will repent and return unto me, saith the Father, behold they shall be numbered among my people, O house of Israel.*"[16]

This additional reference from the teachings of Christ concerning the last days makes it clear that the phrase **"times of the Gentiles"**, in the *Book of Mormon*, refers to the restoration of the Church of Jesus Christ among the Gentiles, or the American people. The reference to the "light" which shall "*break forth among them that sit in darkness*" appears to mean the revelation of God to mankind in the latter days, a portion of which was given to the Gentiles through Joseph Smith. (It could also partially apply to the adventist scholars, to the transcendentalists, to the Disciples of Christ, and to other enlightened groups who arose to purify the Christian church at the time of the Great Awakening.) It is also apparent that if the Latter-day Saints fail to recognize the fulness of that light, as it is given to all mankind, the fulness of the light which they have received will be taken from them. This is confirmed by another prophecy to be found in the *Book of Mormon*, referred to here only in part:

"**Wo be unto him that shall say: We have received the word of God, and we need no more of the word of God, for we have enough!** *For behold, thus saith the Lord God: I will give unto the children of men line upon line, precept upon precept, here a little and there a little; and blessed are those who hearken unto my precepts, and lend an ear unto my counsel, for they shall learn wisdom; for unto him that receiveth I will give more;* **and from them that shall say, We have enough, from them shall be taken away even that which they have.** *Cursed is he that putteth his trust in man, or maketh flesh his arm, or shall hearken unto the precepts of men, save their precepts shall be given by the power of the Holy Ghost.*"

16. 3 Nephi 16:6-7, 10-13; Reorganized Edition 7: 30-31, 34-38; See also 1 Nephi 22:7-9; Reorganized Edition, 7:15-20, 2 Nephi 30:3-5; Reorgznied Edition,12: 79-82; *D. & C.* 109:60-67, Utah Edition.

The next verse tells us clearly what was meant by Christ's warnings that the Gentiles would reject the *"light"* or *"fullness of the gospel"*, and also what is their promise if they repent of this sin and return unto God:

> "Woe be unto the Gentiles, saith the Lord God of Hosts! *For notwithstanding I shall lengthen out mine arm unto them from day to day,* **they will deny me;** *nevertheless, I will be merciful unto them, saith the Lord God, if they will repent and come unto me; for mine arm is lengthened out all the day long, saith the Lord God of Hosts".* [17]

The chapters following clarify the dual revelation of God in the last days, first through the restoration of the Gospel of Jesus Christ in America, and then through the coming of the *"Lord God"* to Israel, whence His word will roll forth to judge all people after which universal peace and the golden age of mankind will be established.[18]

Is it not likely that the full meaning of the reference to the *"light"* that **"shall break forth among them that sit in darkness, and it shall be the fulness of my gospel"**, is in fact a reference to the coming of the Lord? Has the Day of God actually begun in the year 1844 while Latter-day Saints and Adventists alike failed to perceive this great event? Remember that some two thousand years earlier the Messiah, foretold in the Jewish Torah, or the Old Testament, came to the Jews but they *"perceived Him not"* and denied the Son of God!

Concerning the second coming of the Son of Man in the Glory of the Father the apostle Peter warned us:

> *"But the day of the Lord will come as a thief in the night; in the which the heavens shall pass away with a great noise, and the elements shall melt with fervent heat, the earth also and the works that are therein shall be burnt up."*[19]

In the Revelation of Saint John there is a simplicity in another clear warning:

> *"Remember therefore how thou hast received and heard, and hold fast, and repent. If therefore thou shalt not watch, I will come on thee as a thief, and thou shalt not know what hour I will come upon thee."*[20]

---

17. 2 Nephi 28:21, 24-26, 29-32; Reorganized Edition; 2 Nephi 12:25, 30-31, 35-41.
18. 2 Nephi, Chapter 30; Reorganized Edition 2 Nephi 12:75-100.
19. II Peter 3:10.
20. Revelation 3:3.

Chapter 5

SIGNS OF THE TIMES

The Necessity of Earnest Search

The question returns: Are our times somehow different than those in the days of Jesus? Has the plan of God to allow man his free agency to investigate truth for himself been set aside so that we will now be shown without question who the Son of Man is? Are we now actually supposed to expect the literal return of Elijah, after which Jesus Christ will come down from heaven seated upon a cloud, with all the angels trumpeting His coming? If we are to believe this then why did Jesus need to urge us to use our strong reasoning concerning the signs of the second coming?

"Hearken, O ye people of my church, and ye elders listen together, and hear my voice while it is called today, and harden not your hearts; for verily I say unto you that I am Alpha and Omega, the beginning and the end, the light and the life of the world—a light that shineth in darkness and the darkness comprehendeth it not. I came unto mine own, and mine own received me not; but unto as many as received me gave I power to do many miracles, and to become the sons of God; and even unto them that believed on my name gave I power to obtain eternal life.

"And even so I have sent mine everlasting covenant into the world, to be a light to the world, and to be a standard for my people, and for the Gentiles to seek to it, and to be a messenger before my face to prepare the way before me. Wherefore, come ye into it, and **with him that cometh I will reason as with men in days of old, and I will show unto you my strong reasoning.** . . .

"Wherefore, hearken and I will reason with you, *and I will speak unto you and prophesy,* **as unto men in days of old. And I will show it plainly as I showed it unto my disciples as I stood before them in the flesh.** . .*I will show unto you how the day of redemption shall come, and also the restoration of the scattered Israel.*"[1]

---

1. *D. & C.* 45:6-10, 15-16a, 17b; Reorganized *D. & C.* 45:2a-c, i-j, l.

Why did Christ warn us against looking for visible signs just as He had earlier warned His disciples in Jerusalem?

"Wherefore, beware lest ye are deceived; and that ye may not be deceived seek ye earnestly the best gifts, always remembering for what they are given; for verily I say unto you, they are given for the benefit of those who love me and keep all my commandments, and him that seeketh so to do; that all may be benefited that seek or that ask of me, that ask not for a sign that they may consume it upon their lusts." [2]

Surely the adventists of the period 1843-1844 were looking for *"signs and wonders"*. They expected the self-same Jesus, who had lived in Israel some eighteen hundred years earlier, to descend from heaven on a cloud, with a multitude of angels blowing their trumpets to proclaim his coming.

Some True Signs to Look for to Discern the Second Coming

If we are not to look for such visible signs of the coming of the Lord, what are the signs we must watch for in order to recognize Him? This was the same question that Jesus' disciples asked Him when He stood before them in ancient Judea. (See Luke 21:17-31; Matthew 24:3-28.) The latter chapters of this book give a listing of nearly all of the prophecies concerning the signs of the coming of the Lord and the beginning of the Millennial Dispensation. In this chapter I will only summarize a few of these signs and perhaps thus present a key to the understanding of other prophecies contained in our holy scriptures.

We have already seen some of these signs. We have observed that before the actual coming of the Manifestation of God who will bring in the laws and principles which will transform this world into a *"new heaven and a new earth"*, another Great Prophet must come to prepare the way before Him. This Forerunner is to come *"in the spirit and power of Elias, to turn the hearts of the fathers to the children, and the disobedient to the wisdom of the just, to make ready a people prepared for the Lord."* [3] Joseph Smith and Sidney Rigdon were told that they were sent forth to prepare the way for both of the Divine Messengers. [4]

A second sign we have uncovered of the coming of the Lord is that He will not come bearing the name Jesus Christ. Nor are we to interpret the prophecies of the *"second coming"* in a strictly literal sense. Just as

2. *D. & C.* 46:8-9; Reorganized *D. & C.* 46:4.
3. Luke 1:17.
4. *D. & C.* 35:4, 13-18; Reorganized *D. & C.* 34:2, 4.

the Voice who is to prepare the way before Him will not be the literal return of Elijah, but another Holy Being who will come with a similar mission as that of Elijah, so will the second Prophet not be the literal return of Jesus of Nazareth. It will be the same Word of God, the same Spirit of Truth, but this divine power will be manifest through a new human tabernacle, and **in the full glory of the Father.**[5]

A third sign which Jesus gave us to look for in connection with the coming of the two new Messengers, was that we must judge whether or not they are true Prophets of God through their lives and teachings.[6] This is the same sign which He gave John who had sent his disciples to Jesus to ask whether or not He was the promised Messiah.[7] Surely then we must look for Persons with a Christ-like character and with a message for the world which would bear out Jesus' prophecy: **"Thy kingdom come. Thy will be done on earth, as it is in heaven"**,[8] in other words, we should look for Messengers of God who will bring in principles essentially the same as those which Jesus taught but adapted to the needs of a new age, an age marking the full maturity of mankind.[9]

The Light of the Morning Cometh Out of the East

There is still another sign which we have not yet mentioned, although some of you might have recognized it from what was said concerning the fulness of the gospel coming to the house of Israel. In the same revelation in which Jesus told His disciples that they should not look for someone bearing the name of Christ, He also gave this sign concerning the place of His coming:

"Behold, I have told you before; wherefore, if they say unto you: Behold, he is in the desert; go not forth; Behold, he is in the secret chambers; believe it not; for **as the light of the morning cometh out of the east, and shineth even unto the west, and covereth the whole earth, so shall the coming of the Son of Man be.**"[10]

He then went on to give a symbolic reference to the exact land to which the Son of Man would come:

"And now I show unto you a parable. Behold, wheresoever the

---

5. See John 16:12-15; Matthew 16:27; 24:4,5,23-24.
6. Matthew 7:13-20; see also Moroni 7:4-19.
7. Matthew 11:3-6.
8. Matthew 6:10.
9. See 2 Nephi 30:16-18; Reorganized Edition 12:96-100; *D. & C.* 128:18b, 24-22; Reorganized *D. & C.* 110: 18d-e, 22-24.
10. Joseph Smith 1:24-26; see also Matthew 24:25-27.

carcass is, there will the eagles be gathered together; so likewise shall mine elect be gathered from the four quarters of the earth."[11]

In another revelation, already cited, Jesus referred us to the prophecies of Isaiah and the other prophets concerning the gathering of Israel to the Holy Land of Israel in the last days where the Lord would dwell in their midst.[12]

When the angel Moroni appeared to Joseph Smith he cited some of the prophecies of Isaiah and other Old Testament prophets concerning the coming of the two Great Prophets in the last days to the land of Israel. Was either of these two Holy Persons the Lord of Hosts or Son of Man who was promised to come in the full glory of the Father to usher in the Millenial Kingdom? Let's look to another prophecy of Isaiah for an answer to this question. Remember that the Latter-day Saints had been told that *"when the times of the Gentiles is come in, a light shall break forth among them that sit in darkness, and it shall be the fulness of my gospel; but they receive it not; for they perceive not the light".*[13] They were even told that many among them had sinned a very grievous sin *"in that they are walking in darkness at noonday."* [14] Hear now the words of Isaiah concerning the people of Israel in the last days:

"The people that walked in darkness have seen a great light: they that dwelt in the land of the shadow of death, **upon them hath the light shined....** *For unto us a child is born, unto us a son is given: and the government shall be upon his shoulder: and his name shall be called Wonderful, Counselor, The mighty God, The everlasting Father, The Prince of Peace.*

"Of the increase of his government and peace there shall be no end, upon the throne of David, and his kingdom, to order it and to establish it with judgment and with justice from henceforth even forever. The zeal of the Lord of Hosts will perform this. **The Lord sent a word into Jacob, and it hath lighted upon Israel."** [15]

There can be little doubt that Isaiah was here speaking of the Manifestation of God who would come to Israel in the last days and there set up His kingdom, which kingdom would increase until it had filled

11. Joseph Smith 1:27; Matthew 24:28.
12. 3 Nephi 23:1-5; Reorganized Edition 10:26-32; Examples are to be found in such prophecies as Isaiah 35:1-2, 10; 40:1-11; 42:1-10; 49:1-23; 52:1-15; *D. & C.* 133:13, 21-26, 35; Reorganized *D. & C.* 108:4b, 5e-6a, 6f; etc.
13. *D. & C.* 45:28-29; Reorganized *D. & C.* 45:4b-c.
14. *D. & C.* 95:6; Reorganized *D. & C.* 92:1e.
15. Isaiah 9:2, 6-8.

the whole earth and would endure **"henceforth and forever"**. Zechariah said similarly concerning the coming of the Lord to Israel:

"Sing and rejoice, O daughter of Zion: for, lo, I come, and I will dwell in the midst of thee, saith the Lord. And many nations shall be joined to the Lord in that day, and shall be my people: and I will dwell in the midst of thee, and thou shalt know that the Lord of hosts hath sent me unto thee. And the Lord shall inherit Judah his portion in the holy land, and shall choose Jerusalem again."[16]

The Lord Sent a Word Unto Jacob and It Hath Lighted Upon Israel

In still other prophecies Isaiah is even more specific concerning the exact localities in Israel where this mighty Prophet should come to dwell:

"The wilderness and the solitary place shall be glad for thee; and the desert shall rejoice, and blossom as the rose. It shall blossom abundantly, and rejoice even with joy and singing: the glory of Lebanon shall be given unto it, the excellency of **Carmel and Sharon, they shall see the Glory of the Lord,** *and the excellency of our God. And* **Sharon shall be a fold of flocks, and the valley of Achor (Acca) a place for the herds to lie down in, for my people that have sought me."**[17] Acca, Sharon, and Carmel! Should we not search to see if one called *"The Glory of God"* came here?

The Children of Israel to Return to the Holy Land With Their Prophets

In section 45 of the *Doctrine and Covenants,* not only were the Saints told that the times of the Gentiles would be fulfilled if they failed to perceive the *"Light"* of God or the *"fulness of the gospel"*, but that the times of the Gentiles would be fulfilled **prior** to the gathering of a remnant of Israel to the land of Jerusalem: *"And this I have told you concerning Jerusalem; and when that day shall come,* **shall a remnant be scattered among all nations; but they shall be gathered again; but they shall remain until the times of the Gentiles be fulfilled".**[18]

This is another important clue concerning the time of the coming of the Glory of God. If the *"light"* of God refers to the Manifestation who was to come in the full glory of the Father, and if He was to come after the fulfillment of the *"times of the Gentiles"* but prior to the gathering of the Jews to Israel, then this second Great Prophet must

16. **Z**echariah 2:10-12
17. Isaiah 35:1-2; 65:10
18. Verses 24 and 25 in Utah Edition; verse 3f in Reorganized Edition.

have come sometime after 1844 but prior to the issuance of the Balfour Declaration in 1917, since it was in that declaration that the government of Great Britain declared that it viewed with favor *"the establishment in Palestine of a national home for the Jewish people".*[19] The return of the Jews to Israel following that declaration marks one of the most significant migrations of a people in the modern world. The rise of Hitlerism and the subsequent persecution of the Jews was one of the important contributing influences to this modern exodus.

Elam and Assyria (Modern Persia) to First See the New Day of God

The adventist scholars of the early 1800s appear to have expected the appearance of the Lord in the visible heavens, to be seen almost instantaneously by men around the world, but even if they had looked to Israel for this great event in the year 1844, they would not have seen the coming of the Son of Man. Jesus was standing in Israel when He told His disciples: **"For as the light of the morning cometh out of the east, and shineth even unto the west, and covereth the whole earth, so shall also the coming of the Son of Man be"**.[20] In other words, the earliest dawning of the new day of God was to be in a land to the east of Israel, after which it would shine *"even unto the west"* and eventually cover *"the whole earth"*.

Isaiah, who spoke of the coming of the Glory of God to northern Israel, also spoke of Him as gathering the tribes of Israel from Assyria, from Elam, from Shinar and from other nations, whithersoever the Lord had led them (see Isaiah 11:10-13; 51:17-20).

Finally, the *Book of Mormon* records Jesus' testimony that after He visited the Jews in the land of Israel and the Nephite-Lamanite peoples on this continent, He would then manifest His word *"unto the Gentiles"* and last of all unto the *"lost tribes of Israel."*[21] (As we have seen in an earlier chapter, the ten northern tribes of Israel were carried away captive into what was then Assyria and Media or what is now northern Persia.) Jesus then told these descendants of Israel in America that *"in the latter days shall the truth come unto the Gentiles"* until such day that *"the Gentiles shall sin against my gospel, and shall reject the fulness of my gospel, behold, saith the Father, I will bring the fulness of my gospel from among them, but I will remember my*

19. See Seymour Weinberg, *"The Lord is One"*, a pamphlet published by the National Spiritual Assembly of the Baha'i's of the United States, 1963.
20. Joseph Smith 1:26.
21. 3 Nephi 16:1-6; 17:2-4; Reorganized Edition, 3 Nephi 7:24-30; 8:2-4.

covenant unto you, O house of Israel, and ye shall come unto the knowledge of the fulness of my gospel." [22]

It was left for Joseph Smith to tell us that the two Major Prophets of the new day of God would first appear among the exiles of Israel and Judah in the lands to which they had been led into captivity, the northern ten tribes to Assyria and Media and the two remaining tribes, Judah and Benjamin, to Shinar and Elam.

In an amazing prediction in which Joseph Smith tells of the revelation of God in the last days first among the Gentiles in America and secondly among the Jews in the land of Jerusalem, he speaks also of the return of the ten tribes of Israel and the tribe of Judah, to the land of Israel with their **Prophets:**

"**Let them, therefore, who are among the Gentiles flee unto Zion. And let them who be of Judah flee unto Jerusalem, unto the mountains of the Lord's house....** *For behold, the Lord God hath sent the angel crying through the midst of heaven, saying: Prepare ye the way of the Lord, and make his paths straight, for the hour of his coming is nigh— when the Lamb shall stand upon Mount Zion, and with him a hundred and forty-four thousand,* **having his Father's name written on their foreheads.** *Wherefore, prepare ye for the coming of the Bridegroom; go ye, go ye out to meet him....* **And he shall utter his voice out of Zion, and he shall speak from Jerusalem,** *and his voice shall be heard among all people....* **And the Lord, even the Savior, shall stand in the midst of his people, and shall reign over all flesh.**

"**And they who are in the north countries** [23] **shall come in remembrance before the Lord: and their prophets shall hear his voice, and shall no longer stay themselves....** And *in the barren deserts there shall come forth* **pools of living water;** and *the parched ground shall no longer be a thirsty land.* **And they shall bring forth their rich treasures unto the children of Ephraim, my servants.... And they also of the tribe of Judah, after their pain shall be sanctified in holiness before the Lord, to dwell in his presence day and night, forever and ever.**" [24] (Please read

---

22. See 3 Nephi 16:7-13; Reorganized Edition, 7:31-38.
23. The ten tribes of Israel were taken northward and then eastward from Israel and planted in colonies in northern Assyria and Media. The Prophets of Israel thereafter always spoke of them as being carried into the lands of the north, and prophesied their return from the lands of the north in the last days. We should not read such prophecies in terms of our modern understanding of geography but in terms of the geography of the known world in the times of the Hebrew prophets.
24. *D. & C.* 133:12-13, 17-19, 21, 25-26, 29-30, 35; Reorganized *D. & C.* 108:4a-b, 5b-e, g, 6b-c, f.

the entire of section 133 in the *Doctrine and Covenants,* or the comparable revelation in section 108 of the Reorganized Church edition, and you will find many more clues concerning the coming of the two Great Prophets in the lands of the east after the restoration of the Gospel of of Jesus Christ in America. Remember to read with a spiritual eye that you might understand the real meaning and not merely the external literal interpretation.)

Chapter 6

THE GATE TO THE KINGDOM

I Will Set My Throne in Elam

Jesus said that we must search diligently and use our *"strong reasoning"* in order to recognize the true Prophets of God.[1] Had the adventist scholars and their followers searched the prophecies of holy scripture diligently and used their strong reasoning they would have found not only the date of the coming of the Son of Man (1844) but also the place of this earliest appearance. That same prophet, Daniel, who revealed this date as the time of the beginning of the mission of the first of the twin Manifestations of God who would come in the latter days, also said that these visions which he had of the last days took place in **Elam**, that province of southern Persia to which the Jews had been carried captive by the Babylonians. Daniel likewise spoke of a struggle between the princes of Persia and a *"great Prince"* among the Persians *"which standeth for the children of thy people:..."*[2]

Earlier in his writings Daniel had related how the great king Nebuchadnezzar of Babylonia had had a dream in which he saw a great image whose head was of fine gold, whose breast and arms were of silver, whose belly and thighs were of brass, whose legs were of iron and whose feet part iron and part clay. He then saw that a stone was cut out, without hands, which smote the image upon the feet and broke it into pieces: *"Then was the iron, the clay, the brass, the silver, and the gold, broken to pieces together, and became like the chaff of the summer threshing floors; and the wind carried them away: and the stone that smote the image became a great mountain, and filled the whole earth".*[3]

1. Matthew 6:33; 7:7-8; *D. & C.* 45:9-16; 88:118; Reorganized *D. & C.* 45:2d-k; 85:36a.
2. Daniel 12:1. Susa, called in the *Bible* Shushan, was the capital of the kingdom of Elam and later, of the great Persian Empire.
3. Daniel 2:31-36.

After all of the wise men had been summoned by the king and each had been unable to interpret the meaning of this dream, Nebuchadnezzar then called Daniel to him and asked him to interpret the meaning of this vision. In his inspired interpretation Daniel related how the great image represented a succession of ancient empires from that of Nebuchadnezzar (the head of gold) down to the times of today. Our own period is represented by the feet *"part of iron and part of clay"* symbolizing the many separate nations and races of our time, some of whom are strong and others weak, but just as iron and clay cannot mix, neither can these contending nations and peoples find unity until a new Teacher appears who will establish the principle of oneness of mankind and the unity of all races, nations and religions. This is the stone which will roll forth and break in pieces the nationalism, racism, sectarianism and materialism which characterises the world of the latter days. Daniel then concludes with this prophecy:

"And in the days of these kings shall the God of heaven set up a kingdom, which shall never be destroyed: and the kingdom shall not be left to other people, but it shall break in pieces and consume all these kingdoms, and it shall stand forever." [4]

Daniel gave us the key to undertand when this kingdom would first appear.[5] The promised year was 1844, the very year of the martyrdom of Joseph Smith,promised by him as the time of the appearance of *"One mighty and strong, holding the scepter of power in his hand, to set in order the house of God".* [6]

An even more direct reference to Elam as the place of the earliest beginning of God's kingdom of the last days is found in the forty-ninth chapter of Jeremiah, verse thirty-eight, which reads: *"And I will set my throne in Elam, and will destroy from thence the King and the princes, saith the Lord."*

One Mighty and Strong, Holding the Scepter of Power

What did happen in Elam in the year 1844? The reader will be interested in a beautifully written history of this period, entitled *The Dawn Breakers*, which contains a first hand account of the beginning of an important religious movement. It began in the city of Shiraz, in the ancient province of Elam. **The date was May 23, 1844.**

4. Daniel 2:44.
5. Also see chapter 16.
6. *D. & C.* 85:7, Utah edition.

A young man, just twenty-four years of age, declared that He was the Promised One foretold in all the holy books. He said that He was the *"Báb"*, which in Persian means *"door"* or *"gate"*, and declared that His teachings were the gateway into a new age of unity; one in which the world would be as one country and minkind its citizens, in which there would be one religion uniting the word of God through all the prophets. This was the cornerstone upon which the house of God could be built.

As Jesus first spoke to Peter, the fisherman, so the Báb spoke to Mullá Husayn, His first disciple. Mullá Husayn's own words can best describe the depth of that experience:

> *"I sat enraptured by the magic of His voice and the sweeping force of His revelation. At last I reluctantly arose from my seat and begged to depart. He (the Báb) smilingly bade me be seated and said, 'If you leave in such a state, whoever sees you will assuredly say; 'This poor youth has lost his mind'....*
>
> *"I sat spellbound by His utterance, oblivious of time....This Revelation so suddenly and impetuously thrust upon me, came as a thunderbolt which, for a time, seemed to have benumbed my faculties. I was blinded by its dazzling splendour and overwhelmed by its crushing force. Excitement, joy, awe and wonder stirred the depths of my soul. Predominant among these emotions was a sense of gladness and strength which seemed to have transfigured me."* 7

Whose Mouth Shall Utter Words, Eternal Words; While His Bowels Shall Be a Fountain of Truth, to Set in Order the House of God.

Mullá Husayn was the first of eighteen disciples whom the Báb called the *"Letters of the Living."* Just as Jesus had instructed His twelve apostles and sent them forth to proclaim His message so did the Báb instruct these eighteen *"Letters of the Living"* and send them forth throughout the land of Persia. Here are the words, the eternal words, which this One mighty and strong delivered to His apostles in sending them on their missions:

> *"O My beloved friends! You are the bearers of the name of God in this Day. You have been chosen as the repositories of His mystery. It behooves each one of you to manifest the attributes of God, and to exemplify by your deeds and words the signs of His righteousness, His*

---

7. *The Dawn-Breakers,* pp. 61-65; cited in William B. Sears, *The Martyr Prophet of a World Faith,* Bahá'í Publishing Trust, Wilmette, Illinois, 1950.

power and glory. The very members of your body must bear witness to the loftiness of your purpose, the integrity of your life, the reality of your faith, and the exalted character of your devotion. For verily I say, this is the Day spoken of by God in His Book: 'On that day will We set a seal upon their mouths; yet shall their hands speak unto Us, and their feet shall bear witness to that which they shall have done.'"

"Ponder the words of Jesus addressed to His disciples, as He sent them forth to propogate the Cause of God. In words such as these, He bade them arise and fulfill their mission: 'Ye are even as the fire which in the darkness of the night has been kindled upon the mountain-top. Let your light shine before the eyes of men. Such must be the purity of your character and the degree of your renunciation, that the people of the earth may through you recognize and be drawn closer to the heavenly Father who is the Source of purity and grace. For none has seen the Father who is in heaven. You who are His spiritual children must by your deeds exemplify His virtues, and witness to His glory. You are the salt of the earth, but if the salt has lost its savour, wherewith shall it be salted? Such must be the degree of your detachment, that into whatever city you enter to proclaim and teach the Cause of God, you should in no wise expect either meat or reward from its people. Nay, when you depart out of that city, you should shake the dust from off your feet. As you have entered it pure and undefiled, so must you depart from that city. For verily I say, the heavenly Father is ever with you and keeps watch over you. If you be faithful to Him, He will assuredly deliver into your hands all the treasures of the earth, and will exalt you above all the rulers and kings of the world!'

"O My Letters! Verily I say, immensely exalted is this Day above the days of the apostles of old. Nay, immeasurable is the difference! You are the witnesses of the Dawn of the promised Day of God. You are the partakers of the mystic chalice of His Revelation. Gird up the loins of endeavour, and be mindful of the words of God as revealed in His Book: 'Lo, the Lord thy God is come, and with Him is the company of His angels arrayed before Him! Purge your hearts of worldly desires and let angelic virtues be your adorning. Strive that by your deeds you may bear witness to the truth of these words of God, and beware lest, by 'turning back', He may change you for another people, who, 'shall not be your like', and who shall take from you the kingdom of God.

"The days when idle worship was deemed sufficient are ended. The time is come when naught but the purest motive, supported by deeds of stainless purity, can ascend to the throne of the Most High

and be acceptable unto Him. 'The good word riseth up unto Him, and the righteous deed will cause it to be exalted before Him.' You are the lowly, of whom God has thus spoken in His Book 'And We desire to show favour to those who were brought low in the land, and to make them spiritual leaders among men, and to make them Our heirs'. You have been called to this station; you will attain to it, only if you arise to trample beneath your feet every earthly desire, and endeavour to become those 'honored servants of His who speak not till He hath spoken, and who do His bidding.'

"You are the first letters that have been generated from this Primal Point, the first Springs that have welled out from the Source of this Revelation. Beseech the Lord your God to grant that no earthly entanglements, no worldly affections, no ephemeral pursuits, may tarnish the purity, or embitter the sweetness, of that grace which flows through you.

"I am preparing you for the advent of a mighty Day. Exert your utmost endeavour that, in the world to come, I, Who am now instructing you, may, before the mercy-seat of God, rejoice in your deeds and glory in your achievements. The secret of the Day that is to come is now concealed. It can neither be divulged nor estimated. The newly born babe of that Day excels the wisest and most venerable men of this time, and the lowliest and most unlearned of that period shall surpass in understanding the most erudite and accomplished divines of this age.[8]

"Scatter throughout the length and breadth of this land, and, with steadfast feet and sanctified hearts, prepare the way for His coming. Heed not your weaknesses and frailty; fix your gaze upon the invincible power of the Lord, your God, the Almighty. Has He not, in past days, caused Abraham, in spite of His seeming helplessness, to triumph over the forces of Nimrod? Has He not enabled Moses, whose staff was His only companion, to vanquish Pharaoh and his hosts? Has He not established the ascendancy of Jesus, poor and lowly as He was in the eyes of men, over the combined forces of the Jewish people? Has He not subjected the barbarous militant tribes of Arabia to the holy and transforming discipline of Muhammad, His Prophet? Arise in His name, put your trust wholly in Him, and be assured of ultimate victory."[9]

"With such words the Báb quickened the faith of His disciples and launched them upon their missions. He assigned each to his own native

8. Compare *D. & C.* 38:7-9; 128:18b; Reorganized *D. & C.* 38:2; 110:18d-e; 2 Nephi 30:15-18; Reorganized Edition 12:96-100.
9. *The Dawn-Breakers,* pp. 92-94. Because of the length of the paragraph in the *Dawn-Breakers* the above quotations used are broken down into smaller paragraphs for ease in reading.

province as the field of his labors." He directed them each to refrain from specific references to His own name and person. Rather they were to raise the call that the Gate to the Promised One has been opened, that His proof is irrefutable, and that His testimony is complete. To Mullá Husayn, the Báb addressed these additional parting words:

"*My hope is that you may, by the aid of God, be enabled to remove the veils from the eyes of the wayward and to cleanse the minds of the malevolent....The hosts of the invisible Kingdom, be assured, will sustain and reinforce your efforts. The essence of power is now dwelling in you,...His almighty arms will surround you, and His unfailing Spirit will ever continue to guide your steps. He that loves you, loves God; and whoever opposes you, has opposed God. Whoso befriends you, him will God befriend; and whoso rejects you, him will God reject.*" [10]

It was Mullá Husayn's privilege not only to have been the first to recognize the Messenger Who was to prepare the way for the Manifestation of God Who would come after Him, but also to bear the tidings of the Báb to that Glorious Personage. The Báb directed Mullá Husayn to carry a message to Teheran, "*that city which enshrines a Mystery of such transcendent holiness as neither Hijaz nor Shiraz can hope to rival...*" [10] There, one who became known as Bahá'u'lláh received him graciously, and after reading only one page from the scroll containing the revealed message of the Báb, recognized its Divine origin immediately and arose to become one of His followers.

The Ministries of the Báb and of Joseph Smith Compared

In every dispensation the prophets and Manifestations of God have been rejected by the religious and political leaders of their day. Their followers are always few in number but show a similar valor in the face of intense persecution. While we cannot parallel the stations of the Báb and Joseph Smith, yet there is a close parallel between the brief turbulent ministry of the Báb and that of the Mormon prophet. There is a remarkable similarity in the distinguishing features of their careers. Both were youthful and had little formal education, and yet each dared to challenge the time-honored conventions, laws and rites of the religions into which they were born. The dramatic swiftness with which their mission moved toward its climax, the role that the religious ministry played as chief instigators of the outrages they were made to suffer, the indignities heaped upon them, their final arrest and execution by the bullets of their enemies, the similarity of these and countless other

10. Ibid., p. 96.

details of their lives and teachings are apparent to anyone studying the history of these two parallel religious movements on opposite sides of the globe, as they each sought to pave the way for the Great Prophet who was to come after them to usher in the glorious Kingdom.

The Báb was publicly executed before a firing squad at high noon on Sunday, July 9, 1850, thirty years from the time of His birth in Shiraz. Within three years, the Cause for which He gave His life seemed on the verge of extinction. Over twenty-thousand of His followers suffered martyrdom in His path. Yet this abyss of darkness and despair was the very hour for which the Báb had long been preparing His followers. Repeatedly He had told them that He was but the humble forerunner of a Messenger of imcomparable greatness yet to follow. In His holy book, the Bayán, the Báb had written: *"Of all the tributes I have paid to Him who is to come after Me, the greatest is this, My written confession that no words of Mine can adequately describe Him, nor can any reference to Him in My book the Bayán do justice to His Cause."* [11]

---

11. Cited in Sears, op. cit. p. 18.

Chapter 7

THE GLORY OF THE FATHER

Thou Wast Sent Forth to Prepare the Way Before Me and Before Elijah

Joseph Smith and William Miller had each set the year for the appearance of the first of the two Prophets who would arise in the East, at the time of the restoration of the Gospel of Jesus Christ in the West. Joseph Smith had been told by direct revelation that he was called to prepare the way for these two Messengers. In this same revelation he was promised the *"keys of the mystery of those things which have been sealed,..."* until the coming of the Lord.[1] In another divine disclosure he was told that he would *"fall by the shaft of death"* and that the Lord God would *"send One mighty and strong, holding the scepter of power in his hand, clothed with light for a covering, whose mouth shall utter words, eternal words; while his bowels shall be a fountain of truth"*. The purpose of this Great One's mission was *"to set in order the house of God, and to arrange by lot the inheritances of the saints whose names are found, and the names of their fathers, and of their children, enrolled in the book of the law of God."* A further warning was given that *"all they who are not found written in the book of remembrance shall find none inheritance in that day, but they shall be cut asunder, and their portion shall be appointed them among unbelievers, where are wailing and gnashing of teeth".* [2]

The footnotes at the bottom of the page, where this revelation is found in the *Doctrine and Covenants*, refers the reader back to several prophecies in the Old Testament. One of these, the Book of Joshua, chapters 14 through 19, describes how Joshua anciently divided Israel among the tribes of Israel by casting lots. Another refers to the Book of Ezra, chapter 2, verses sixty-one and two, which describes how some of the children of Israel had lost the priesthood or authority to act in God's name, through disobedience to God's commands.

In this prophecy concerning the coming of *"One mighty and strong"*

1. *D. & C.* 35:3-4, 17-18, 25-27; Reorganized *D. & C.* 34:2a-b, 4e-f, 6c-d.
2. *D. & C.* 85, especially verses 7-12, Utah edition.

the Lord appears also to be referring back to the revelation of the prophet Daniel concerning what would happen in the latter days in the lands of Elam and Assyria, then called Persia and now Iran:

"*Then I lifted up mine eyes, and looked, and behold a certain man clothed in linen, whose loins were girded with fine gold of Uphaz....Then said he unto me, Fear not, Daniel: for from the first day that thou didst set thine heart to understand, and to chasten thyself before thy God, thy words were heard, and I am come for thy words.*

"*But the prince of the kingdom of Persia withstood me one and twenty days: but, lo,* **Michael, one of the chief princes, came to help me;** *and I remained there with the kings of Persia.*

"*Now I am come to make thee understand* **what shall befall thy people in the latter days:** *for yet the vision is for many days....And at that time* **shall Michael stand up, the great prince which standeth for the children of thy people:** *and there shall be a time of trouble, such as never was since there was a nation even to that same time:* **and at that time thy people shall be delivered, every one that shall be found written in the book.**" [3]

The very name Michael is translated into English as "*The Glory of the Lord*" or "*The Glory of God*" or "*one who looks like God*". [4] The prophet Daniel was among the exiles of Judah who had been taken captive into Elam or southern Persia.

The Prophet Micah spoke of another Great One who would come to Israel in the last days from Assyria or northern Persia where the ten tribes of northern Israel had been taken captive by the Assyrian armies:

"*In that day also he shall come even from Assyria, and from the fortified cities, and from the fortress even to the river, and from sea to sea, and from mountain to mountain. Notwithstanding the land shall be desolate because of them that dwell therein, for the fruit of their doings.*

"*Feed thy people with thy rod, the flock of thine heritage, which dwell solitarily in the wood, in the midst of Carmel: let them feed in Bashan and Gilead, as in the days of old. According to the days of thy coming out of the land of Egypt will I shew unto him marvelous things. The nations shall see and be confounded at all their might: they shall lay their hand upon their mouth, their ears shall be deaf. Thou wilt perform the truth to Jacob, and the mercy to Abraham, which thou hast sworn unto our fathers from the days of old.*" [5]

3. Daniel 10:5, 12-14; 12:1.
4. See p. 77 of *Thief in the Night* by William Sears.
5. Micah 7:7, 12-16, 20.

These two prophecies from the *Old Testament* help to explain the meaning of the revelations to Joseph Smith concerning the two Prophets for whom he was preparing the way. Since Joseph Smith was to hold the *"keys of the mystery of those things which were sealed"* until the coming of these holy Messengers it seems to follow that the first of these Divine Personages would first appear in the year 1844. This is also the same year given by Daniel and by John the Revelator as the year of the coming of the Lord, as pointed out by William Miller and the adventist scholars of the early eighteen hundreds. In the previous chapter we have seen that One claiming to be the first of these Promised Ones did arise in 1844 in the land of Elam, in the city of Shiraz in southern Persia. He declared that he was the Gate to *"One Whom God shall make manifest,"* and implied that this next Divine Messenger would appear nineteen years from the date of His own declaration. This would be in the year 1863.

Did Joseph Smith, or any of the *Bible* prophets, have any similar intimation of the time of the ministry of this second Great Prophet, who, according to Micah, would come to Israel *"from Assyria"*, from *"mountain to mountain"*, from *"fortified cities"*, from *"the fortress even to the river"* and from *"sea to sea"*? Indeed Micah goes on not only to tell the locality in Israel to which this Prophet would come, i.e. *"in the midst of Carmel"*, but also the length of His ministry, in these words: *"According to the days of thy coming out of the land of Egypt will I show unto him marvelous things"*. The children of Israel dwelt in the wilderness for forty years after coming out of the land of Egypt before they were permitted by God to enter the promised land.

There is an interesting prophecy recorded in section 130 of the *Doctrine and Covenants*. Beginning with verse eleven we read:

"And a white stone is given to each of those who come into the celestial kingdom, whereon is a new name written, which no man knoweth save he that receiveth it. The new name is the key word.

"I prophesy, in the name of the Lord God, that the **commencement of the difficulties** *which will cause much bloodshed* **previous to the coming of the Son of Man** *will be in South Carolina. It may probably arise through the slave question. This a voice declared to me, while I was praying on the subject, December 25th, 1832.*

"While I was praying earnestly to know the time of the coming of the Son of man, when I heard a voice repeat the following: 'Joseph

my son, **if thou livest until thou art eighty-five years old, thou shalt see the face of the Son of Man;** *therefore let this suffice, and trouble me no more on this matter.*"[6]

What an amazing prophecy! Since this revelation applies to the coming kingdom of God, we can safely assume that the *"new name"* applies to those who recognize the Lord and enter His heavenly kingdom. And just as the date 1844 applied not to the time of the birth of the first of the two High Prophets but to the time of that Prophet's declaration of His ministry, so also would the two dates referred to in the above prophecy, concerning the coming of the *"Son of Man"*, apply to the period of the active ministry of the second of the two Messengers of the new Day of God.

These two dates are implied in the **bold-faced** portions of the foregoing prophecy. After the symbolic reference to the *"new name"* to be given to those who enter the divine kingdom, Joseph's prophecy then speaks of the **beginning** of those *"wars and rumors of wars"* which Christ had earlier said was to be one of the signs of the coming of the kingdom.[7] **These difficulties which would cause much bloodshed previous to the coming of the Son of Man** would begin in South Carolina and probably arise over the slave question.[8]

We have now seen the exact fulfillment of this portion of Joseph's prophecy. The American Civil War, which was fought over the slave question, began in South Carolina in the year 1860. This year then marks the *"***commencement*** of the difficulties which will cause* **much bloodshed previous** *to the coming of the Son of Man"*. The war dragged on until 1865, but in 1863 a very significant thing happened. On January 1st of that year Abraham Lincoln issued the Emancipation Proclamation ending human slavery, and declaring the basic equality of all men before God without regard to their race, nationality or previous condition of servitude. America was the first nation to take this important step, although Great Britain had preceded her in ending the slave trade. The other nations, one by one, followed the lead of these two, until most of the people of the world are now finding freedom. Thus 1863 marks a most important turning point in human history. It is certainly the most important date in that long struggle to put an end to human slavery.

6. *D. & C.* 130:11-15, Utah edition.
7. See *D. & C.* 45:24-33; Reorganized *D. & C.* 45:3f,4a-f.
8. See also Joseph Smith's explanation of this disclosure in Section 87, Utah edition.

The Civil War itself was the beginning of a long series of wars and internal revolutions which have gradually won the freedom of those peoples who were once subject peoples of the great colonial empires. And still the struggle for civil rights and the equality of all men everywhere goes on. Nevertheless, America, that nation which led the world in putting an end to human bondage, is now similarly leading the world in putting an end to industrial bondage as well. The right to work, the right to an equal education, the right to an equal use of public facilities, the right to live whereever one chooses without regard to race, nationality or religion, all of those rights and many more are in the process of being won in America. However, the movement for the equality and oneness of all humankind is taking place in all of the continents and islands of the globe.

A Great Prince Among the Persians

The real impetus for this movement began in the ancient land of Persia. As with all other important cultural changes, this great social revolution began with the teachings of a Prophet of God. In the same year that Abraham Lincoln issued the Emancipation Proclamation, i.e. in April 1863, outside of the city of Baghdad, nineteen years from the evening in Shiraz when the Báb had spoken to Mullá Husayn, Bahá'u'lláh declared to the followers of the Báb, and to the world, that He was the One whom the Báb had foretold. He was the One who had come to fulfill all history and to usher in the glorious Kingdom of the Father. He was the Son of Man come in the full Glory of the Lord to usher in the age of unity, the age of the oneness of all mankind. His very name Bahá'u'lláh means in Persian, the *"Glory of God"*.

Bahá'u'lláh was born in Teherán, in that region of Persia anciently known as Assyria. He was of noble lineage. His father was a governor over the province surrounding Teheran, the capital city of all Persia. Not only was He a direct descendant of the ancient King Yasdigirid III, last of the Sasanyan Dynasty of Persia but also of the Major Prophets Abraham, through His wife Katurah, and Zoroaster. (He also came through the lineage of Jesse as foretold by Isaiah.) While we cannot in this brief summary examine each of the prophecies of holy scripture applying to the life and teachings of Bahá'u'lláh, we can look at just a few of those outstanding ones which were fulfilled in remarkable detail in the course of this Great Prophet's earthly ministry. Many additional prophecies have already been cited in preceding sections of this book.

Bahá'u'lláh came from that same region of Persia where the children of Israel had been planted as colonies by the Assyrian armies in 721 B.C., and from whence Isaiah and other prophets foretold that a faithful remnant would return to Israel in the last days. I am sure that the Lord had reference to this same land when He told Joseph Smith that, *"they who are in the north countries shall come in remembrance before the Lord; and their prophets shall hear His voice, and shall no longer stay themselves...."*[9] Assyria was to the north and east of ancient Israel and it was this land of which the ancient Hebrew prophets spoke when they foretold that the children of Israel would be taken captive into the lands of the north and from whence a faithful remnant would return in the last days.[10]

The prophet Daniel had a whole series of visions concerning the latter days, when the Kingdom of God would be established upon the earth. Concerning one of these he said:

"I saw in the night visions, and, behold, one like the Son of man came with the clouds of heaven, and came to the Ancient of days, and they brought him near before him.

"And there was given him dominion, and glory, and a kingdom, that all people, nations, and languages, should serve him: his dominion is an everlasting dominion, which shall not pass away, and his kingdom that which shall not be destroyed."[11]

In some prophecies He is spoken of as Michael, which means *"one who looks like God"*. In still others He is spoken of as a *"Chief Prince among the Persians"* and a *"deliverer"* of Israel.

He Will Come to Thee From Assyria

Now let's turn back to the prophecy of Micah quoted at the beginning of this chapter:

"In that day also he shall come even to thee from Assyria, and from fortified cities, and from the fortress even to the river, and from sea to sea, and from mountain to mountain".

As we have seen, Bahá'u'lláh joined the religious movement of the Báb. In so doing He gave up His right of governorship of the leading province of Persia and sacrificed all of His earthly possessions. In the persecutions which followed the martyrdom of the Báb, He was imprisoned in a *"black pit"* four stories underneath the city of Teheran. He was bound with heavy chains, around His feet and wrists and around

---

9. D. & C. 133:26; Reorganized D. & C. 108:6a.
10. See the prophetic reference in chapter 20.
11. Daniel 7:13-14.

His neck. Most of His friends who were put in prison with Him were taken away one by one to be killed. Bahá'u'lláh was Himself fed poisoned food in a vain attempt to kill Him.

While He was in this loathsome dungeon, deep underneath the old fortress city of Teheran, the voice of Heaven came to Him, calling Him to His mission:

"*Verily, We shall render Thee victorious by Thyself and by Thy pen. Grieve Thou not for that which hath befallen Thee, neither be Thou afraid, for Thou art in safety. Erelong will God raise up the treasures of the earth—men who will aid Thee through Thyself and through Thy name, wherewith God hath revived the hearts of such as have recognized Him.*" [12]

This vision was in the year 1852, but just as Joseph Smith was told to wait until the appropriate time before declaring his mission, so did Bahá'u'lláh wait for the appropriate time before declaring His mission. This set time was just three years after the beginning of the American Civil War, or "*the commencement of the difficulties which will cause much bloodshed previous to the coming of the Son of Man....*", as Joseph Smith had foreseen.

Bahá'u'lláh's imprisonment in the "*black pit of Teheran*" lasted four months but He and His companions remained zealous and enthusiastic, in the greatest happiness. Bahá'u'lláh was so ill from the ordeal that it was thought that He would die, so instead of sentencing Him to death the Shah ordered that He be exiled to Baghdad in what was anciently Shinar and still later Babylonia, by the river Tigris. He was accompanied on this long arduous winter journey by His family and a number of other believers, a "*faithful remnant*" of the once numerous host of followers of the Báb. Twenty thousand had been martyred with terrible tortures in the streets of Persia.

About a year after coming to Baghdad, He departed alone into the wilderness of Sulaymaniyyih in the mountains of Kurdistan, to fast and pray in contemplation of the great mission which lay before Him. There He remained for two years.

The period following this retirement is described by Dr. Esslemont in his world-renowned volume entitled, **Bahá'u'lláh and the New Era.**

"*After His return from this retirement, His fame became greater than ever and people flocked to Baghdad from far and near to see Him*

---

12. Bahá'u'lláh, *Epistle to the Son of the Wolf*, pp. 20-21.

and hear His teachings. Jews, Christians, and Zoroastrians, as well as Muhammadans, became interested in the new message. The 'Ullma* (Muhammadan doctors), however, took up a hostile attitude and persistently plotted....His overthrow. On a certain occasion they sent one of their number to interview Him and submit to Him certain questions. The envoy found the answers of Bahá'u'lláh so convincing and His wisdom so amazing, although evidently not acquired by study, that he was obliged to confess that in knowledge and understanding Bahá'u'lláh was peerless. In order, however, that the 'Ullma who had sent him should be satisfied as to the reality of Bahá'u'lláh's prophethood, he asked that some miracle should be produced as a proof. Bahá'u'lláh expressed His willingness to accept the suggestion on certain conditions, declaring that if the 'Ullma would agree regarding some miracle to be performed, and would sign and seal a document to the effect that on performance of this miracle they would confess the validity of His mission and cease to oppose Him, He would furnish the desired proof or else stand convicted of imposture. Had the aim of the 'Ullma been to get at the truth, surely here was their opportunity; but their intention was far otherwise. Rightly or wrongly, they meant to secure a decision in their own favor. They feared the truth and fled from the daring challenge. This discomfiture, however, only spurred them on to divise fresh plots for the eradication of the oppressed sect. The Consul-General of Persia in Baghdad came to their assistance and sent repeated messages to the Shah to the effect that Bahá'u'lláh was injuring the Muhammadan religion more than ever, still exerting a malign influence in Persia, and that He ought therefore to be banished to some more distant place." 13

Two of Bahá'u'lláh's best known books of revelation were written during this *"Babylonian exile"*. These are, the **Hidden Words**, those lyric gems of wise counsel which have brought help and healing to thousands of aching and troubled hearts, and the **Katáb-i-Iqan (The Book of Certitude)**, that long foretold key to unlock the *"hidden mysteries"* of scripture and to unloose the meaning of every *"sealed"* revelation. 14

Upon receiving the news of Bahá'u'lláh's subsequent banishment to Turkey, His followers beseiged the house of their beloved Leader to such an extent that the family encamped in the Garden of Ridván 15

13. J.E. Esslemont, *Bahá'u'lláh and the New Era*, Revised Edition, pp. 42-43; *God Passes By*, pp. 144.
14. See for example 2 Nephi 30:16-18. Daniel 12:4, 8, 9; *God Passes By* pp. 138-139.
15. Pronounced Riswan and meaning *"Paradise"*.
* 'Ullma plural for Mulla.

outside the city. Here He remained, with a small company of His disciples, for twelve days. It was during these twelve days beginning April 21, 1863, nineteen years after the Báb's declaration, that He announced that He was the One whose coming had been foretold by the Báb and by all of the prophets of the past, the Promised One of all Faiths, the Glory of the Lord, the Prince of Peace, the return of Christ in the Glory of the Father.

Bahá'u'lláh and His companions now continued that long 40 year series of exiles and imprisonments foretold by Micah (7:15). This little band of exiles made the journey all the way from Baghdad to Constantinople *"most of them on foot"**, a distance comparable to that of the exodus of the Latter-day Saints across the plains and mountains to Utah. Constantinople had been the ancient capital of the Eastern Roman Empire, and, after Rome, the greatest city of the Mediterranean world. Now it was the capital of the Turkish Empire. It lay on the narrow Strait of Bosphorus which separate Europe and Asia while connecting the Mediterranean and Black Seas by the way of the Sea of Marmara and the Aegean Sea.

After four months' imprisonment in Constantinople, they were again banished, this time in the city of Adrianople, at the foot of the Istranca Mountains. Although lasting only a few days, the journey from Constantinople to Adrianople was the most terrible journey they had yet encountered. Snow lay heavily upon the ground. They were destitute of clothing and food and suffered in the extreme.

It was during this episode of imprisonments that Bahá'u'lláh wrote His famous series of proclamations to the crowned heads of Europe, the Sultan of Turkey, the Shah of Iran, to the Pope. In the *Kitab-i-Aqdás* is found the message to the Government of the United States. In these epistles Bahá'u'lláh announced His mission and called upon each of these leaders or representatives of the people to lend their energies to the establishment of true religion, just government and international peace. He asked the heads of governments to send representatives to a great world convention to be assembled for the purpose of laying the foundation of a federation of mankind.

Needless to say, these appeals went unheeded. Bahá'u'lláh then sent out a second series of letters. These were much sharper in tone, and in them the King of kings instructed His vassals. In these tablets He foretold the history of the modern period: the downfall of the second Napoleonic empire, then at the height of its power, 1870; the fall of the

---

* *God Passes By*, p. 156.

Hapsburg monarchy and the break-up of Austria-Hungary Empire, 1918, into many nations; wars in which Germany would be reduced to ruins 1918-1945; the overthrow of the Russian czardom, 1917, and much more. He called upon the Pope of Christendom and the Caliph of Islam to give up their temporal power and prophecied that if they did not do so this power would be seized from them by force. He foretold the discovery of atomic energy and warned of imminent destruction unless the world united to control aggression and *"after Him, His son, Abdú'l Bahá, knew of it and spoke of it to the Japanese Ambassador, Viscount Arakawa".* *

After four and a half years, further trouble ensued, as resentments and fears of Bahá'u'lláh among the Muslim leaders were fanned to a fury by those jealous of His power and wisdom. Eventually, Bahá'u'lláh and His followers were banished by the Turkish government to Akka (Acre) in Palestine, where they arrived on August 31, 1868.

Imprisonment in Akka

Again turning to Dr. Esselmont's excellent introduction to Bahá'í history we read:

"At that time Akka (Acre) was a prison-city to which the worst criminals were sent from all parts of the Turkish Empire. On arriving there, after a miserable sea journey, Baha'u'lláh and His followers, about eighty to eighty-four in number, including men, women and children, were imprisoned in the army barracks. The place was dirty and cheerless in the extreme. There were no beds or comforts of any sort. The food supplied was wretched and inadequate, so much so that after a time the prisoners begged to be allowed to buy their food for themselves. During the first few days the children were crying continually, and sleep was almost impossible. Malaria, dysentery and other diseases soon broke out, and everyone in the company fell sick, with the exception of two. Three succumbed to their sickness, and the sufferings of the survivors were indescribable.

"This rigorous imprisonment lasted for two years, during which time none of the Bahá'is were allowed outside the prison door, except four men, carefully guarded, who went out daily to buy food.

"During the imprisonment in the barracks, visitors were rigidly excluded. Several of the Bahá'í's of Persia came all the way on foot for the purpose of seeing their beloved leader, but were refused admittance

* *The Chosen Highway,* p. 184.

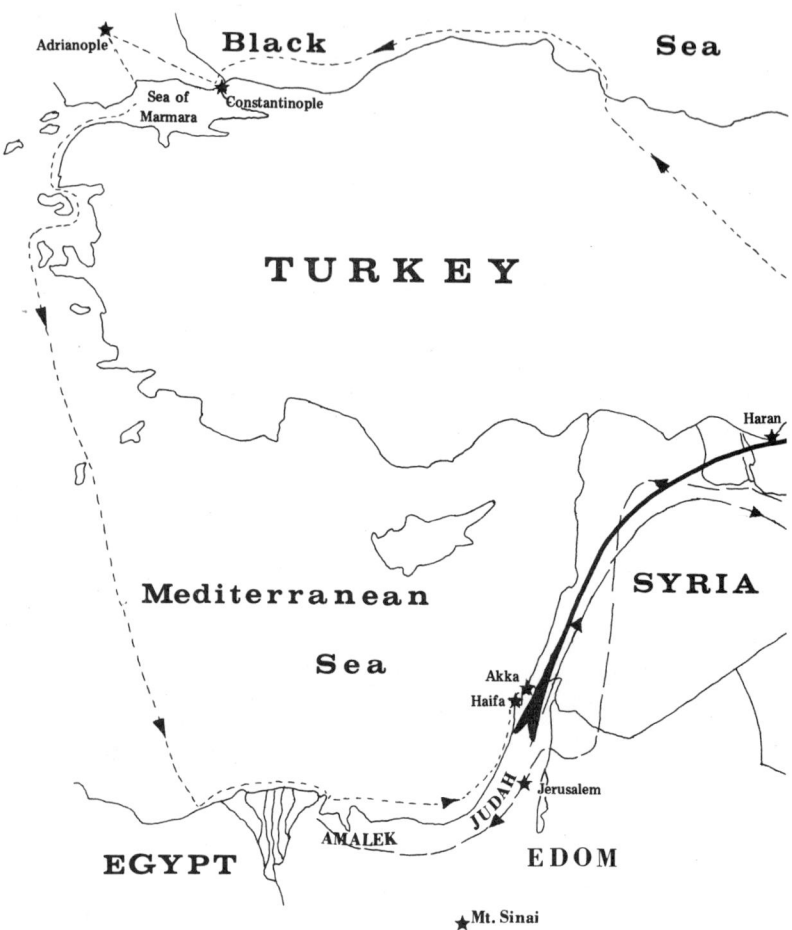

Map III showing the travels of Abraham, The Báb, and Bahá'u'lláh and the Dispersion and Return of a Faithful Remnant of Israel From the *"Lands of the North"*, i.e. Assyria and Media.

  Mt. Sinai (where Moses received His call).
  Judah (where Jesus received His call).
  Ancient Padan Aram, Halah and Nineveh (Cities where the Israelites were held captive after 722 B.C. (1,2,3).
  Media (This region is where the ten tribes were taken into captivity).
  Modern Tehran (Birthplace of Bahá'u'lláh). (4)
  Modern Baghdad (Where Bahá'u'lláh declared His mission).
  Elam (Where most of the Jews were taken into captivity).
  Shiraz (Modern), (Where the Báb declared His mission).
  Ancient Ur (Where Abraham received His call). (5)
  Ancient Babylonia.
  Ancient Assyria.

"The Lord shall set His hand the second time to recover the remnant of His people which shall be left, from Assyria..." — Isaiah 11:11

"In that day He shall come to thee from Assyria.... Feed thy people with thy rod...in the midst of Carmel let them feed...as in days of old." — Micah 7:12,14.

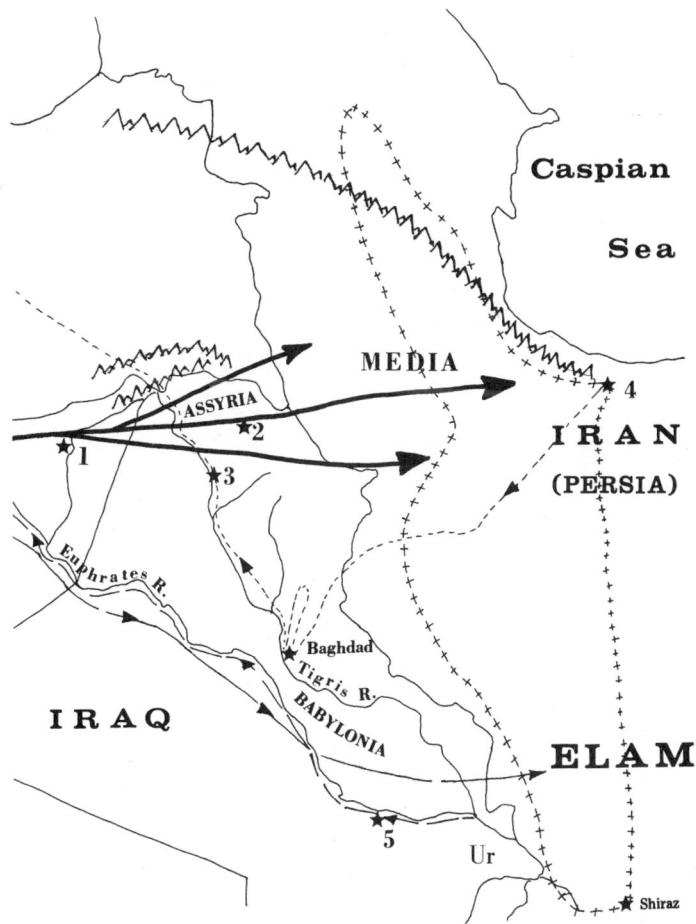

——▶—— General route of the travels of Abraham in ancient times from Ur to Jerusalem and to Egypt.

▬▬▶ Captivity and deportation of *"Ephraim"* or the ten tribes of Israel to Assyria and Media, after 721 B.C. (now northern Iraq and Persia).

—▶— Captivity and deportation of *"Judah"* or the Jews to Babylonia and Elam, after 600 B.C. (now southern Iraq and Persia).

++++++ General route of the travels of the Báb or *"Gate to the Kingdom"*, who first declared His mission in Shiraz, in what was anciently Elam. See Jeremiah 49: 38-39; Daniel 8:1-2, 10:13-14.

------▶- General route of the travels of Bahá'u'lláh or *"Glory of God"*, who first received His divine call in Tehran, was exiled to Baghdad where He declared His mission, and then to prisons in Constantinople, Adrianople and, finally, to Akka in Israel. He thus fulfilled prophecies found in Isaiah 11:11; Micah 7:12-14; *Doctrine and Covenants* 133:26-30; Reorganized *D. & C.* 108:6.

"And they who are in the northern countries shall come in remembrance before the Lord; and their Prophets shall hear His voice, and shall no longer stay themselves. . . .And they shall bring forth their rich treasures unto the children of Ephraim my servants." — D. & C. 133:26-30; (Missouri Edition 108:6a,6c)

within the city walls. They used to go to a place on the plain outside the third moat, from which they could see the windows of Bahá'u'lláh's quarters. He would show Himself to them at one of the windows and after gazing on Him from afar, they would weep and return to their homes, fired with new zeal for sacrifice and service.

Restrictions Relaxed

"At last the imprisonment was mitigated. A mobilization of Turkish troops occurred and the barracks were required for soldiers. Bahá'u'lláh and His family were transferred to a house by themselves and the rest of the party were accomodated in a caravanserai (hotel) in the town. Bahá'u'lláh was confined for seven more years in this house. In a small room near that in which He was imprisoned, thirteen of His household, including both sexes, had to accomodate themselves as best they could! In the earlier part of their stay in this house they suffered greatly from insufficiency of accommodation, inadequate food supply and lack of the ordinary conveniences of life. After a time, however, a few additional rooms were placed at their disposal and they were able to live in comparative comfort. From the time Bahá'u'lláh and His companions left the barracks, visitors were allowed to see them, and gradually the severe restrictions imposed by the Imperial firmans (orders) were more and more left in abeyance, although now and then reimposed for a time." [16]

While in the fortress of Akka, Bahá'u'lláh wrote to some friends:

"Fear not. These doors shall be opened. My tent shall be pitched on Mount Carmel, and the utmost joy shall be realized." In due course this declaration was literally fulfilled. He was permitted to live in a private house at Bahji in the valley of Sharon and often times would pitch His tent on Mount Carmel, there to pray and meditate, to teach His followers, and to receive revelations from God. His total ministry lasted for exactly forty years as Micah had foretold:

"Notwithstanding the land shall be desolate because of them that dwell therein, for the fruit of their doings. Feed thy people with thy rod, the flock of thine heritage, which dwell solitarily in the wood, in the midst of Carmel: let them feed in Bashan and Gilead, as in the days of old.

"According to the days of thy coming out of the land of Egypt (forty years) will I shew unto him marvellous things. The nations shall

---

16. Esslemont, op. cit., pp. 46-48.

see and be confounded at all their might: they shall lay their hand upon their mouth, their ears shall be deaf.

"Thou wilt perform the truth to Jacob, and the mercy to Abraham, which thou hast sworn unto our fathers from the days of old."[17]

And in the words of Isaiah:

"The excellency of Carmel and Sharon, they shall see the glory of the Lord and the excellency of our God. . . . And I will bring forth a seed out of Jacob, and out of Judah an inheritor of my mountains: and mine elect shall inherit it, and my servants shall dwell therein. And Sharon shall be a fold of flocks, and the valley of Achor a place for the herds to lie down in, for my people that have sought me."[18]

Thus did Bahá'u'lláh literally fulfill many *Bible* prophesies!

---

17. Micah 7:13-16,20.
18. Isaiah 35:2; 65:9-10.

Chapter 8

THE GLORIES WHICH WERE TO BE REVEALED

A Great and Marvelous Work

Bahá'u'lláh revealed over a hundred Books and Tablets. Besides those already mentioned we have in English His **Seven Valleys** which trace the journey of the true seeker and **Four Valleys** which describes the four stages of the heart. **Prayers and Meditations**, is a group of revealed prayers and meditations for all occasions. His letters to the crowned monarchs of Europe and the Middle East and to the Presidents of the American republics have been collected and published together in a volume entitled: **Proclamations to the Kings**.

In addition there are several compilations from the Writings of Bahá'u'lláh and His son and successor Abdu'l-Bahá. Those most easily obtainable are **Gleanings From the Writings of Bahá'u'lláh, Glad Tidings of Bahá'u'lláh, Bahá'i World Faith, The Bahá'i Revelation, The Reality of Man, The Divine Art of Living, and Some Answered Questions**.

Bahá'u'lláh's greatest work is not yet published in English, and this for a special reason—we are not yet ready to receive and live it fully. This is His **Kitab-i-Aqdás—The Book of Laws** wherewith mankind will establish a universal government under the direct and infallible guidance of a Universal House of Justice, inspired in all of its decisions through Bahá'u'lláh.

Of all the descriptions of the life and work of Bahá'u'lláh I consider one of the most beautiful to be a prophetic utterance originally revealed through Isaiah and repeated to the Nephite-Lamanite disciples of Jesus Christ upon the American continent nearly two thousand years ago, as follows:

"And then shall be brought to pass that which is written: *Awake, awake again, and put on thy strength, O Zion; put on thy beautiful garments, O Jerusalem, the holy city, for henceforth there shall no more come into thee the uncircumcised and the unclean. Shake thyself from the dust; arise, sit down, O Jerusalem; loose thyself from the bands of thy neck, O captive daughter of Zion. For thus saith the Lord: Ye have sold yourselves for naught, and ye shall be redeemed without money.*

"Verily, verily, I say unto you, that my people shall know my name; yea, in that day they shall know that I am he that doth speak. And then shall they say: How beautiful upon the mountains are the feet of him that bringeth good tidings unto them, that publisheth peace; that bringeth good tidings unto them of good, that publisheth salvation; that saith unto Zion: Thy God reigneth!

"Behold, my servant shall deal prudently; he shall be exalted and extolled and be very high. As many were astonished at thee—his visage was so marred, more than any man, and his form more than the sons of men—so shall he sprinkle many nations; the kings shall shut their mouths at him, for that which had not been told them shall they see; and that which they had not heard shall they consider.

"Verily, verily, I say unto you, all these things shall surely come, even as the Father hath commanded me. Then shall this covenant which the Father hath covenanted with his people be fulfilled; and then shall Jerusalem be inhabited again with my people, and it shall be the land of their inheritance." [1]

Christ then went on to tell these ancient Americans, and indirectly we of the latter days when His prophecy is being fulfilled, that when His gospel should be restored to earth among the Gentiles, and when this same gospel should begin to be carried forth by the Gentiles to the seed of the Nephite and Lamanite peoples scattered among the American Indians, this would be a sign unto them that—*"I shall gather in, from their long dispersion, my people, O house of Israel, and shall establish again among them my Zion."* Returning then to Jesus' description of this work of the Father among the children of Israel, immediately following the restoration of the Gospel of Jesus Christ in this continent, we read:

"For in that day, for my sake shall the Father work a work, which shall be a great and a marvelous work among them; and there shall be among them those who will not believe it, although a man shall declare it unto them. But behold, the life of my servant shall be in my hand; therefore they shall not hurt him, although he shall be marred because of them. Yet I will heal him, for I will show unto them that my wisdom is greater than the cunning of the devil. . . .

---

1. 3 Nephi 20:36-40, 43-46; Reorganized Edition 9:74-78, 81-85.

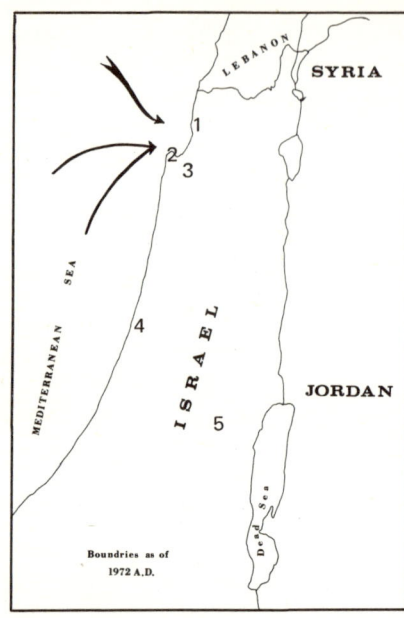

Map IV: The Return of a Remnant of Israel from Assyria, and of Judah from all nations, 1868 to the present.

1. Bahá'u'lláh and company of exiles arrive in Akká from Assyria (northern Iran) 1868 A.D.
2. The Jews return from all nations through Haifa after the Balfour Declaration in 1917 A.D.
3. Mount Carmel.
4. Tel Aviv.
5. Jerusalem.

"I will look unto the Lord. . . . In that day also he shall come to thee even from Assyria. . . . Feed thy people with thy rod, . . . in the midst of Carmel . . . . According to the days of thy coming out of the land of Egypt will I shew unto him marvelous things."

—Micah 7:7-15

"The exellency of Carmel and Sharon, they shall see the Glory of the Lord. . . . And Sharon shall be a fold of flocks and the valley of Achor a place for the herds to lie down in."

—Isaiah 35:1-2; 65:9-10

"And there shall be a highway for the remnant of his people which shall be left from Assyria. . . . And it shall come to pass that my people shall be gathered home unto the lands of their possessions; and my word also shall be gathered in one."

—Isaiah 11:16; 2 Nephi 29:14; Reorganized 12:73

"Behold, thy God reigneth; As the dews of Carmel, so shall the knowledge of God descend upon them."

—D. & C. 128:19; Reorganized D. & C. 110:19b

"And then shall the work of the Father commence at that day, even when this gospel shall be preached among the remnant of this people. Verily I say unto you, at that day shall the work of the Father commence among all the dispersed of my people, yea, even the tribes which have been lost, which the Father hath led away out of Jerusalem. Yea, and then shall the work commence, with the Father, among all nations, in preparing the way whereby his people may be gathered home to the land of the inheritance. And they shall go out from all nations; and they shall not go out in haste, nor go by flight, for I will go before them, saith the Father, and I will be their rearward". [2]

And thus, as foretold, the Glory of God, Bahá'u'lláh, the Redeemer of Israel, entered the Holy Land to prepare the way before His chosen ones. Beginning with the little band of faithful followers accompanying Bahá'u'lláh, the children of Israel have been gathered from their long dispersion among the nations, to dwell in His presence forever and ever.[3]

After having begun as a prisoner and an exile, His neck marred by the chains of His enemies, Baha'u'llah was healed by the mercy of God in order that He might become the redeemer, not only of Israel, but of all mankind. His healing message of love and justice has sprinkled many nations. Kings and rulers were called upon to carry out His world administrative order, yet they shut their mouths at Him and turned a deaf ear to His Tablets. Now His people, those who know His name and recognize that it is God who speaks through Him, are carrying His healing message of unity and peace to all mankind, bringing good tidings to them of good, publishing salvation, and saying to Zion: Thy God reigneth! The covenant of God through His chosen messengers and Prophets is being fulfilled. The land of Jerusalem is being inhabited again with His people, as the new Holy Land, not just of the Jews, the Christians and the Muslims, but of all peoples and religions. "*As the dews of Carmel so shall the knowledge of God descend upon them!*"[4] And truly, from Carmel, comes to us words like beautiful dew, the Message of God through Bahá'u'lláh!

Thou Shalt See the Face of the Son of Man

It was while at Bahji that Baha'u'llah had His only interview with anyone from the so-called *"western world"*. Professor Edward G. Browne, the distinguished orientalist of the University of Cambridge visited Bahá'u'lláh at Bahji. The year was 1890, that year foretold in

2. 3 Nephi 21:1, 9-10, 26-29; Reorganized Edition 9:95-97; 10:4-8.
3. See *D. & C.* 133:25-35; Reorganized *D. & C.* 108:5g-6f.
4. *D. & C.* 128:19; Reorganized *D. & C.* 110:19b.

the revelation given to Joseph Smith: "*Joseph, my son, if thou livest until thou art eighty-five years old, thou shalt see the face of the Son of Man;...*"[5] Obviously, if Joseph Smith had lived to be eighty-five and in good health, he also could have seen the "*Face of the Son of Man*". Here, in brief, are some of Professor Browne's recorded impressions of that meeting:

"*The face of Him on Whom I gazed I can never forget, though I cannot describe it. Those piercing eyes seemed to read one's very soul; power and authority sat on that ample brow; while the deep lines on the forehead and face implied an age which the jet-black hair and beard flowing down in indistinguishable luxuriance almost to the waist seemed to belie. No need to ask in Whose presence I stood, as I bowed myself before One Who is the object of a devotion and love which kings might envy and emperors sigh for in vain!*

"*A mild dignified voice bade me be seated, and then continued: 'Praise be to God that thou hast attained!...Thou hast come to see a prisoner and an exile....We desire but the good of the world and the happiness of the nations; yet they deem Us a stirrer-up of strife and sedition worthy of bondage and banishment....That all nations should become one in faith and all men as brothers; that the bonds of affection and unity between the sons of men should be strengthened; that diversity of religion should cease, and differences of race be annulled—what harm is there is this?...Yet so it shall be; these fruitless strifes, these ruinous wars shall pass away, and the* **Most Great Peace** *shall come...Do not you in Europe need this also? Is not this that which Christ foretold?...Yet do We see your kings and rulers lavishing their treasures more freely on means of destruction of the human race than on that which would conduce to the happiness of mankind....These strifes and this bloodshed and discord must cease, and all men be as one kindred and one family....Let not a man glory in this, that he loves his country; let him rather glory in this, that he loves his kind....'*

"Such, so far as I can recall them, were the words which besides many others, I heard from Bahá. Let those who read them consider well with themselves whether such doctrines merit death and bonds, and whether the world is more likely to gain or lose by their diffusion."[6]

World Unity the Goal

We cannot begin to examine every fruit of the teachings of Bahá'u'lláh in this brief introduction.[7] These you must search out for yourselves.[8]

---

5. *D. & C.* 130:15, Utah edition. Joseph Smith born December 23, 1805.
6. Introduction to "*A Traveller's Narrative Episode of the Bab*", p. 39; cited in Esslemont, op. cit., pp. 52-53.
7. See Revelation 22:1-14.
8. See *D. & C.* 88:63-68, 73-83, 118-120, 126; Reorganized *D. & C.* 85:16-18, 20-22, 36, 38c.

So .Great A Cause 115

The prophet Zechariah predicted a future Day when the Manifestation of God would again speak from the land of Jerusalem. In that Day all nations would be joined in one, worshipping one Lord and be called by His name: *"Sing and rejoice, O daughter of Zion: for, lo, I come, and I will dwell in the midst of thee, saith the Lord. And many nations shall be joined to the Lord in that day, and shall be my people: and I will dwell in the midst of thee, and thou shalt know that the Lord of hosts hath sent me unto thee. And the Lord shall inherit Judah his portion in the holy land, and shall choose Jerusalem again. . . . And the Lord shall be king over all the earth: in that day shall there be one Lord, and his name one."*9

Perhaps a few excerpts from the concluding pages of a book written by the great grandson of Bahá'u'lláh, Shoghi Effendi, **The World Order of Bahá'u'lláh,** will serve to show how thoroughly Zechariah's prophecy has been fulfilled in the Teachings and Administrative Order of Bahá'u'lláh:

"Unification of the whole of mankind is the hall-mark of the stage which human society is now approaching. Unity of family, of tribe, of city-state, and nation have been successively attempted and fully established. World unity is the goal towards which a harassed humanity is striving. Nation-building has come to an end. The anarchy inherent in state sovereignty is moving towards a climax. A world, growing to maturity, must abandon this fetish, recognize the oneness and wholeness of human relationships, and establish once and for all the machinery that can best incarnate this fundamental principle of its life. . . .

"The unity of the human race, as envisaged by Baha'u'llah, implies the establishment of a world commonwealth in which all nations, races, creeds and classes are closely and permanently united, and in which the autonomy of its state members and the personal freedom and inititive of the individuals that compose them are definitely and completely safeguarded. This commonwealth must as far as we can visualize it, consist of a world legislature, whose members will, as the trustees of the whole of mankind, ultimately control the entire resources of all the component nations, and will enact such laws as shall be required to regulate the life, satisfy the needs and adjust the relationships of all races and peoples. A world executive ,backed by an international Force, will carry out the decisions arrived at, and apply the laws enacted by, this world legislature, and will safeguard the organic unity of the whole commonwealth. A world tribunal will adjudicate and deliver its

9. Zechariah 2:10-12; 14:9.

compulsory and final verdict in all and any disputes that may arise between the various elements constituting this universal system. A mechanism of world inter-communication will be devised, embracing the whole planet, freed from national hindrances and restrictions, and functioning with marvelous swiftness and perfect regularity. A world metropolis will act as the nerve center of a world civilization, the focus towards which the unifying forces of life will converge and from which its energizing influences will radiate. A world language will either be invented or chosen from among the existing languages and will be taught in the schools of all the federated nations as an auxiliary to their mother tongue. A world script, a world literature, a uniform and universal system of currency, of weights and measures, will simplify and facilitate intercourse and understanding among the nations and races of mankind.

*"In such a world society, science and religion, the two most potent forces in human life, will be reconciled, will co-operate, and will harmoniously develop. The press will, under such a system, while giving full scope to the expression of the diversified views and convictions of mankind, cease to be mischievously manipulated by vested interests, whether private or public, and will be liberated from the influence of contending governments and peoples. The economic resources of the world will be organized, its sources of raw materials will be tapped and fully utilized, its markets will be co-ordinated and developed, and the distribution of its products will be equitably regulated.

"National rivalries, hatreds, and intrigues will cease, and racial animosity and prejudice will be replaced by racial amity, understanding and co-operation. The causes of religious strife will be permanently removed, economic barriers and restrictions will be completely abolished, and the inordinate distinction between classes will be obliterated. Destitution on the one hand, and gross accumulation of ownership on the other, will disappear. The enormous energy dissipated and wasted on war, whether economic or political, will be consecrated to such ends as will extend the range of human inventions and technical development, to the increase of the productivity of mankind, to the extermination of disease, to the extension of scientific research, to the raising of the standard of physical health, to the sharpening and refinement of the human brain, to the exploitation of the unused and unsuspected resources of the planet, to the prolongation of human life, and to the furtherance of any other agency that can stimulate the intellectual, the moral, and spiritual life of the entire human race.

"A world federal system, ruling the whole earth and exercising unchallengeable authority over its unimaginably vast resources, blending

---

* Paragraph indentation for ease in reading.

THE TWELVE PRINCIPLES

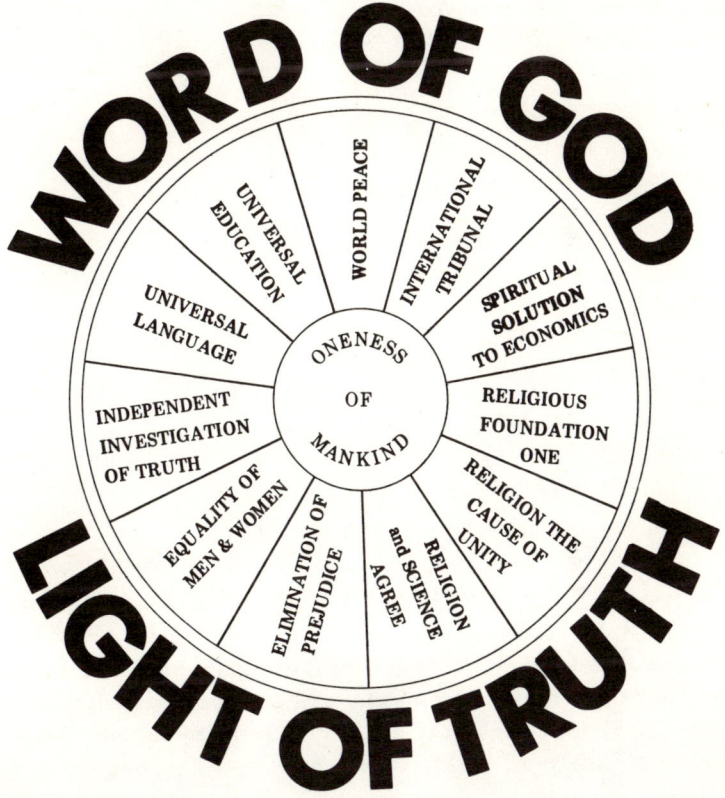

and embodying the ideals of both the East and the West, liberated from the curse of war and its miseries, and bent on the exploitation of all the available sources of energy on the surface of the planet, a system in which Force is made the servant of Justice, whose life is sustained by its universal recognition of one God and by its allegiance to one common Revelation—such is the goal towards which humanity, impelled by the unifying forces of life is moving."[10]

Long has the world waited for this message. No wonder Joseph Smith exclaimed to his followers, just a few months before his martyrdom:

"I will give you a quotation from one of the prophets, who had his eye fixed on the restoration of the priesthood, the glories to be revealed in the last days,...for Malachi says, last chapter, verses 5th and 6th: 'Behold, I will send you Elijah the prophet before the coming of the great and dreadful day of the Lord: And he shall turn the heart of the fathers to the children, and the heart of the children to their fathers, lest I come and smite the earth with a curse'

"For it is necessary in the ushering in of the dispensation of the fulness of times, which dispensation is now beginning to usher in, that a whole and complete and perfect union, and welding together of dispensations, and keys, and powers, and glories should take place, and be revealed from the days of Adam even to the present time. And not only this, but those things which never have been revealed from the foundation of the world, but have been kept hid from the wise and prudent, shall be revealed unto babes and sucklings in this, the dispensation of the fulness of times.

"How beautiful upon the mountains are the feet of those that bring glad tidings of good things, and that say unto Zion: Behold, thy God reigneth! As the dews of Carmel, so shall the knowledge of God descend upon them!" +

There then follows a description of those things which had already been revealed through the restored gospel of Jesus Christ, after which Joseph Smith then went on to urge his followers, and we who read his message:

"Brethren, shall we not go on in so great a cause? Go forward and not backward. Courage, brethren; and on, on to the victory! Let your hearts rejoice, and be exceedingly glad. Let the earth break forth into

---

10. World Order of Baha'u'llah, pages 202 through 204.
+ D. & C. 128:17,18,19; Reorganized D. & C. 110:17a-b, 18d-e, 19b.

singing....Let the mountains shout for joy, and all ye valleys cry aloud; and all ye seas and dry lands tell the wonders of your Eternal King! And ye rivers, and brooks, and rills, flow down with gladness. Let the woods and all the trees of the field praise the Lord; and ye solid rocks weep for joy!...And let the eternal creations declare his name forever and ever! And Again I say, **how glorious is the voice we hear from heaven, proclaiming in our ears, glory, and salvation, and honor, and immortality, and eternal life; kingdoms, principalities, and powers!**

"Behold, the great day of the Lord is at hand; and who can abide the day of his coming, and who can stand when he appeareth? *For he is like a refiner's fire, and like fuller's soap; and he shall sit as a refiner and purifier of silver, and* he shall purify the sons of Levi, and purge them as gold and silver, that they may offer unto the Lord an offering in righteousness."

Only your own heart can answer this plea! Are you ready to go on in so great a cause? Joseph Smith's message was given on September 6, 1842, just slightly over one and a half years before the declaration of the Báb to Mullá Husayn that He was the Promised One, that He was the Messenger of God who had come in the power and mission of Elijah, to *"turn the heart of the fathers to the children, and the heart of the children to their fathers"* before the coming of the great and dreadful day of the Lord. May we conclude with Joseph Smith that we are ready:

"Let us, therefore, as a church and a people, and as Latter-day Saints, offer unto the Lord an offering in righteousness; and let us present in his holy temple, when it is finished, a book containing the records of our dead, which shall be worthy of all acceptation." [11]

That Men Might be Made Partakers of the Glories Which Were to be Revealed

In this brief summary I have quoted but a few of the prophecies contained in Latter-day Saint scripture, and in other scriptures common to all Christians alike, **concerning the times and places, and the other signs to look for if We would discern the coming of the two new Prophets of the Day of God, for Whom Joseph Smith, William Miller, and others were preparing the way. I have introduced you to two Wondrous Figures Who appeared in those lands and at the times foretold in these prophecies.** Are they the two Prophets for Whom the world has long been waiting and Who Joseph Smith declared, must come to

---

11. Please read the entire portion of this section of the *Doctrine and Covenants* pertaining to the coming Kingdom of God. The quotations are from *D. & C.* 128, verses 17, 18b, 19b, 22a, 23-24; Reorganized *D. & C.* 110: 17, 18d-e, 19b, 22a-b, 23-24.

Israel *"at the time of the restoration"?* [12] The chance of this being the case is certainly worth the investigation! If they are, then certainly we must study their lives and deeds and judge them aright:

"*And for this cause, that men might be made partakers of the glories which were to be revealed,* **the Lord sent forth the fulness of his gospel, his everlasting covenant, reasoning in plainness and simplicity—to prepare the weak for those things which are coming on the earth,** *and for the Lord's errand in the day when the weak shall confound the wise, and* **the little one become a strong nation, and two shall put their tens of thousands to flight.** *And by the weak things of the earth the Lord shall thrash the nations by the power of his Spirit'.* [13]

Let us follow the admonition of our beloved prophet who gave his life for so great a cause:

"*We believe all that God has revealed, all that He does not reveal, and we believe that He will yet reveal many great and important things pertaining to the Kingdom of God.*"

"*We Believe in being honest, true, chaste, benevolent, virtuous, and in doing good to all men; indeed, we may say that we follow the admonition of Paul—We believe all things, we hope all things, we have endured many things, and hope to be able to endure all things. If there is anything virtuous, lovely, or of good report or praiseworthy, we seek after these things.*" [14]

Courage, brethren; and on, on to the victory!

---

12. *D. & C.* 77:15, Utah edition.
13. *D. & C.* 133: 57-59; Reorganized *D. & C.* 108: 11a-b
14. Articles of Faith, nos. 9, 13.

Section II

"SEEK YE DILIGENTLY
OUT OF THE BEST BOOKS WORDS OF WISDOM"

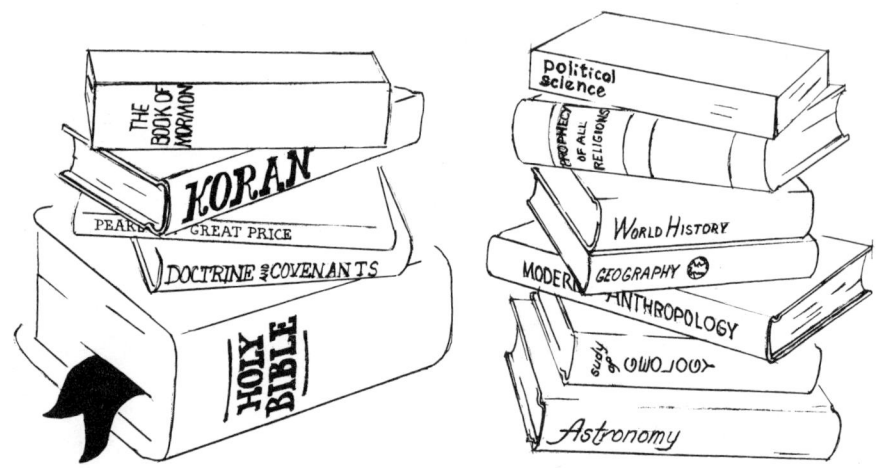

"Teach ye diligently and my grace shall attend you. . . in all things pertaining unto the Kingdom of God. . .

Of things both in heaven and in earth, and under the earth; things which are, things which must shortly come to pass; things which are at home, things which are abroad; the wars and perplexities of the nations, and the judgements which are on the land; and a knowledge also of countries and of kingdoms that ye may be prepared in all things. . ."

D. & C. 88:118, 78-79; Reorganized D. & C. 85; 36a, 216-c.

INTRODUCTION TO SECTION II

The Truth Shall be Distinguished From Error and the Wisdom of Every Command Shall be Tested

In chapters 2 through 4 these questions continually arose: Did Joseph Smith and William Miller really know the identity of the two Prophets for whom they were preparing the way? Did Joseph Smith believe that the self-same Jesus, who was born in Bethlehem and grew up in the village of Nazareth, would descend from heaven upon a cloud with all of the eyes of men turned heavenward to behold His coming? Or is this simply our own interpretation of what was to happen? Could it be that the Son of Man did return in the Glory of the Father, as a *"thief in the night"*, and took men unawares?

From the cited references where Miriam and Aaron spoke against Moses, and John put a question to Jesus (Numbers 12:1-2,5-9; Matthew 11:2-6) we have found that even lesser prophets or seers are given only a partial knowledge of the mysteries of God. Obviously, from the above Bible quotes, they had little feeling of surety and were filled with doubts at times. They, like ourselves, were left the free agency to investigate the meaning of the truth of the revelations which were given through themselves. In the words of the Lord through Joseph Smith:

"Behold, I am God and have spoken it; these commandments are of me, and were given unto my servants in their weakness, after the manner of their language, that they might come to understanding. And inasmuch as they erred it might be made known; and inasmuch as they sought wisdom they might be instructed; and inasmuch as they sinned they might be chastened, that they might repent; and inasmuch as they were humble they might be made strong, and blessed from on high and receive knowledge from time to time". [1]

Sometimes, too, the lesser prophet knows far more than he is permitted to reveal to his followers because of their own limitations of understanding:

"Behold, ye are little children and ye cannot bear all things now; ye must grow in grace and in the knowledge of the truth." [2]

1. *D. & C.* 1:24-28; Reorganized *D. & C.* 1:5a-c.
2. *D. & C.* 50:40; Reorganized *D. & C.* 50:8d.

"Therefore, marvel not at these things, for ye are not yet pure; ye can not yet bear my glory; but ye shall behold it if ye are faithful in keeping all my words that I have given you."[3]

And we must be careful in this spiritual quest, not to seize upon a passage or two of sacred writings, which somehow impresses itself firmly in our minds, and forget everything else that has been said on that subject. An isolated passage of scripture taken by itself and interpreted in a grossly literal sense may yield an interpretation completely distorted from the facts. All too often a partial truth, misunderstood and misinterpreted becomes no truth at all. This might be seen in the following poem by John Godfrey Saxe:

THE BLIND MEN AND THE ELEPHANT

It was six men of Indostan,
 To learning much inclined,
Who went to see the Elephant
 (Though all of them were blind,)
That each by observation
 Might satisfy his mind.

The First approached the Elephant,
 And happening to fall
Against his broad and sturdy side,
 At once began to bawl:
"God bless me! but the Elephant
 Is very like a wall!"

The Second, feeling of the tusk,
 Cried, "Ho! what have we here
So very round and smooth and sharp?
 To me 'tis mighty clear
This wonder of an Elephant
 Is very like a spear!

---

3. *D. & C.* 136:37a, Utah Edition.

The Third approached the animal
    And happened to take
The squirming trunk within his hands,
    Thus boldly up and spake:
"I see," quoth he, "the elephant
    Is very like a snake!"

The Fourth reached out his eager hand,
    And felt about the knee.
"What most this wondrous beast is like,
    Is mighty plain," quoth he;
"Tis clear enough the Elephant
    Is very like a tree!"

The Fifth, who chanced to touch an ear.
    Said: "E'en the blindest man
Can tell what this resembles most;
    Deny the fact who can,
This marvel of an Elephant
    Is very like a fan!"

The Sixth no sooner had begun
    About the beast to grope,
Than, seizing on the swinging tail
    That fell within his scope,
"I see," quoth he, "the Elephant
    Is very like a rope!"

And so these men of Indostan
    Disputed loud and long,
Each in his own opinion
    Exceeding stiff and strong,
Though each was partly in the right,
    And all were in the wrong.[4]

---

4. Cited in Bennion, Lowell L., *The Religion of the Latter-day Saints,* L.D.S. Department of Education, Salt Lake City, Utah, 1940, pp. 19-20.

If we search the holy scriptures we will find that each of the Divine Messengers came in a way that was different from that which the people of their day expected. For this reason each was rejected and maligned by the majority of their own generation. Jesus clearly foretold that when the Son of Man comes again in the Glory of the Father He will come *"as a thief in the night"* and will *"take men unawares"*.[5] He warned us to reject those who come in His name saying, *"Then if any man shall say unto you, Lo, here is Christ, or there; believe it not"*;[6] rather, we must judge the new Prophets by the fruits of their lives and teachings.[7]

There are some things which are facts in the testimony of Joseph Smith concerning the Millennial Dispensation for which he was sent to prepare the way. First, he was shown that he was sent to prepare the way for two Holy Messengers.[8] Second, he was told that these two Prophets would speak to Israel, at the time of the restoration.[9] Third, he was also told that the Jews would be gathered to the land of Jerusalem but not *"until the times of the Gentiles be fulfilled"*.[10] Fourth, he was informed that in that day *"a light"* should *"break forth among them that sit in darkness, and it shall be the fulness of my gospel"* but that they would reject this light and say that *"Christ delayeth his coming until the end of the earth"*; *"And in that generation shall the times of the Gentiles be fulfilled"*.[11] Fifth, the emphasis given in all of Joseph Smith's prophecies was that the two Great Prophets would come quickly, even that *"I am living in your midst and ye cannot see me."*[12] The earliest date implied in the writings of Joseph Smith was 1844, i.e. the year of the martyrdom of Joseph Smith.[13] The latest date was 1890, i.e. the year in which he would have been 85 years old had he lived.[14] There are many other prophecies. In fact, the next section contains a listing of many of them.

Progressive Revelation Through a Series of Dispensations

The problem of getting the greatest understanding out of such an

5. See references (under item "B", Chapter 18).
6. Matthew 24:23.
7. Matthew 7:15-20.
8. *D. & C.* 35:4; Reorganized *D. & C.* 34:2b.
9. *D. & C.* 77:15; Utah Edition.
10. *D. & C.* 45:24-25; Reorganized *D. & C.* 45:3f.
11. Ibid., verses 26-30; 4a-d.
12. *D. & C.* 38:7-8; Reorganized *D. & C.* 38:2b.
13. See especially *D. & C.* 85:7-8; 112:14-15; 34; Reorganized *D. & C.* 105:6, 13b.
14. *D. & C.* 130:14-15, Utah Edition.

abundance of prophecy concerning the last days is a very real one. In order to assist you in this endeavor I have organized these prophecies in a logical sequence. This has been a real task, believe me, one which has consumed many years of study and research, of meditation and prayer.

I finally decided to organize my findings in a question and answer format. I took those questions which I had asked myself concerning God's great plan and the unfoldment of this plan in the cycles of human history, referred to in scripture as *"dispensations of the gospel".* These were the questions for which I knew I must find answers unless I was to forever remain in a state of perplexity and bewilderment concerning the coming Kingdom of God.

I learned that the word *"gospel"* means *"good news"* or *"glad tidings"* and has reference to the reappearance at regular intervals in human history of a Great Prophet, or Heavenly Manifestation, each of whom renews the divine message and restores the knowledge and power of God, after a long night of spiritual darkness. The coming of each of these Holy Messengers to usher in a new dispensation is like a new divine springtime. With His coming the world is reawakened spiritually and from the hearts of mankind a new spiritual and material civilization springs into being.

Such a heavenly florescence can be seen in the coming of Moses and the emergence of the great Israelite culture, first in Palestine in the eastern hemisphere and then, by direct transplantation, in the Nephite-Mulekite civilization in the western world. In both hemispheres this original religious resurrection or resurgence was followed by an eventual decline and spiritual apostasy from the word of God.

A second example of this spiritual renaissance is that of the rapid rise of the Christian civilization following the ministry of Jesus Christ. Here again, for several hundred years there was a spiritual regeneration. Peoples of many diverse languages, cultures, and races were brought together into harmony and love through their common allegiance to one God through His Holy Messenger. This brilliant rise of civilization occurred both in the Old World in and around the Mediterranean Sea, and in the New World throughout the region of what is now Central America and southern Mexico.

This Christian civilization deteriorated into what is known as the *"dark ages"* of European history, which enshrouded the nations of Europe in the darkness of ignorance and error for a period of approximately a full thousand years. However, six hundred years after

PROOFS... of Prophethood

- **The MAN** — PERFECTION, INNATE KNOWLEDGE
- **the BOOK** — REVELATION
- **The CIVILIZATION**

the ministry of Jesus Christ, another Great Prophet arose from the seed of Abraham. Muhammad, the Apostle of God, came to the earth in perhaps the darkest most deteriorated outreaches of the Christian dispensation. He came to the barbaric tribes of the Arabian peninsula, an area to which Ishmael (the father of the Arabs), the first born son of Abraham, had been cast out. Nevertheless, in the Great Covenant of God this son had been promised a great birthright, that he would be the father of a great nation and that "twelve princes" would arise through his lineage.[15]

Under the guidance of these *"twelve princes"* this Islamic civilization developed with marvelous swiftness. It spread its influence across the African continent to the shores of the Atlantic Ocean. To the east it came to encompass all of the Semitic nations, Central Asia, Persia, much of India and finally, touched the shores of the Pacific Ocean through the conversion of the barbarous tribes of the East Indies. It even spread northward across the Mediterranean Sea into Sicily, the Balkans and the Iberian Peninsula, or what is now Spain and Portugal. Throughout this vast region great libraries and universities sprang up in which scholars came to develop the beginnings of our present system of mathematics and such sciences as astronomy, medicine and scientific agriculture. In the natural course of events, Islam too became perverted and divided. But ultimately this civilization came to spread the last rays of its light, like a brilliant sunset, to set ablaze the dark clouds of Europe and to cause the emergence of the Renaissance and Reformation in the Christian world.[16]

The Great or Ancient Covenant of God

These are but a few examples of progressive revelation and the subsequent emergence of ever higher and higher civilizations. Each of these great civilizations of the past had their origin in the appearance on earth of one of these noble Spiritual Founders. What of the generation in which we now live? If these past civilizations were the result of the coming of a Holy Prophet of God, what of the present day? It is well known that in the past one hundred and thirty years (since around 1844) there has been a new spiritual florescence. In terms of our material progress, mankind has advanced more rapidly in this brief period than in all of the dispensations of the past combined. Must we

15. Genesis 17:20. The twelve princes were the Imams or Great Arab Spiritual Leaders who succeeded Muhammad.
16. For an excellent short treatise on this subject I would recommend Stanwood Cobb's *Islamic Contributions to Civilization,* Avalon Press, Washington 15, D.C., 1963.

'Abdu'l-Bahá
Center of the Covenant

again look to that revelation, given to Joseph Smith in March of 1831: "*a light shall break forth among them that sit in darkness, but they receive it not...*"? [17]

In studying the revelation of each of the Great Prophets of the past I learned that each not only foretold the coming of His Successor, the next Messenger of God who would arise to renew the Divine Religion, (see p. 27 in Chap. 1), but that each also foresaw the final culmination of this process of ever and ever higher revelations from God in a golden climax referred to variously as the *"end of time"*, the *"New Jerusalem"*, the *"Kingdom of God"* on earth, or a *"New Heaven and a New Earth"*.

We have found that many of the lesser prophets, and all of the Great Prophets or Manifestations, spoke of the coming of the greatest of all Holy Messengers, one most frequently referred to as the *"Glory of God"* or the *"Glory of the Father"*. Preceding His coming there would arise another Great Prophet who would prepare the way before Him, and following after Him there would be a third personage referred to as the *"messenger of the covenant"*.[18] Always these three are spoken of in relation to the restoration of the children of Israel to the lands of their inheritance and the establishment of the Kingly Way of God on earth.

These prophecies speak of the establishment of unity among all the sons and daughters of God, the emergence of universal peace and justice, the coming together of all the truths of God into one, the resolution of the conflicts among the contending religions, and between religion on the one hand and science on the other. We are given to understand in these prophecies that all of the nations of the earth will become one nation and that justice and the word of God will flow forth from Mount Zion in Israel. Perhaps Zechariah has summarized these prophecies most succinctly in these words:

"And it shall be in that day, that living waters shall go out from Jerusalem; half of them toward the former sea, and half of them toward the hinder sea: in summer and in winter shall it be. And the Lord shall be king over all the earth: in that day shall there be one Lord, and his name one." [19]

17. *D. & C.* 45:28-29; Reorganized *D. & C.* 45:4b-d.
18. See especially Malachi 3:1-4; 4:5-6. This was obviously not a third prophet, but a great saint who would guide the new religion during its formative stage.
19. Zechariah 14:8-9.

A Marvelous Work and a Wonder

I came to understand the special role of Joseph Smith in this Divine Plan, the purpose of the restoration of the Gospel of Jesus Christ, and the reason for the renewal of the Aaronic and Melchizedek priesthoods. I learned of the destiny of America in this Creative Plan, and especially of those early inhabitants now commonly called the American Indian, and those *"new-comers"* referred to in the Book of Mormon as *"Gentiles"*.

Through following the guidelines given from holy scripture I came to discover the Twin Prophets of the Millennial Dispensation, the Center of the Covenant and the Divine Administrative Order which is, like the Word and Power of God in the dispensations of the past, transforming this world into a New Heaven and a New Earth. I came to discover the marvelous teachings of God revealed in this new age and the Kingdom of God which is now enthroned in the hearts of millions of followers among all races, nations and peoples. I learned of a great new Revelation which is transforming this age of darkness into Light, this age of confusion and bloodshed into one of peace and harmony among all of the children of God.

Seek Learning Even by Study and Also by Faith

For those of you who have not trodden the path which I have followed I would not insist that every revelation and every prophecy of Joseph Smith applied specifically to the coming of the two Great Prophets who, I discovered, first appeared in Persia and then came to Israel, as foretold. I am convinced in my own mind that this is true. Nevertheless, God alone is the All Knowing, the All Wise. I urge only that you become sincere seekers. One of the principle truths revealed by the New Prophets is that in this age of maturity every man must investigate truth for himself. Each must use his strong reasoning and then ask for the guidance of the Holy Spirit. Many who have prayed to God and asked if this were true, have been given an answer. You too could try this!

In the following section I have listed those questions which I asked myself in my search for the Kingdom of God. Following each of these questions I have then given the references in the scriptures which either answer the question directly or which point to the places in the world, the time in history, and the signs to look for in order to recognize the Truth.

I have listed first those verses which give the most immediate and direct answer to each question. Following these references I have then listed, within brackets, additional verses which further substantiate or add to the first references.

It may not be necessary that you look up all of these references. Sometimes by looking up one of them your memory will be refreshed as to other revelations bearing on the same subject. There may be other passages of scripture which you will want to read in their full context in the holy writings.

On the other hand, many of you may have found sufficient *"road signs"* given in Section I to lead you to go on from there to investigate the Word of God now streaming forth from the Holy Land **"as the dews of Carmel"**.

I pray, brothers and sisters, that you will examine the evidence presented in this book with an open mind. If you do this in all sincerity, following the guidance of the Holy Spirit, I assure you that your prayers will be answered and that the mysteries of God will be unfolded unto you.

May God bless you in your search.

There are many more additional references than those used in this book and which are listed in the Bibliography. You may wish to write to either the author or the publisher for these.

Part A

GOD HAS A PLAN

Chapter 9

HOW DO WE KNOW GOD AND HIS WILL?

A. **The Great Prophets and Messengers of God Each Revealed His Oneness**

> QUESTION: IS THERE MORE THAN ONE GOD? THE ANSWER FROM HOLY SCRIPTURE:

Abraham Fled From the Idolatrous Land of Chaldea to Become the Founder of a Purely Monotheistic Religion:

See Abraham 1:5, 7, 15, 17, 18, 19

In the Mosaic Dispensation in Both Israel and America Mankind Was Taught the Oneness of God:

See Moses 1:6, 15; Alma 11:26-31 (Reorganized Edition—Alma 8:79-84)

Other references: Exodus 20:3-6; Deuteronomy 6:4-5; Isaiah 43:10-12; 45:21-23; 46:9-10

Jesus Directed Us to Worship God Only:

See Mark 12:28-30; Matthew 19:16-17; See also Mark 10:17-18 and Luke 18:18-19

Muhammad Similarly Taught That There Is But One God:

Koran 2:158

The Only Living and True God:

D. & C. 20:16-19 (Reorganized D. & C. 17:3d-4b)

B. **The Meaning of the Word *"Gods"* and *"Sons of God"***

> QUESTION: IF THERE IS ONLY ONE GOD, THEN WHAT IS THE MEANING OF THE WORD *"GODS"* AND OF THE PHRASE *"SONS OF GOD"*, AS USED IN HOLY SCRIPTURE?

Those Who Receive the Fulness of God's Revelation;

D. & C. 76:55-56, 57 (Reorganized D. & C. 76:5f-h); 1 John 3:1-2
See also Moses 6:8; 7:1; D. & C. 45:7-8; 132:20-23, 24-37 (Reorganized D. & C. 45:2b-c)

The Great Prophets or Heads of Each Dispensation of Divine Religion Were Frequently Spoken Of as The "Son of God" or as "Sons of God" Because Each Received His Revelation Directly From God:

Moses 6:22; Abraham 1:17; Moses 1:3-5; Exodus 33:11, Alma 11:32-35 (Reorganized Edition Alma 8:85-89); John 10:34-38

C. Ways of Knowing God and His Will

QUESTION: CAN MAN COMPREHEND THE ESSENCE OF GOD?

God Is the First Cause and the End of All Things:

Genesis 1:1; Psalms 90:2; Hebrews 1:10-12

None Can Find Out the Extent of His Doings:

Jacob 4:8; Alma 40:8 (Reorganized Edition Jacob 3:9-11; Alma 19:38); D. & C. 88:41-44; 76:1-4 (Reorganized D. & C. 85: 10c-11b; 76:1a-c)

QUESTION: IF WE CANNOT COMPREHEND THE ESSENCE OF GOD, THEN HOW CAN WE KNOW HIM?

All Nature Manifests the Glory of God's Creation:

Psalm 24:1-2; Moses 6:63; D. & C. 88:45-47 (Reorganized D. & C. 85;12a-c) See also Psalms 8:1-6, 9; 19:1-2; Isaiah 40:12-31, 41:1; 44:24.

God Guides the Destiny of Nations:

Amos 9:7-9; Jonah 4:11. See also Isaiah 44:24-28; 45:1; 4-9, 12-13.

The Holy Prophets are Emissaries of the Will of God:

Amos 3:7; 2 Peter 1:19-21; John 4:34; 10:37-38; 12:49-50; *Koran* 10:48.

See also Deuteronomy 29:29; Isaiah 48:9-10; 40:8; Moses 1:31-35; Hebrews 1:1-2.

The PERFECT MIRROR

138 ... *So Great A Cause*

D. The Dispensations of Divine Truth

QUESTION: IN JOHN 14:9 JESUS IS QUOTED AS SAYING: *"HE THAT HATH SEEN ME HATH SEEN THE FATHER".* MANY OF THE PROPHETS SPOKE AS THOUGH GOD HIMSELF WERE SPEAKING TO THE PEOPLE. ARE THE PROPHETS OR IS ANY ONE OF THE HOLY MESSENGERS THE SAME AS GOD?

They Are the Voice of God in the Message Which They Bring to Mankind:

Jeremiah 2:1-2; Ezekiel 36:1-2; *D. & C.* 1:1-2 (Reorganized *D. & C.* 1:1a-b); John 7:14-18

The Attributes or Qualities of God are Revealed Through the Lives and Teachings of the Prophets and Messengers:

The Universal Love of God— See Jeremiah 31:3; John 3:16; 2 Nephi 26:28, 33 (Reorganized Edition—2 Nephi 11:104-105, 111-115)

Spiritual Cleanliness—(See Alma 7:19-25 Reorganized Edition—Alma 5:33-42)

Inner Righteousness—(See Isaiah 1:11-17)

Sincerity and Holiness—(Matthew 6:5-8)

Justice—Amos 5:21-24, Micah 6:8

Forgiveness and Mercy—(Luke 15:25-32)

Intelligence—(Abraham 3:19; *D. & C.* 88:41; 93:36; (Reorganized *D. & C.* 85:10c; 90:6a)

Universality—(Psalm 139:7-12)

Perfection—(3 Nephi 12:48 (Reorganized Edition—3 Nephi 5:92)

God Called His Prophets and Messengers in Each Dispensation to Reveal His Will in Accordance to the Needs and Conditions of That Age:

Jeremiah 1:4-9; Exodus 3:2-4; John 3:31-36; *D. & C.* 1:24-28 (Reorganized *D. & C.* 1:5a-c); Alma 29:4,8 (Reorganized Edition Alma 15:55,59)

Chapter 10

PROGRESSIVE REVELATION AND THE INDEPENDANT INVESTIGATION OF TRUTH

A. The Eternal Creative Word of God

QUESTION: WHAT IS THE HOLY SPIRIT OR HOLY GHOST?

The Creative Power of God:

John 1:1-3, 10; D. & C. 93:8-10 (Reorganized D. & C. 90-1d-f). See also Proverbs 8: 22-31.

The Inspiration of God in Each Dispensation Through His Prophets and Messengers:

John 1:4-9; 1 Corinthians 12:4-7; D. & C. 8:2-3; 68:3-5 (Reorganized D. & C. 8:1c-2a; 68:b-c; 1 Nephi 22:1-2 (Reorganized Edition— 1 Nephi 7:1-5); Jacob 4:13 (R.E. Jacob 3:19-21)

See also Proverbs 8:32-36; Galatians 1:10-12; 1 Nephi 10:17-19; Moroni 10:4-7 (Reorganized Edition —1 Nephi 3:23-32; Moroni 10:4-7); D. & C. 18:34-36; 39:6; 76:114-117; 88:3-7 (Reorganized D. & C. 16:5f-g; 39:2b; 76:8a-b; 85:1c-2b)

The Sustaining Power of God in the Universe:

D. & C. 88:3; 8-13 (Reorganized D. & C. 85:1c, 2c-3b)

B. Divine Revelation Is Continuous and Progressive

QUESTION: HAVE WE RECEIVED A FULNESS OF REVELATION CONCERNING GOD AND HIS CREATIVE PLAN?

God Will Grant Further Revelation Only According to Our Willingness to Receive It:

D. & C. 6:1-5, (also 11:1-5; 12:1-5; 14:1-5)—(Reorganized D. &C. 6:1-2; 10:1-2; 11:1-2; 12:1-2) Alma 12:9-11 (R.E.—Alma 9:15-19)

We Must Grow Spiritually in Order to Recognize God's Messenger:

D. & C. 38:5-9; 50:40,44-46 (Reorganized D. & C. 38:1d-2c; 50:8d,f,g)

The New Messenger of God Will Reveal All Mysteries to Those Who Endure Valiantly:

D. & C. 121:26-31; 128:18b, 19b (Reorganized Edition 110:18d, 3, 19b)

See also D. & C. 76:5-10 (Reorganized D. & C. 76:2)

A Warning Against Following the Precepts of Others and Denying Further Revelation From God:

2 Nephi 28:16-21, 24-30 (Reorganized Edition—2 Nephi 12:19-20, 23-26, 30-38

Those Who Deny Further Revelation Will Deny the Lord When He Comes:

2 Nephi 28:31-32 (Reorganized Edition—2 Nephi 12:39-41)

C. Man Possesses the Free Agency to Investigate Truth for Himself

QUESTION: DOES MAN POSSESS A FREEDOM OF CONSCIENCE TO THINK, STUDY AND ACT FOR HIMSELF?

Man's Intelligence Is From God:

D. & C. 131:7-8; 93:26-33, 36, 37, 39-40 (Reorganized D. & C. 90:4c-5d,6a,c-d)

The Knowledge of Good and Evil Was Given to the First Prophet:

Moses 6:55-57; 2 Nephi 2:26b-27 (Reorganized Edition—2 Nephi 1:116-121)

Free Agency Is Inherent in the Plan of God for the Progress of Man:

Moses 4:3; Jeremiah 7:19; 17:10, 2 Nephi 10:23 (Reorganized Edition—2 Nephi 7:40); John 8:31-32; D. & C. 58:26-29; 98:8; (Reorganized D. & C. 58:6c-f; 95:2c)

QUESTION: SINCE MAN IS A FREE AGENT, SHOULD HE BE COMPELLED IN HIS RELIGIOUS BELIEFS?

The Spirit of the Lord Withdraws When Religion Becomes Authoritarian:

Koran 2:256-257; *D. & C.* 121:34-40 (Utah Edition)

Love and Charity Are the Principles of True Religion:

D. & C. 121:41-46 (Utah Edition); Mosiah 23:7 (Reorganized Edition—Mosiah 11:7)

The Priesthood Was Given to Man in Order that He might Use it to Serve God and His Fellow Men More Effectively:

Mark 8:34-36; Matthew 20:24-28; (Also Luke 22:24-27; *D. & C.* 4:1-7 (Reorganized *D. & C.* 4:1-2)

Individual Spiritual Guidance Given to Those Who Have Faith:

D. & C. 18:18-20 (Reorganized *D. & C.* 16:4c-d)

D. The Greatest Goals of Life

QUESTION: WHAT IS THE PURPOSE OF OUR LIVES?

To Gain Knowledge:

D. & C. 6:6-7; 130:18-19; 131:6 (Reorganized *D. & C.* 6:3); Proverbs 3:13-22

To Progress Eternally Through All the Worlds of God:

Abraham 3:24-26; *D. & C.* 130:20-21 (Utah Edition)

To Teach and Serve Our Fellow Men:

D. & C. 18:10-16 (Reorganized *D. & C.* 16:3e-4a); John 21:15-17; Mosiah 2:17 (Reorganized Edition—Mosiah 1:49)

To Reflect in Our Lives the Attributes of God:

Genesis 1:26,27; John 4:23-24; Matthew 5:48. See also Psalms 51:3, 6-10; 2 Nephi 2:24-25 (Reorganized Edition—2 Nephi 1:114-115)

To Seek the Lord and His Kingdom:

Matthew 6:33; 7:7-8; *D. & C.* 6:13 (Reorganized *D. & C.* 6:5e)

To Gain Immortality and Eternal Life:
Moses 1: (33-36), 37-39

QUESTION: WHAT DO THE SCRIPTURES MEAN BY ETERNAL LIFE?

To Know God and to Recognize His Manifestations or Prophets:
John 17:3; (see also *D. & C.* 132:24, Utah Edition); *D. & C.* 101:38-40; 45:9-10 (Reorganized *D. & C.* 98:5k-l; 45:2d-e)

To Accept the New Revelation of God Is to Have Eternal Life:
D. & C. 42:61; 14:7; 68:10-12 (Reorganized *D. & C.* 42:17a; 12:3b; 68:1g-h)

Our Lives Should be Devoted to Seeking the Son of Man When He Comes in the Glory of the Father:
Matthew 10:37-42; 16:24-27

Genealogy OF ABRAHAM

- =SARAH
  - ISAAC
    - MOSES
      - JESUS CHRIST
- =HAGAR
  - ISHMAEL
    - MUHAMMAD
      - IMAMS (12)
        - BAB
- =KATURAH
  - MIDIAN
    - BAHÁ'U'LLÁH

Chapter 11

THE CREATIVE PLAN OF GOD

A. God's Promises to Mankind if They Obey Him

QUESTION: WHAT IS THE GREAT OR *"ANCIENT"* COVENANT OF GOD? WHAT ARE ITS PROMISES TO MANKIND IF WE OBEY THIS COVENANT?

THE FIRST PROMISE: God Would Renew the Divine Religion Through a Series of Great Prophets or Manifestations of the Will and Attributes of God, Each One to Head Up a New Dispensation of the Gospel:

Moses 5:58-59; 7:42, 45a, 47; Abraham 3:22-23; Deuteronomy 18:17-19; John 16:12-14

The Dawning Place of the New Suns of God Shown Unto Moses:

Deuteronomy 33:1-3

THE SECOND PROMISE: That God Would Raise Up a Choice Lineage Through the Great Prophets:

D. & C. 107:55 (Reorganized D. & C. 104:28c); Moses 7:51-52; Genesis 9:1, 7-9; Abraham 2:9-10 (see also Genesis 12:2-3; 18:18; 22:18)

This Great Covenant Was Renewed Through the Sons of Abraham:

Genesis 17:18-20; 25:1-2; Exodus 18:1, (2-8), 9-10, 11-12, (13-27),24

THE THIRD PROMISE: That the Lands of the Near East Would be Given to the Descendants of Abraham, With the Land of Israel Promised as the Homeland of the Descendants of Jacob:

Genesis 15:18; 17:(2), 4-8; 22:17-18; 21:(9-13), 17-18, 20-21; 26:2-5; 28:(10-12), 13-15; 32:28; Exodus 19:1-8

See also Exodus 31:16-18; Deuteronomy 9:15; I Chronicles 16:13-24; Joshua 1:1-9; Psalms 89:3-5, 15-37; 105:6-15; II Samuel 23:1-5; Jeremiah 11:1-8

So Great A Cause 145

THE FOURTH PROMISE: That the Kingdom of God Would Be Set Up at the End of the Age:

Moses 7:58, 60-62a, 64b-67; 1:40-41; John 16:12-14; Matthew 16:27

B. The Renewal of the Religion of God Through a Series of Great Prophets

QUESTION: WAS CHRISTIANITY A RENEWAL OF THE RELIGION OF ABRAHAM AND MOSES?

Christ's Own Answer:

John 8:56; 5:45-47; 3 Nephi 20:23-24 (Reorganized Edition—Nephi 9:60-62)

See also John 5:39-44

QUESTION: WAS THE RELIGION OF ISLAM SIMILARLY A RENEWAL OF THE RELIGION OF GOD AS REVEALED PROGRESSIVELY THROUGH ABRAHAM, MOSES AND JESUS?

Muhammad Acknowledged His Oneness With Abraham, Moses and Jesus:

Koran 2:81-83, 86-88, 109, 129-131

C. The Universality of God's Revelation

QUESTION: IS GOD'S REVELATION CONFINED TO ONE OR A FEW CHOSEN PEOPLE OR IS IT UNIVERSAL?

All Flesh is One:

Acts 17:24, 26-27, 28b; 1 Nephi 17:35a, 36 (Reorganized Edition 1 Nephi 5:121-122, 126-127)

There is Only One God and One Relgion:

Koran 23:53-56; 4:67

God Grants Unto All Nations After the Manner of Their Language, All of His Word That He Seeth Fit That They Should Have:

Alma 29:1-3, 4b, 5, 8 (Reorganized Edition—Alma 15:52-54 , 55-56,59) See complete context—verses 1 through 8, or 52 through 59 in Reorganized Edition.
D. & C. 1:24-28, 34-35a; (Reorganized D. & C. 1:5a-c, 6a); 2 Nephi 31:3 (Reorganized Edition—2 Nephi 13:4-5)

QUESTION: SINCE GOD REVEALS HIS WORD TO ALL NATIONS, ACCORDING TO THE WORDS OF THE PROPHETS, THEN IS THE FOUNDATION OF ALL TRUE RELIGION ONE AND THE SAME?

All Good Comes From God:

Moroni 7:12, 14-15 (Reorganized Edition—Moroni 7:10, 12-13); Matthew 7:20

God Gives the Same Message Unto All Nations:

2 Nephi 29:7-11 (Reorganized Edition 2 Nephi 12:55-660)

QUESTION: IS ANYONE DENIED THE FULL SALVATION OF GOD BECAUSE OF RACIAL, NATIONAL, SOCIAL, OR SEX DIFFERENCES?

God Is No Respector of Persons:

Acts 10:34-35; 15:8-9; 1 Corinthians 12:12-13; Romans 2:10-11

None Are Forbidden the Full Salvation of God:

2 Nephi 26:23-28, 30, 33 (Reorganized Edition—2 Nephi 11:95-105,107b-108a, 111b-115)

God's Teachers May be of Any Race of Nation:

Romans 10:11-15

Racial, Religious, Sex and Class Prejudices Are Not of God:

Amos 9:7-9; Galatians 3:28-29; Colossians 3:9-11, (12-25); Matthew 25:45

QUESTION: GOD PROMISED ABRAHAM THAT THROUGH HIS SEED ALL NATIONS OF THE EARTH WOULD BE BLESSED. DID HE MEAN ONLY THE LITERAL DESCENDANTS OF THE

PROPHET OR DID HE MEAN ALL OF THOSE
WHO FOLLOW THE DIVINE TEACHINGS AND
COVENANT OF GOD?

As Many as Receive and Live the Religion of God Are Accounted as Abraham's Seed:

Abraham 2:10; Matthew 3:1, 7-10; Romans 9:6-8. (See also Luke 3:1-9; Galatians 3:7-9)

All Those Who Repent and Recognize the Coming of the Lord Are His Seed:

Romans 2:28-29; 2 Nephi 6:13-14; 10-16; 30:1-2 (Reorganized Edition—2 Nephi 5:33-38; 7:23-25; 12:75-78)

God Will Raise Up a Pure People From Among All People, Who Will Serve Him in Righteousness:

2 Nephi 31:15, 20 (Reorganized Edition 2 Nephi 13:19-20, 29 - 30); D. & C. 100 :15-17 (Reorganized D. & C. 97:4c-d); Isaiah 56: (1-2), 6-8

There Shall Be One Lord Over All the Earth, and His Name Shall Be One:

1 Nephi 22:24-28, (31) (Reorganized Edition 1 Nephi 7:55-64, (68-70); Zechariah 14:8-9; John 10:14-16; 3 Nephi 16:(1-6), 7, 11-13 [Reorganized Edition 3 Nephi 7:(24-30), 31, 36-37]. See also 1 Nephi 13:41 (Reorganized Edition 1 Nephi 3: 195-197)

Part B

THE SPECIAL ROLES
OF ISRAEL AND AMERICA

Chapter 12

GOD'S PLAN UNFOLDS
THE SPECIAL MISSION OF JOSEPH SMITH

A. A New Covenant Promised for the Age of Maturity

>QUESTION: THE GREAT OR ANCIENT COVENANT OF GOD WAS TO FIND ITS FULFILLMENT IN THE ESTABLISHMENT OF THE KINGDOM OF GOD ON THE EARTH. DID GOD PROMISE THAT HE WOULD MAKE A NEW COVENANT WITH MANKIND AT THAT TIME?

The End of the Priestly Functions of Religion and the Beginning of an Independent Investigation of Truth:

Jeremiah 31:31-34; John 4:19-21, 23,24; D. & C. 13; 128:24 (Reorganized D. & C. 110:24)

Each Individual Will Be Held Accountable for His Own Acts and Not for the Acts of Another:

Ezekiel 18:1-5, 9, 10-20, 31-32

Men Should Do Things of Their Own Free Will:

D. & C. 58:26-29 (Reorganized D. & C. 58:6c-f)

Science and Religion Must Agree; Search All Things:

D. & C. 88:73-83, 117-119; 121:26-31 (Reorganized D. & C. 85:20-21, 36)

Each Must Investigate Truth for Himself or Perish in Darkness:

2 Nephi 28: (24-30),31-32; 32:4 (Reorganized Edition—2 Nephi 12:(30-38), 39-41; 14:5)

B. Prepare Ye the Way of the Lord

>QUESTION: SINCE THE CHURCH OF JESUS CHRIST WAS ESTABLISHED IN THE LATTER DAYS IN

ORDER TO PREPARE MEN'S MINDS AND HEARTS FOR THE COMING KINGDOM OF GOD, WHAT WAS ITS ROLE IN RELATIONSHIP TO THIS NEW AGE OF FULFILLMENT?

A Falling Away Foretold Before the Coming of the Lord:

Amos 8:11-12; Micah 3:5-7; 2 Timothy 3:1-7; 4:3-4; Revelation 13:7. See also Isaiah 24:1-6; 2 Thessalonians 2:1-4; 2 Peter 2:1-2; 1 Nephi 13:24-26 (R. E. 1 Nephi 3:164-169)

The New Manifestation Would Send His Angels (Forerunners) Before Him:

Mark 13:27; Joseph Smith 1:37-39; Revelation 7:1-3, 9-10; 8:2 See also Matthew 13:36-43; D. & C. 29:7-11; 33:2-10, 17-18 (Reorganized D. & C. 28:2c-g; 32:1c-2f, 3e)

Joseph Smith Came to Restore the Original Pure Teachings of Christ Prior to the Coming of the Lord in the Full Glory of the Father:

Joseph Smith 2:18-19; D. & C. 14:1-4, (5-7), 8-10; 24:19 (Reorganized D. & C. 12:1-2, (3), 4a-5b; 23:7c-d)
See also 2 Nephi 28:3-5, 9-12 (Reorganized Edition—2 Nephi 12:3-7, 12-14; D. & C. 1:14-16; 10:57-63; 18:41-47; 20:1-2, 8-15 (Reorganized D. & C. 1:3c-e; 3:14a-15d; 16:6d-7e; 17:1a-b, 2c-3c)

The Restored Gospel of Jesus Christ Contains Much But Not All of the Revelation of God to Be Given in the Latter Days:

1 Nephi 13:34, (35-36), 37; 2 Nephi 3:6-8, (11-18a), 18b-21, 24 (Reorganized Edition—1 Nephi 3:181-183, (184-186), 187-189; 2 Nephi 2:10-14, (17-36), 37-43, 46-47); D. & C. 10:49-52; 6:26-29 (Reorganized D. & C. 3:11; 6:12a-14a)
See also D. & C. 19:21-24, 31-32; 128:18b-24 (Reorganized D. & C. 18:2l-o, 4d-5a; 110:18d-24c)

QUESTION: THE GREAT OR ANCIENT COVENANT OF GOD PROMISED THE CONTINUITY OF REVELATION AND THE SUCCESSION OF HIGH PROPHETS UNTIL THE LORD SHOULD COME TO USHER IN THE MILLENIAL DISPENSATION OR KINGDOM OF GOD ON EARTH: WHAT

So Great A Cause . . . 151

WAS THE RELATIONSHIP OF THE CHURCH OF JESUS CHRIST OF LATTER-DAY SAINTS TO THE COMING KINGDOM, OR WHAT WERE ITS PURPOSES FOR MANKIND?

FIRST: It Was a Voice of Warning to All Nations and Peoples of a Coming Judgement:

D. & C. 1:(1-10), 11-15, (32-33, 37-38); 43:17-21, (22), 23-24, (25), 26-30; 63:57-59; 84:87 (Reorganized *D. & C.* 1:(1-2), 3, (5f-g, 7-8) 43:5-6b, (6c), 6d-7c; 63:15a-c; 83:15b)

SECOND: It Was a Proclamation to the Peoples and Rulers of the Earth of the Imminent Return of the Lord:

D. & C. 33:2-3, 10-11, 16-18; 34:5-8, (9-10), 11-12; 124:3, 8-11 [Reorganized *D. & C.* 32:1e-d, 2f-g, 3d-e; 33:1c-e, (2a), 2b-e; 107:1c, 2b-3]
See also *D. & C.* 58:63-65 (Reorganized *D. & C.* 58:15c-d)

THIRD: Its Intent Was to Teach Men to Reason as in Days of Old, in Order That They May Be Able to Discern the Signs of His Coming:

1 Peter 3:15; 1 Thessalonians 5:21; Acts 17:2; 18:4; *D. & C.* 45: (1-7), 9-10, 15-16; 50:10-12; 68:1, 10-11; 71:7-9 (Reorganized *D. & C.* 45:(1a-2b), 2d-e, 2i-k, 50:4a-b; 68:1a, g-h; 71:2e-g)
See also Luke 12:22-31; *D. & C.* 66:2, 5, 7, 9 (Reorganized *D. & C.* 66:1b, 2b, 5c)

Relationship of the Restored Gospel of Christ to the Coming Kingdom of the Father:

Ephesians 1:9-10; Acts 3:19-21; 3 Nephi 20:26-27, 29-30; 21:7-11, 22-23 (Reorganized Edition—3 Nephi 9:64-65, 67-69, 93-98; 1-2; *D. & C.* 65:1-6 (Reorganized *D. & C.* 65:1a-f)

He That Understands the Gospel Fully Will Receive the Lord When He Comes in the Glory of the Father:

D. & C. 39:5-6, 11-13, 17-24 (Reorganized *D. & C.* 39:2, 3d-4b, 5-6)

FOURTH: The Revelations Which Were Given Were to Open Men's Minds That They Might be Receptive to the Greater Revelations Which the New Prophet Would Bring to Mankind:

D. & C. 11:22-27; 42:15; 58:3-6, 9-14a, (14b-15); 63:66; 64:32-33; 71:1-6; 76:5-10 (Reorganized *D. & C.* 10:10c-11c; 42:5c; 58: 2a-3b, 3d-4a, (4b); 63:16c; 64:6c; 71:1-2d; 76:2a-d)

See Joseph Smith 2:30, 34, 36, 40-41, 54. The scriptures which he quotes all pertain to **the coming of two Great Prophets after the restoration of the Gospel of Jesus Christ.** See also Alma 34: 26-41 (Reorganized Edition—Alma 16:221-239)

Joseph Smith Urged Us to Go Forward to Receive the Fulness of the Gospel of Which the Church of Jesus Christ of Latter-day Saints Was But the Beginning or Forerunner:

D. & C. 38:7-9; 101:22-23, 32-36; 128:17, 18b-19, (20-21), 22-24; 133:57-59, 63-64, 71 (Reorganized *D. & C.* 38:2b; 98:5a, 5g-i; 110:17, 18d-19, (20-21), 22-24; 108:11a-b, 11e-12b, 13a)

C. **Joseph Smith Was a Forerunner to the Coming of the Two Great Prophets of the New Day of God, Similar to John the Baptist and Samuel the Lamanite in the Dispensation of Christ**

QUESTION: IS THERE A SIMILARITY BETWEEN THE MISSION OF JOSEPH SMITH AND OF THOSE FORERUNNERS WHO PREPARED THE WAY THE COMING OF JESUS CHRIST?

In Ancient Israel John the Baptist Taught Repentance, Baptism, and Faith in the Coming Messiah, Who Was Already Living on the Earth During His Own Ministry:

Matthew 3:1-3, 5-7, 11-12 (See also Mark 1:1-18 and Luke 3:1-20)

Samuel the Lamanite Warned of Judgements to Come Upon the Nephites Except They Repent and Live Up to God's Commandments Prior to the Coming of Jesus Christ:

Helaman 13:1-3, (5-8); 14:2 (Reorganized Edition—Helaman 5:1-4, (6-10); 55)

Joseph Smith and Sidney Rigdom Were Called Upon to Prepare the Way for Two Great Prophets Who Were to Come in Rapid Succession to Usher in the Kingdom of God on Earth:

D. & C. 35:3-6, 10-12, 15-18; 77:14-15 (Reorganized *D. & C.* 34: 2, 3d-e, 4d-f)

Chapter 13

WHAT HAPPENED TO ZIONISM AND UNITED ORDER?

A. Keys to the Kingdom

QUESTION: WERE ANY OF THE PRINCIPLES OF THE COMING KINGDOM, UPON WHICH A NEW WORLD ORDER MIGHT BE BUILT, REVEALED TO THE LATTER-DAY SAINTS?

The Oneness of Mankind Was Enjoined in the Dispensations of Enoch, Moses and of Christ and Rerevealed Through Joseph Smith:

Moses 7:17-18; Omni 18, 19; 4 Nephi 2-3, (7-8), 15-18 (Reorganized Edition—Omni 32, 34; 4 Nephi 1:3-4, (9), 17-21); John 12:11, 20-21; 15:12-14

The Lord Revealed to Joseph Smith That Human Bondage is Contrary to the Will of God:

D. & C. 101:78-80 (Reorganized D. & C. 98:10:e-h)

John the Revelator Predicted That There Would Be Twelve Principles of Unity Upon Which the Kingdom of God Would Be Built:

Revelation 21:1-7, 10-14, 21-27; 22:1-2, 4-5, 17

Joseph Smith Likewise Foresaw Twelve Principles of Unity, the Chief of Which is the Oneness of Mankind:

D. & C. 38:23-28 (Reorganized D. & C. 38:5c-6b)

Joseph Smith Urged the Saints to Seek a Spiritual Solution for Economic Problems:

Material Means should Be Sought Only to Do Good:
D. & C. 6:7 (Reorganized D. & C. 6:3b-c); Jacob 2:17-19 (Reorganized Edition—Jacob 2:22-24); Matthew 6:19-24

Equality in Temporal Things Is a Prerequisite to Equality in Spiritual Things:

D. & C. 70:14, (15-18); 78:3-7 (Reorganized D. & C. 70:3d, (4); 77:1c-g)

Beware of Pride and Covetousness:

2 Nephi 9:30; Jacob 2:12-16, 20-21; 4 Nephi 23-26, 43-45; Mormon 6:16-20, 22 (Reorganized Edition—2 Nephi 6:62-64; Jacob 2:14-21, 25-28; 4 Nephi 1:26-28, 51-53; Mormon 3:18-20, 23); D. & C. 38:39, 42; 88:123 (Reorganized D. & C. 38:9a-c; 85:38a) See also D. & C. 56:14-20 (Reorganized D. & C. 56:4c-5c)

Work in the Spirit of Service is Worship of God:

D. & C. 42:40-42; 70:12-13; 82:14-19, 24;88:124-126 (Reorganized D. & C. 42:12a-b; 70:3c; 81:4c-g, 6e; 85:38a-c)

The Law of Consecration or United Order:

D. & C. 42:29-39; 70:7-11; 82:20-21, 24 (Reorganized D. & C. 42:8-11; 70:2b-3c; 81:5, 6c)

See also D. & C. 51:1-5, 7-9, 13-20; 78:11-15; 104:67-77 (Reorganized D. & C. 51:1, 2, 4-5; 77:2d-3e; 101; 12a-j)

The Law of Tithing—All Surplus Property to Be Given:

D. & C. 119:1-7 (Reorganized D. & C. 106:1-2); Mark 10:17-22, (23-27)

The Principles of Common Consent and Consultation Were Revealed in Part to Joseph Smith:

D. & C. 20:65, 71; 26:2; 88:122; 121:40-46 (Reorganized D. & C. 17:16a, 20; 25:1b; 85:37b)

See also D. & C. 28:13; 104:21, 64, 67, 70-71 (Reorganized D. & C. 27:4c; 101:3c, 10d, 12a, 12d-e)

B. God Said That the Saints Were Not Yet Ready to Receive the Kingdom

QUESTION: SINCE THESE PRINCIPLES WERE GIVEN AS A PART OF THE NEW AND EVERLASTING COVENANT, ARE THEY BEING PRACTICED IN THE CHURCH TODAY? IF THEY ARE NOT NOW BEING PRACTICED, WHEN AND WHY WERE THEY ABROGATED?

A Covenant Is a Solemn Promise Between God and Man.

D. & C. 25:13-15; 82:7-10 (Reorganized D. & C. 24:3c-4a, 4b; 81:2-3)

So Great A Cause ... 155

The Alternate Results of Covenant Keeping and of Covenant Breaking:

D. & C. 1:31-35; 38:13-19, 21-22; 63:1, (2-4), 5-9, 13, 15, 20-23; 54:3-6, 10; 56:1-4; 95:11-12 (Reorganized *D. & C.* 1:5f-6b; 38: 4a-e, 5a-b; 63:1a, (b-c), 2a-3a, 4a, 4c, 6-7; 54:1b-e, 3; 56:1a-2a; 92:3a)

The Church Was Made to Be a Judge of the Nations:

D. & C. 64:29-43 (Reorganized *D. & C.* 64:6b-8b)

Zion is Not to Be Removed But the People Constituting Zion May Be Changed:

D. & C. 97:7-9, 18-28 (Reorganized *D. & C.* 94:2e-g, 5a-g); See also *D. & C.* 105:35-37; 113:7-10; 133:17-21, 57-74 (Reorganized *D. & C.* 102:10c-d; 108:5a-e, 11-13); 3 Nephi 16:10-13; 20:29-30; 2 Nephi 29:14 (Reorganized Edition 3 Nephi 7:34-38; 9:67-69; 2 Nephi 12:73-74)

Repeated Warnings Given to the Saints to Repent:

D. & C. 3:1-11; 20:32-34; 41:1-6; 50:4-6, (7-9); 68:30-32, 33-35; 88:121; 121:34-38 (Reorganized *D. & C.* 2:1-4; 17:6d-e; 41:1-2; 50:2, (3); 68:4e-g,i; 85:37a)
See also *D. & C.* 63:12-23, 32-34, 53-64, 66; 75:28-29; 90:35-37; 100:13; 101:16-19; 112:23-28, 34 (Reorganized *D. & C.* 63:4-7, 9a-c, 13c-16a, c; 75:5a-b, 87:8b-d; 97:4a; 98:4f-g; 105:9a-11b, 13b)

The Sin of Omission—Failure to Seek the Lord and His Kingdom:

D. & C. 38:7-9; 45:7, 9, 26-30, 36-39, 44, 47-50, 56-59 (Reorganized *D. & C.* 38:2; 45:2b, d, 4a-d, 5c-6a, d-e, 8a-c, 10b-d); Joseph Smith 1:46-53; *D. & C.* 50: (17-22), 23-26, 34, 40, 44-46; 95:1-6; 106:4-5; 1:11-16, 38; (Reorganized *D. & C.* 50:(5-6a), 6b-c, 7d, 8d, g; 92:1a-e; 103:2; 1:3, 8a-b) 2 Nephi 7:10-11; 9:27-29, 31-33, 42-43, (44-52); 28:32 (Reorganized Edition—2 Nephi 5:67-69; 6:56-61, 65-67, 83-85, (86-103; 12:40-41)

Afflictions Permitted to Befall the Saints Because of Their Transgressions:

D. & C. 101:1-5, (6-12), 40-42; 103:4, 8-10 (Reorganized *D. & C.* 98:1-2, (3-4d, 5k-m; 100:1b, 2c-d)

The United Order Dissolved; the Saints Driven From the Land of Zion:

D. & C. 52:14-21; 104:1-9, 18, 51-57; 105:1-10 (Reorganized D. & C. 52:4b-5b; 101:1, 2g, 9e-10c; 102:1-3c)

C. The Ancient Priesthood Was Restored in Order to Prepare the Saints for the Administrative Order of the Lord of the Kingdom

QUESTION: WHY WAS THE PRIESTHOOD OF FORMER DISPENSATIONS RESTORED? HOW LONG WAS IT PROMISED THAT THE PRIESTHOOD WOULD CONTINUE?

John the Baptist Restored the Aaronic Priesthood to Joseph Smith and Oliver Cowdery With the Promise that It Would Endure Until the Sons of Levi Again Offer an Offering Unto the Lord in Righteousness:

D. & C. 13 Utah Edition; Joseph Smith 2:67-75 and footnote

The Priesthood Was Promised to Remain Until the Restoration of All things:

D. & C. 86:8-11 (Reorganized D. & C. 84:3-4)

QUESTION: TO WHAT PEOPLE DID JOHN THE BAPTIST REFER WHEN HE SAID *"UNTIL THE SONS OF LEVI DO OFFER AGAIN AN OFFERING UNTO THE LORD IN RIGHTEOUSNESS"*?

Three Holy Persons Promised: A Messenger Who Will Prepare the Way, The Lord, and a Messenger of the Covenant—All Three to Purify the Sons of Levi in the Land of Jerusalem:

Malachi 3:1-4

Who Will Accept These Three Messengers and Abide the New Day of the Lord? Will You Be Among This Chosen People?

D. & C. 133:10-13, 21, 33-35; 128:23-24 (Reorganized D. & C. 108:3c-4b, 5e, 6d-f; 110:23-24)

Chapter 14

THE FULNESS OF
THE GOSPEL TO GO TO THE HOUSE OF ISRAEL

A. Israel to Be Redeemed—The Glory of the Lord to Come to the Land of Jerusalem

QUESTION: WHAT PROMISES DID THE LORD MAKE CONCERNING ISRAEL IN THE LAST DAYS?

The Descendants of Jacob to be Again Remembered By the Lord:

Isaiah 65:8-10

A New Dispensation Promised—The Lord to Come to Israel:
Isaiah 65:17-19, (20-24), 25

The Land of Jerusalem to be Redeemed:

Isaiah 66:5, 10; (11-12, 13-15, 16)

All Nations and Tongues to See the Glory of the Lord—His Servants to be Called by a New Name:

Isaiah 66:18; 65:14-16

The Children of Israel to Offer an Offering Unto the Lord in Righteousness:

Isaiah 66:19-23

B. Judgements of the Lord Upon the Saints—The Fulness of the Gospel to Be Taken From Them and to Go to the Seed of Abraham

QUESTION: SINCE THE LATTER-DAY SAINTS FAILED TO FULLY OBEY THEIR COVENANT WITH THE LORD WERE THEY PERMANENTLY REJECTED BY HIM AS A PEOPLE OF PROMISE?

The Times of the Gentiles Fulfilled Because the Gentiles Failed to Accept the Fulness of the Gospel, and the New Light of God Dawning in the East:

D. & C. 45:22-32, 39, 44 (Reorganized D. & C. 45:3e-4e, 6a, d)

158 . . . *So Great A Cause*

The Fulness of the Gospel to Go to the Lost Tribes of Israel and to the Jews in the Land of Israel:

1 Nephi 13:41-42; 15:18-20; (Reorganized Edition 1 Nephi 3:194 - 200, 4:28-33); 2 Nephi 29:12-14; (Reorganized Edition 2 Nephi 12:67-74) 3 Nephi 16:(8-9), 10-12, (13-15a), 15b, (16-20); 20: 27-33, (34-46); (chapter 21)(Reorganized Edition 3 Nephi 7:(32-33), 34-37, (38-40), 41, (42-45); 9:65-71, (72-106); (10:1-8)

The Gentiles to be Numbered Among the Covenant People if They Repent:

3 Nephi 16:13-15; 21:14-25; (Reorganized Edition 3 Nephi 7:38-40; 10:1-4)

QUESTION: DO THESE PROPHECIES CONCERNING WHAT IS GOING TO HAPPEN TO THE GENTILES APPLY TO THE LATTER-DAY SAINTS?

Latter-day Saints Are Spoken of as Gentiles in the Book of Mormon:

2 Nephi 30:3-5; 3 Nephi 16:6-7; (Also 1 Nephi 22:7-9); (Reorganized Edition 2 Nephi 12:79-82; 3 Nephi 7:30-31; (Also 1 Nephi 7:15-20)

Joseph Smith Makes a Clear Distinction Between the Latter-day Saints and the Descendants of Israel:

D. & C. 109:60-65, Utah Edition

QUESTION: DOES THE BOOK OF MORMON FORETELL WHAT WOULD HAPPEN TO THE LATTER-DAY SAINTS AS A CONSEQUENCE OF THEIR REJECTION OF THE FULNESS OF THE REVELATION OF GOD?

Materialism, Racism and Priestcraft Condemned:

2 Nephi 26:19-22, 23-24, 25, 28-29, 32-33; 28:12-16; (Reorganized Edition 2 Nephi 11:89-93a, 95-99, 104-106, 110-115; 12; 14-20)

Failure to Seek the Further Revelation of God Foretold:

2 Nephi 28:21, 24-32, (29:7-11); [Reorganized Edition 2 Nephi 12:25-26, 40-41, (55-66)]

So Great A Cause . . . 159

"I Will Hide Up Their Treasures When They Shall Flee Before Their Enemies": *

Helaman 13:17, 20, (21-23), 24-26, (27-28, 29-31) (32-39); (Reorganized Edition—Helaman 5:22, 26-27, (28-32), 33-36, (37-39), 40-43, (44-53)

QUESTION: WERE THESE PROPHECIES FULFILLED?

The Latter-day Saints Were Led Out of Bondage Like the Children of Israel, to Dwell in the Wilderness of Confusion Until They Are Ready to Receive the Glory of God and the Revelation He Will Bring:

D. & C. 103:15-20; 136:1-4, 11, 16-18, 22, 30-33, 37-42; (Reorganized Edition 100:3d-f). (Compare Exodus 18-20; Deuteronomy 5-6)

C. The Work of God in Human History

> QUESTION: WHAT IS THE MEANING OF THE ALLEGORY OF THE TAME AND WILD OLIVE TREES AS RELATED IN JACOB CHAPTERS 5 AND 6 (Chapters 3 and 4 in Reorganized Edition)?

Israel is Scattered Among the Nations:

Jacob 5:3-8, 13-14; (Reorganized Edition—Jacob 3:31-39, 46-48)

Gentile Nations Are Grafted Onto the Tree of Israel:

Jacob 5:9-12, 17-18; (Reorganized Edition—Jacob 3:40-45, 52-57)

Disunity and Apostasy Overcome the Church of God Among the Gentile Nations:

Jacob 5:29-32, 37; (Reorganized Edition—Jacob 3:72-78, 83-84)

The Foundation of All Prophetic Religions is One:

Jacob 5:34-36; (Reorganized Edition 3:80-82)

The Religion of the Descendants of Israel Scattered Among the Nations Also Became Corrupted:

Jacob 5:38-42; (Reorganized Edition—Jacob 3:85-92)

---

* This address was given by the prophet Samuel, concerning the Nephites, just six years prior to the birth of Jesus Christ. Would this same warning apply to the Latter-day Saints who are similarly living in the days of the coming of two Great Prophets or Manifestations of God?

Map V: **TESTIMONY OF TWO NATIONS**—The Revelations of God in the Latter-days or in the Dispensation of the Fulness of Times.

"After He has manifest Himself unto the Jews and also unto the Gentiles, then He shall manifest Himself unto the Gentiles and also unto the Jews, and the last shall be first and the first shall be last. . . . Wherefore murmur ye, because that ye shall receive more of My word? Know ye not that the testimony of two nations is a witness unto you that I am God, that I remember one nation like unto another? And when the two nations shall run together the testimony of the two nations shall run together also."

1 Nephi 13:42b; 2 Nephi 29:8; Reorganized Edition, 1 Nephi 3:199-200; 2 Nephi 12:58-61

So Great A Cause . . . 161

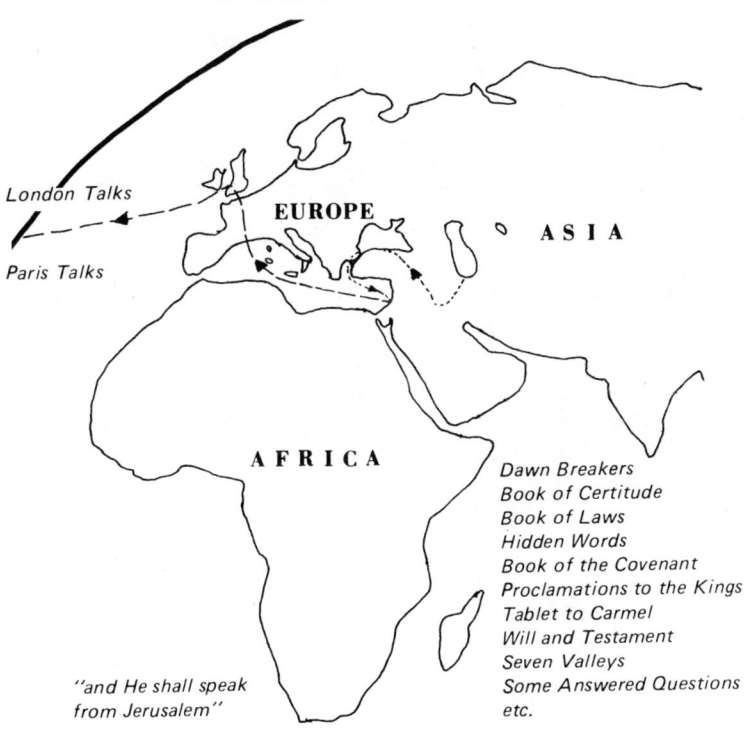

"and also unto the Jews"

Historic Journeys
◀┅┅┅ Exile of Bahá'u'lláh from Teheran to Akka.
◀━━ Journey of Abdu'l-Bahá from Akka (Acre) to America.
◀━·━ Exodus of the Latter-day Saints.

"*And He shall utter His voice out of Zion, and He shall speak from Jerusalem. . . And they who are in the north countries shall come in remembrance before the Lord; and their prophets' shall hear His voice, and shall no longer stay themselves. . . And they also of the tribe of Judah, after their pain shall be sanctified in holiness before the Lord, to dwell in His presence day and night, forever and ever.*"

D. & C. 133:21, 26a, 35; Reorganized D. & C. 108:52, 6a, 6f

The Revelation of God to be Taken Away From the Gentiles and Given Again to the House of Israel:

Jacob 5:52-56, 60-62, 68; (Reorganized Edition Jacob 3:112-119, 123-126, 133-134)

The Lord to Appear Among the Children of Israel in the Last Days:

Jacob 5:71-76; (Reorganized Edition Jacob 3:137-150)

D. The Day of Judgement; to Be Followed by the Kingdom of God on Earth

Jacob 6:1-4; 1 Nephi 10:12-14, 18-19; 13:42; (Reorganized Edition Jacob 4:1-7; 1 Nephi 3:16-19, 29-32, 27-28, 198-200)

Chapter 15

THE DESTINY OF AMERICA
LATTER-DAY SAINTS AND AMERICAN INDIANS

A. The Latter-day Saints to Be Redeemed if They Return Unto the Lord

> QUESTION: WHAT IS THE FUTURE DESTINY OF THE LATTER-DAY SAINTS?

Redemption of the Saints Promised After a Season:

D. & C. 43:27-31; 98:18; 100-13, 15-17; 103:11-14; 105:9-10, (27-29), 34-37, (38-41); [Reorganized D. & C. 43:7a-c; 95:3f; 97: 4a, c, d; 100:3; 102:3c, 8b, 10b-d, (11)]

A Prayer by Joseph Smith Both for the Redemption of the Saints and Also for the Redemption of Israel:

D. & C. 109:46-49, 60-67, 77, 80, Utah Edition

The Book of Mormon Promises That if the Gentiles Repent and Return Unto the Father They Shall Be Numbered Among His Chosen People:

1 Nephi 14:1-2; 2 Nephi 6:12-14, 17; 30:1b-2; 3 Nephi 16:13-14; (Reorganized Edition 1 Nephi 3:201-205; 2 Nephi 5:30-38, 42b; 12:76b-78; 3 Nephi 7:38-39)

America is a Land of Promise for the Righteous:

2 Nephi 10:19; Ether 2:10-11; (Reorganized Edition 2 Nephi 7: 30-32; Ether 1:32-33)

B. Indian Peoples of America Are Promised Great Blessings

> QUESTION: WHAT IS THE DESTINY OF THE AMERICAN INDIAN?

An Ancient American Scripture to Come Forth Through the Gentiles to the Indians:

Isaiah 29:4, 11-12; Psalm 85:11; 1 Nephi 13:35-37, (38-41); 2

Nephi 26:14-17; Title Page to Book of Mormon; [Reorganized Edition 1 Nephi 3:184-189, (190-197); 2 Nephi 11:80-86; Title Page]
See also 1 Nephi 1:1-3; 6:1-6; 19:23-24; Omni 1:15-16, 19; (Reorganized Edition 1 Nephi 1:1-2; 2:1-6; 4:3-7; Omni 1:26-27, 34)

The Nephites and Lamanites Were Descendants of Israel Through Joseph and Judah and Were Thus Heirs to the Covenant of God With This People:

1 Nephi 5:14-16; 15:12-14; 2 Nephi 3:3-5, (22-24); Omni 15, 19; [Reorganized Edition 1 Nephi 1:164-168; 4:14-19; 2 Nephi 2:4-9, (44-47); Omni 1:26, 34] D. & C. 10:57-62, 65-67; (Reorganized D. & C. 3:14a-15b,c, 16)

The Seed of Joseph Was Promised a Choice Land Across the Ocean From the Land of Israel:

Genesis 35:9-11; 49:22, 25-26; Deuteronomy 33:13-16; 1 Nephi 18:23-25; 2 Nephi 10:10-14, 19-20; 3 Nephi 15:12-17; (Reorganized Edition 1 Nephi 5:212-217; 2 Nephi 7:17-21, 30-36; 3 Nephi 7:13-16)
See also 1 Nephi 13:30; 2 Nephi 1:5-12;   (Reorganized Edition 1 Nephi 3:176-177; 2 Nephi 1:6-26)

C. **The Gentiles and Indians May Together Build a New Divine Civilization in America**

    QUESTION: WHY ARE THE LATTER-DAY SAINTS INTERESTED IN THE AMERICAN INDIAN? ARE THE DESTINIES OF THESE TWO SEPARATE PEOPLES IN ANY WAY RELATED?

The Gentiles Are Promised That They Shall Assist the Remnant of Jacob, and the Other Inhabitants of Ancient America Who Mingled With Them to Become What is Now Known as the American Indian, in Building a New Jerusalem in America:

Isaiah 49:6; Ether 13:4, 7-12; 3 Nephi 20:21-22; 21:22-25; (Reorganized Edition Ether 6:4a, 6-13; 3 Nephi 9:57-59; 10:1-4a; D. & C. 84:1-3; (Reorganized D. & C. 83:1)
[See also D. & C. 57:1-5, (Reorganized D. & C. 57:1);Articles of Faith, no. 10]

D. The Sacred Scriptures of the Church of Jesus Christ of Latter-day Saints Have Many Valuable Guidelines to Assist the Sincere Seeker After Truth

QUESTION: SINCE THE SPECIAL MISSION OF THE CHURCH AND PRIESTHOOD WAS TO STIMULATE MEN'S MINDS AND HEARTS TO SEEK THE LORD AND HIS KINGDOM: WHAT SPECIAL GUIDELINES DOES IT OFFER TO ASSIST US IN PURSUING THIS GREAT QUEST?

We Should Give Diligent Heed to Every Word From God, Believing That He Will Yet Reveal Many Great and Important Things Pertaining to the Kingdom of God:

D. & C. 84:43-50, 54-58, 76, 119; 101:32-35; (Reorganized D. & C. 83:7a-h, 8a-c, 12c-d, 24c; 98:5g-h); *The Articles of Faith* nos. 9 and 13

We Should Pray to God for the Spirit of Inspiration, Have Faith That He Will Fulfill His Covenants, and Earnestly Seek His Revelation:

James 1:5-6; D. & C. 8:1-3, 10-11; 88:126, 131; 90:24; 98:1-3, 11-15; 136:32-33; (Reorganized D. & C. 8:1c-2a, 3d-f; 85:38c, 40; 87:6c; 95:1, 3a-d) Mark 10:14-15

We Should Nourish the Word of God, Desiring to Believe:

Alma 32:27-28, 41-43; (Reorganized Edition Alma 16:151-154, 170-173)

We Should Search the Scriptures Diligently, and Study All Things Out in Our Minds:

3 Nephi 23:1, 5; (Reorganized Edition 3 Nephi 10:26-27, 32:) D. & C. 9:7-8; (Reorganized D. & C. 9:3a-c;) Jeremiah 29:13; Deuteronomy 4:29; John 8:31-32; Matthew 7:7-8; Moroni 10:3-8, 19-22, 24-25; (Reorganized Edition Moroni 10:3-9, 14-16, 18-20)

We Should Study All Things Which Pertain to the Kingdom of God, and Sincerely Seek for Guidance and Enlightenment Out of the Best Books:

2 Nephi 9:28-29; (Reorganized Edition 2 Nephi 6:57-61); D. & C. 88:77-80, 83, 118, 126; (Reorganized D. & C. 85:21b-e, 22b, 36a, 38c)

Part C

THE PROMISED DAY HAS COME

Chapter 16

THE TIME OF THE LORD'S ADVENT FORETOLD

A. The *"Lord"* or *"One Mighty and Strong"* to Come in the Year 1844

> QUESTION: SINCE THE PURPOSE OF THE CHURCH OF JESUS CHRIST OF LATTER-DAY SAINTS WAS TO PREPARE THE WAY FOR THE COMING OF THE LORD OF THE KINGDOM AND THE BEGINNING OF THE MILLENNIAL DISPENSATION, WERE THE SAINTS GIVEN ANY CLUES TO AID THEM TO KNOW THE TIME THAT THIS GREAT EVENT WOULD OCCUR?

The Restoration of the Gospel Was Itself a Sign That the Lord's Coming Was Imminent:

2 Nephi 30:3-11; 3 Nephi 16:7; (21:1-7); 21:26-29; (Reorganized Edition 2 Nephi 12:79-91; 3 Nephi 7:31; (9:86-95); 10:4-8); *D. & C.* 45:9, (Reorganized *D. & C.* 45:2d.)

The Saints Were Told That the Jews Were to be Gathered to the Land of Jerusalem, But Not Until After the Times of the Gentiles Had Been Fulfilled:

D. & C. 45:25, 28-30, 36-39; (Reorganized *D. & C.* 45:3f, 4b-d, 5c-6a)

They Were Even Told That the Lord Was Already Living on the Earth but Had Not Yet Revealed His Identity:

D. & C. 38:7-9; 50:40, 44-46; 29:5; 61:36-39; (Reorganized *D. & C.* 38:2; 50:8d, f-g; 28:2b; 61:6c-e.)

Joseph Smith Was Given the Keys of Revelation and Commandment For the Church:

D. & C. 5:8-11, 14-15; 28:2, 7; 35:15-18, 20-21; 115:19; 132:7; (Reorganized *D. & C.* 5:2d-3c, d-e; 27:2a, d; 34:4d-f, 5b)

These Keys of Authority Were Not to be Taken From Him Until the Coming of the Lord:

D. & C. 43:1-3, 9-12, 17; 64:4-5; 112:14-15, 30-34; (Reorganized D. & C. 43:1, 3b-d, 5a; 64:2a; 105:6, 12-13)

"One Mighty and Strong" Was to be Given the Scepter of Power and Authority After the One Who Was Called of God and Appointed Would Fall by the Shaft of Death:*

D. & C. 58:20, 22; 38:21-22; 85:6-8, (9-10); 135:1, (4); [Reorganized D. & C. 58:5a-b; 38:5a-b; 113:1, (4a-b)]

The Lord, or "A Mighty and Strong One" Was Promised as the One Who Would be Raised Up in the East to the Residue of the House of Israel:

Isaiah 28:2-6, 9-11, (16-17)

B. The Year 1844 Was Also Given in Both the Old and New Testaments as the Year of the Coming of the Lord and the Beginning of the New Age

QUESTION: DURING THE SAME PERIOD THAT JOSEPH SMITH WAS RECEIVING REVELATION TO PREPARE THE SAINTS FOR THE IMMINENT RETURN OF THE LORD, MANY SINCERE BIBLICAL SCHOLARS, WORKING INDEPENDENTLY OF ONE ANOTHER, ON FIVE DIFFERENT CONTINENTS, ARRIVED AT ALMOST THE SAME EXACT YEAR AS THAT FORETOLD IN HIS PROPHECIES. WHAT PROPHECIES IN HOLY SCRIPTURE DID THESE SCHOLARS READ IN ORDER TO ARRIVE AT THIS CONCLUSION?

The Prophet Daniel Had Foretold the Exact Year of Christ's Crucifixion:

Daniel 9:21-26

An Explanation of Daniel's Prophecy:+

Numbers 14:34; Ezra 7:1, 6-10, 23, 27-28

* Joseph Smith was shot in Carthage jail, on the 27th of June, 1844.
+ Daniel used the symbol of a day to stand for a year, as in the book of Numbers. The "*commandment to restore and to build Jerusalem*" referred to the Decree of

Using the Same Symbolism of a Day for a Year, Daniel Also Foretold the Exact Year When One Like Jesus Christ Would Come to Usher in the Kingdom of God on Earth: #

Daniel 7:13-14; 8:13-14, 17

Jesus Confirmed the Importance of This Prophecy Concerning the Time of the Lord's Coming:

Matthew 24:3-5, 15

John the Revelator, in the New Testament, Also Pointed Out the Year of the Coming of "Michael" and the Ending of the Times of the Gentiles, as the Jews Would Again be Permitted to Return to the Land of Jerusalem. ††

Revelation 12:1-2, 5-13

A Partial Explanation of John's Prophecy:

Genesis 16:3-11, 15; 17:19, 20

The Temple in Jerusalem Was to be Under the Control of the Gentiles (i.e. Muslims) for Two Thousand, Two Hundred and Sixty Years. During This Period Muhammad and Ali Were to be God's Witnesses, Until the Kingdom of the Father Should be Ushered In: **

Artaxerxes for this purpose, given in 457 B.C. From 457 B.C. until the crucifixion of Jesus the Christ was 70 weeks, 490 days, or, in prophecy, 490 years. Daniel thus prophesied that the Messiah would be *"cut off"*, i.e. slain, at the age of 32, or in the year 32 A.D.

\# William Miller, the most noted of the adventist scholars, subtracted the figure 457, the year of Artaxerxes' Decree to rebuild Jerusalem, from the 2,300 days (years), given in Daniel's prophecy, giving him the year 1843 as the year when the abomination of desolation would be ended and the sanctuary of Israel be cleansed of Gentile control. Since Daniel had also said that it would be *"Michael"* or a *"Chief Prince among the Persians"* Who would deliver the children of Israel from their long exile in Persia, this was taken as a prophecy of the second coming of Christ to the children of Israel. (Note Miller's error in failing to add one year to account for the extra year between 1 B.C. and 1 A.D. He later noted this error and correctly set the year for the appearance of the Lord as 1844 A.D.)

†† The Word *"Michael"* means, *"one who looks like God"*, i.e. a Great Prophet or Manifestation of the will and attributes of God, as a mirror reflection.

** Ali was named by Muhammad to be His successor, nevertheless, apostasy broke out among the Muslims immediately upon Muhammad's death, the larger portion refusing to accept the leadership of Ali and the remaining Imams after him. The year 1260 A.H. in the Muslim Calendar is the same year as the year 1844 A.D. in the Christian calendar. The Muslim year begins on March 21st, hence Miller's prophecy that the Lord would return on March 21, 1844. The Muslim Calendar dates from the flight of Muhammad from Mecca in 622 A.D., which year is accepted as the beginning of the Islamic Era. It should be understood that the Islamic year is shorter than the Christian year, having twelve lunar months or three hundred and fifty-four days, except on leap years which have 355 days in a year.

Revelation 11:1-4.

The Calamities and Judgments of the Last Days Foretold, to be Followed by the Kingdom of God on Earth:

Revelation 11:7, (8-9), 10, (11-14), 15.

The Gospel of Jesus Christ to be Restored Before the Coming of the Lord:

Revelation 14:6-7; *D. & C.* 133:16-19, 36-40; (Reorganized *D. & C.* 108:5a-d, 7a-c) 3 Nephi 6:7-12; 20:25-30; 21:1-11; (Reorganized Edition 3 Nephi 7:31-37; 9:63-69a (86-98)

Other Witnesses Also to Arise to Prepare the Way Before Him:

Revelation 14:14-19.

The Religions, or Dispensations, of Moses and Christ Fulfilled:

Revelation 15:2-4, 8 (Compare *D. & C.* 128:18-21; Reorganized *D. & C.* 110:18-21)

A New Dispensation to be Ushered In; All Things to be Made New; The Glory of God to Enlighten All Mankind:

Revelation 21:1-5, 22-27 (Compare *D. & C.* 128:22-24; Reorganized *D. & C.* 110:22-24)

C. Rend the Veil of Unbelief

QUESTION: WERE THE LATTER-DAY SAINTS TOLD TO LOOK TO THESE PROPHECIES IN ORDER TO PERCEIVE THE SIGNS AND TO KNOW THE TIME OF THE COMING OF THE LORD IN THE GLORY OF THE FATHER?

The Book of Mormon Tells Us to Look to the Teachings of John the Revelator and Also That the Hidden Mysteries of His Book Will be Unfolded and Made Manifest in Very Deed:

1 Nephi 14:18-27, Ether 4:14-17; (Reorganized Edition 1 Nephi 3:238-251; Ether 1:110-114)

Jesus Told the Saints to Look to Joseph Smith's Inspired Translation of the New Testament, Concerning the Coming Kingdom of God, That They May be Prepared For the Things to Come:

D. & C. 45:58-62; 93:6, 18-19; Reorganized *D. & C.* 45:11a-b; 90:1c, 3a-b.

So Great A Cause . . . 171

Additional Signs of the Time, Place and Conditions of the World at the Time of the Coming of the Son of Man With a New Name, as Given in the Inspired Revision of the Holy Bible:

Matthew 24; Joseph Smith 1:5-12, 18-20, 24-37.

D. **Two Messengers of God to Usher in the Kingdom**

QUESTION: IN ADDITION TO SETTING THE DATE FOR THE COMING OF THE *"LORD"*, OR *"ONE MIGHTY AND STRONG"*, AS THE YEAR 1844, JOSEPH SMITH FORETOLD THE COMING OF A SECOND MESSENGER. THE PERIOD OF 1860 TO 1890 IS REFERRED TO IN CONNECTION WITH THE COMING OF THIS *"SON OF MAN"*. IS THERE ANY CONFLICT IN THESE TWO SETS OF PROPHECIES?

Two Chosen Messengers to Come, the First to Prepare the Way for the Second; Both to Come in Rapid Succession:

Malachi 3:1; 4:5-6; *D. & C.* 35:4; (Reorganized *D. & C.* 34:2b;) Isaiah 11:1-5, 10-12; *D. & C.* 113:1-6, Utah Edition; Zechariah 4:11-14; 2 Nephi 8:17-20; [Reorganized Edition 2 Nephi 5:100-106(See also Isaiah 51:17-20); *D. & C.* 77:14-15, Utah Edition]

Joseph Smith Prophesied the Coming of the "Son of Man" After the Beginning of the American Civil War, i.e. Some Time After 1860:()

D. & C. 87:1-8; 130:12-13, Utah Edition

Joseph Smith Could Have Seen the Son of Man if He Had Lived Until the Year 1890: **

D. & C. 130:14-15, Utah Edition.

() The Civil War began in the year 1860. In 1863, Abraham Lincoln issued his proclamation freeing the slaves. The war dragged on for another two years, but the year 1863 marks the decisive point in that conflict. Might we therefore look to this date, 1863, as of greatest significance in relation to the coming of the Son of Man?

** Joseph Smith would have been eighty-five years old in the year 1890. Was the Lord actually living on the earth at that time, and could Joseph Smith have seen Him? Is there anything in history to substantiate such a thought? Would the Lord delay His coming simply because Joseph Smith did not live to be eighty-five, especially since Joseph's martyrdom in 1844 had already been foretold, and that *"One Mighty and Strong holding the scepter of power in His hand"* would be raised up to succeed him? Please re-read the revelation given through Joseph Smith in section 85; also section 45, especially verses 24 through 30 (verses 3f through 5b in the Reorganized Edition).

Chapter 17

I AM IN YOUR MIDST AND YE CANNOT SEE ME

A. Why the Jews Failed to Recognize Christ

QUESTION: WHEN JESUS CAME AMONG THE JEWS, VERY FEW OF THEM RECOGNIZED THAT HE WAS THE MESSIAH FORETOLD IN THEIR PROPHECIES: WHY WAS THIS THE CASE?

He Came From an Insignificant Village and to Outward Appearance Was Just an Ordinary Human Being With Nothing Unusual to Attract Attention:

John 1:46; 7:52-53; Mark 6:1-6; 3:20-22; *Koran* 25:8-9

He Was Accused of Being Unholy for Associating With Tax Collectors and Sinners:

Matthew 9:9-13; 11:18-19; Luke 7:36-39, (40-50); Matthew 21: (28-31), 31-32

He Was Also Accused of Breaking the Laws of Moses:

Mark 2:18-20; 23-28; Luke 13:10-14, (15-17)

He Was Rejected by the Leaders of the Jewish Religion, and Even His Death Was Pointed Out as an Evidence Against Him:

John 7:5, 12-13, 43-49; Deuteronomy 21:22-23

QUESTION: THE JEWS HAD BECOME VERY LEGALISTIC IN THEIR INTERPRETATIONS OF THE LAWS OF MOSES. SO ALSO HAD THEY BECOME VERY LITERALISTIC IN THEIR INTERPRETATION OF OLD TESTAMENT PROPHECY RELATIVE TO THE COMING MESSIAH. WHAT WERE SOME OF THE PROPHECIES WHICH THE JEWS FAILED TO UNDERSTAND IN THEIR TRUE SPIRITUAL MEANING AND THUS DENIED THAT JESUS WAS THE CHRIST?

They Had Expected the Literal Return of Elijah to Prepare the Way Before Him:

Malachi 4:5-6; Matthew 17:10-13

They Expected That the Messiah Would be an Earthly King With Royal Power and Glory: Some Were Even Looking for the Literal Return of King David:

1 Chronicles 17:11-15 (See also 2 Samuel 7:12-17); Ezekiel 34: 22-23; 37:24-25 (See also Zechariah 12:6-10); John 6:14-15; Matthew 20:20-21; 21:8-9; 27:11, 29-31, 36-37

The Hebrews Were Looking for Visible Signs Rather Than Trying to Understand the True Inner Spiritual Meaning of the Scriptures:

Isaiah 13:6-10 (See also Joel 2:30-31); Matthew 16:1-4; Mark 8: 10-12

B. **The Meaning of the *"Return"* of a Great Prophet (and of His Forerunner), Who Had Lived in a Previous Dispensation**

> QUESTION: HAVE WE LEARNED ANY LESSONS FROM THIS HISTORY OF ANOTHER *"CHOSEN PEOPLE"* WHO FAILED TO RECOGNIZE THEIR LORD? ARE THE PROPHECIES OF HOLY SCRIPTURE CONCERNING THE RETURN OF A PREVIOUS MESSENGER OR MESSENGERS OF GOD TO BE TAKEN LITERALLY OR ARE THEY TO BE UNDERSTOOD IN A SPIRITUAL OR FIGURATIVE SENSE?

Some Prophecies Are to be Taken Literally, Others in a Figurative Sense.

1 Nephi 22:1-3; (Reorganized Edition 1 Nephi 7:1-6)

Examples of the Literal Return of the Spirit of a Previous Messenger or Messengers of God:

1. **Visions of Moses and Elijah (Elias) to Later Prophets:**

Luke 9:28-31 (See also Matthew 17:1-3 and Mark 9:2-4); *D. & C.* 110:11-16, Utah Edition

2. **The Appearance of Jesus Christ to the Ancient Americans and to Leaders of the Latter-day Saints:**

3 Nephi 11:8-10; (Reorganized Edition 3 Nephi 5:9-11) Joseph Smith 2:16-17; *D. & C.* 110:1-4, Utah Edition (For members of the Reorganized Church see these same accounts of the visions of Jesus to Joseph Smith and Oliver Cowdery in other publications.)

Examples of the Spiritual Return of a Previous Messenger or Messengers, That is, the Appearance of Another Great Prophet in a Similar Station but Bearing the Same Holy Spirit or Word of God; The Same Light Shining Through a New Lamp:

1. Jesus Was the "Return" of Moses:

   3 Nephi 20:23-24; (Reorganized Edition 3 Nephi 9:60-62)

2. John the Baptist Was the "Return" of Elias:

   Luke 1:13-17; Mathew 11:10-11; 17:10-13 (See also Mark 9:11-13)

C. Elijah and Jesus Will Not Return Again in a Literal Sense to Usher in the Kingdom

QUESTION: BOTH JESUS CHRIST AND ELIJAH HAVE RETURNED IN VISION TO JOSEPH SMITH TO RESTORE THE GOSPEL OF THE SON. IT IS NOW TIME FOR THE KINGDOM OF THE FATHER TO APPEAR. ARE WE, LIKE THE JEWS, STILL LOOKING FOR THE LITERAL FULFILLMENT OF GREAT SPIRITUAL PROPHECIES, OR WILL WE JUDGE THE TWO NEW PROPHETS, WHO ARE TO USHER IN THE KINGDOM, BY THEIR FRUITS, RATHER THAN BY VISIBLE SIGNS AND WONDERS?

An "Elias" or Forerunner Would Prepare the Way Before the Lord of the Millennial Day:
Isaiah 40:1-5; 3 Nephi 24:1-2, (3-4); 25:5-6; [Reorganized Edition 3 Nephi 11:2-4, (5-7), 26-27]; *D. & C.* 35:3-4, (7-11), 12, (13-14), 15-16, (17-21); [Reorganized *D. & C.* 34:2a-b, (3a-d), 3e, (4a-c), 4d-e, (4e-5b)]

The New Son of Man Will Not be Jesus of Nazareth But Another Manifestation of the Full Glory of the Father:
Joseph Smith 1:5-6, 9-11, 21-22 (See also Matthew 24:4-5, 11-13, 23-24)

He Will Bear the Same Holy Spirit or Word of God but Will Come Through a New Human Tabernacle and Will be Called by A New Name:
John 16:12-15; Matthew 16:27; Isaiah 9:6; 3 Nephi 20:32-35; 21: 7-10; Reorganized Edition 3 Nephi 9:70-73, 93-97; Isaiah 52:6; 62:1-3; 65:15-16

His Followers Will Also Be Called After His Name:
Revelation 2:17; 3:5, 12, 22; 14:1; *D. & C.* 130:10-11, Utah Edition; Enoch 68:20-22, 38(*) (See also *D. & C.* 107:54-57; Reorganized *D. & C.* 104:28b-29b)

We Must Judge the Two New Revelators by Their Life and Deeds Rather Than By External Signs and Miracles; If Their Message is of God It Will Endure:
Luke 7:19-23; Matthew 7:15-20 (See also Alma 5:40-41; Reorganized Edition Alma 3:67-68); Moroni 7:(3-12), 13-15, (16-26); (Reorganized Edition Moroni 7:(3-10), 11-13, (14-26)

D. The *"Return"* of Michael or Adam

QUESTION: THE SECOND GREAT MANIFESTATION OF GOD, TO COME IN THE LAST DAYS, IS REFERRED TO VARIOUSLY AS THE FATHER, MICHAEL, OR SOMETIMES AS THE *"RETURN"* OF ADAM, THE FIRST RECORDED MESSENGER OF HOLINESS. WHAT IS THE MEANING OF THESE PROPHECIES?

The Promise: Michael, or "Adam," to Come to Gather His Elect in the Latter Days:
Daniel 10:13-14; 12:1, 4; *D. & C.* 107:53-54; 29:26; 88:115-116; 27:5, 11; (Reorganized *D. & C.* 104:28a-b; 28:7a; 85:35e-f; 26:2a,f.

The Meaning: The Second Prophet Will Bring to Mankind the Principles Which Will Unite All Mankind As They Were in Ancient Sumeria in the Days of Adam; He Will be as a "Second Father" or "Adam" to Usher in a New Cycle of Divine Unity;
Daniel 7:9, (9b-13), 14; 1 Nephi 22:24-26, 28; 3 Nephi 20:36,

---

(*) Referred to in *Thief in the Night,* by William Sears, George Ronald Publishing Co., 46 High Street, Kidlington, Oxford, Ox5 2DN England, 1961, p. 131.

40, 43-46[(See also 21:25-29); Reorganized Edition 1 Nephi 7:55-62, 64; 3 Nephi 9:74, 78-85 (10:4-8)]

A Second Meaning Was Given By Jesus Christ Who Foretold That In the Last Days He Would Come First to Restore His Preparatory Gospel, After Which the Father, or One Who Would Come in the Full Glory of God, Would Set Up the Kingdom of God on Earth:

Acts 3:19-21; 3 Nephi 20:26-27, 30, 34; (Reorganized Edition 9: 64-65, 69a, 71-72); Joseph Smith 2:17b (Joseph Smith's Own Story); 3 Nephi 21:25-26; Ether 4:13-17, 19 (See the Full context of these words of the Lord in verses 4 through 19); [Reorganized Edition 3 Nephi 10:4-5; Ether 1:109-114, 116-117 (Full context in verses 98-117)]

Chapter 18

STUDY IT OUT IN YOUR MIND—SEEK AND YE SHALL FIND

A. The Language of Prophecy

QUESTION: WHY IS SO MUCH OF THE PROPHECY CONCERNING THE TIME OF THE TWIN MESSENGERS CHOSEN TO BRING IN THE KINGDOM OF GOD GIVEN IN FIGURATIVE OR VEILED LANGUAGE?

To Sift Out Those Who Are not Yet Ready to Receive God's Revelation:

Matthew 13:10-16 (See also Isaiah 6:9-12)

Those Who are Ready to Receive Will Understand the Hidden Meaning:

Matthew 13:18-23, (3-9), 47-52; Mark 4:21-25, 33-34

Looking Beyond the Mark:

Jeremiah 5:20-21; Jacob 4:14, (15-17); [Reorganized Edition Jacob 3:22-25, (26-28)]

The Word of the Lord is a Judgment Upon Mankind Whereby the Carnally-Minded Are Separated From Those Who are Spiritually Minded:

Jeremiah 6:19; 7:19; Matthew 6:22-23; 15:12-14; John 9:16-21; 9:39-41; 1 Peter 4:5-6; 1 Corinthians 15:46-50; 2 Nephi 29:11; 9:39b; (Reorganized Edition 2 Nephi 12:65-66; 6:74; *D. & C.* 6:1-7; (Reorganized *D. & C.* 6:1-3)

The Letter of the Scripture Killeth, While the Spirit of the Scripture Giveth Life Eternal:

John 3:3-6; 6:63-64a, 66-68 (See also 11:25-26)

Some Things Pertaining to the Kingdom Were Not Intended to be Understood in the Dispensation in Which They Were Given But Were Written that Future Generations Might Understand:

Daniel 12:4, 8-10; John 16:(12-18), 22-23, 25; 1 Corinthians 4:5; 2 Peter 1:19-21; Isaiah 29:(9-12), 13-14, (15-24)
(See also Habakkuk 1:5; 2:1-4; Revelation 22:10-14)

The Preparatory Gospel of Jesus Christ Was But the Beginning of the Dawning of the New Day of God, in Which Day All of the Things Which Are Obscure in Scripture Will Be brought to Light:

2 Nephi 27:5-8, 20-22 (See the entire context of this quotation in chapter 27); [Reorganized Edition 2 Nephi 11:123-128, 142-145 (For full context see verses 116-160)]; D. & C. 50:40, 45-46; 128:17a, 18b-19, 22a, 23-24; (Reorganized D. & C. 50:8d, g; 110: 17a, 18d-19, 22a-b, 23-24) D. & C. 136:31-33, 37-38, 41-42, Utah Edition

The Lord of the Kingdom Will Unlock the Meaning of All of the Hidden Mysteries:

Daniel 7:9-10; John 16:12-14; Revelation 5:5, 9-10; 2 Nephi 27: 11, 14, 28-30; 30:15-18; (Reorganized Edition 2 Nephi 11:131-132, 135, 154-156; 12:95-100) Enoch 46:3

B. Veils of Darkness

> QUESTION: SINCE THE LATTER-DAY SAINTS WERE TOLD THAT JOSEPH SMITH WOULD HOLD THE KEYS OF REVELATION AND COMMANDMENT *"UNTIL THE LORD COMES"* OR, IN ANOTHER PROPHECY, UNTIL *"ONE MIGHTY AND STRONG, HOLDING THE SCEPTER OF POWER IN HIS HAND"* SHOULD BE RAISED UP TO SET IN ORDER *"THE HOUSE OF GOD"*, WHY DID THEY NOT GO OUT IN SEARCH OF THIS PROMISED ONE AFTER JOSEPH'S MARTYRDOM?

Their Own Scripture Had Foretold That Their Minds Would Be Veiled and That Clouds Would Hide the Coming of the Son of Man:

Daniel 7:13; Joseph Smith 1:1; (Matthew 23:39); Matthew 24: 30; Revelation 1:7 (See also Matthew 26:63-64; Luke 21:27); D. & C. 34:7; 38:7-9a; 45:7, 9-10; (Reorganized D. & C. 33:1e; 38: 2a-b; 45:2b, d, e)

Men Will Look for Visible Rather Than for Spiritual Signs:

D. & C. 63:5-13; (Reorganized D. & C. 63:2a-4a); Alma 32:17-18, 21-22; (Reorganized Edition Alma 16:139-140, 143-144); Luke 17: 20-21; Moses 4:3; D. & C. 132:21-23, 25, Utah Edition; 2 Peter 2:1-2, 3:3, 10a, 13

And Men's Hearts Shall Fail Them, and They Shall Say That Christ Delayeth His Coming:

D. & C. 45:24-30, 34-35, 49-50; (Reorganized D. & C. 45:3f-4d, 5a-b, 8b-c) 2 Nephi 28:29-32; (Reorganized Edition 2 Nephi

12:35-41) 2 Thessalonians 2:1-3a; Joseph Smith 1:34-37a, 38-55 (See Matthew 24:34-51) [1]

C. The Lord Will Not Come With Visible Signs and Wonders

QUESTION: WHEN THE LORD COMES IN THE GLORY OF THE FATHER WILL NOT ALL MANKIND BE ABLE TO RECOGNIZE HIM?

He Shall Come as A Thief in the Night and Take Men unawares:

2 Peter 3:10; Revelation 3:3; 16:15; *D. & C.* 61:38-39; 106:4-5; (Reorganized *D. & C.* 61:6d-e; 103:2;) Matthew 24:42; Mark 13:32-37; *D. & C.* 49:7-8; (Reorganized *D. & C.* 49:2b-c)

We Must Prepare Ourselves, Study and Search in Order to Recognize the Lord:

D. & C. 133:1-4, 10-15; (Reorganized *D. & C.* 108:1a-2a, 3c-4b;) Luke 12:20-32, (33), 34-38, (39-48), 48b, 18:7-8; 21:34-36; 1 Thessalonians 5:1-9; Hebrews 2:3

D. The True Signs of the Coming of the Son of Man

QUESTION: WHAT ARE SOME OF THE SIGNS WE ARE TOLD TO LOOK FOR WITH SPIRITUAL UNDERSTANDING IN ORDER TO RECOGNIZE THE LORD OF THE MILLENNIAL DISPENSATION?

He Will Come as a Mortal Man but Not as One Who is Free to Travel (i.e. a Prisoner):

D. & C. 49:22; 130:1-2; (Reorganized *D. & C.* 49:4a) 1 John 3:2; Isaiah 9:6-7

He Will Fulfill the Laws and Ordinances of the Christian Dispensation, Just as Jesus Christ Fulfilled those of the Dispensation of Moses:

2 Nephi 25:24-25, 30; (Reorganized Edition 2 Nephi 11:45-47, 57) 3 Nephi 12:17-20, 46-48; 15:(2-5), 6-10; [Reorganized Edition 3 Nephi 5:64-68, 91b-92; 7:(3-6), 8-12], Hebrews 7:12, 18-19; Matthew 9:16-17; *D. & C.* 29:23-24; 63:49a; 101:23-25; 22:1-4; (Reorganized *D. & C.* 28:6b-c; 63:13c; 98:5a-b; 20:1a-d)

1. The context in this Gospel would show that the phrase *"heaven and earth"* stands for the former laws and ordinances, and the *"powers of the heavens"* stands for those who hold authority among men.

He Will Fulfill the Priesthood and Usher in a New Administrative Order of Universal Participation:

Joseph Smith 2:68-69 (See also D. & C. 13, Utah Edition); D. & C. 86:8-11; 112:14-15; 64:23; (Reorganized D. & C. 84:3-4; 105: 6; 64:5a;) Jeremiah 31:31-34

The New Manifestation of Holiness Will Not Come With Visible Signs but His Signs Will be Apparent Only to Those Who Believe:

D. & C. 46:8-9, 30; 68:10-11; 67:10, 14; (Reorganized D. & C. 46:4, 8b; 68:1g-f; 63:7b; 67:3a-b, 4)

He Will First Arise in the East (East of Israel)—Israel Will See His Glory—His Teachings Will be Carried to the West and Will Come to Fill the Whole Earth:

D. & C. 45:(51-55), 56-59; 133:13, 21, 35; (Reorganized D. & C. 45:(9-10a), 10b-d; 108:4a-b, 5e, 6f) Joseph Smith 1:24-27 (See Matthew 24:25-28)

Since the Coming Messenger of God Was to Reveal All Truth, the Search of the Sincere Seeker Must be All Inclusive:

D. & C. 50:10-12, 17-26, 34; 88:63-68, 77-83, 86, 92, 116-120; 101:32-35; (Reorganized D. & C. 50:4a-b, 5a-6c, 7d; 85:16b-18b, 21-22, 24a, 25c-d, 35f-36c; 98:5g-h.) (Please read the entire of section 88 (85), thoughtfully and prayerfully)

Chapter 19

PERSIA AND BABYLON TO SEE HIS GLORY

A. The Prophets Foretold That the Twin Manifestations of the New Day of God Would First Arise in the East

QUESTION: THE JEWS HAD EXPECTED THAT THEIR LONG-AWAITED MESSIAH WOULD ARISE IN THE GREAT CAPITOL CITY OF JERUSALEM, IN SPITE OF THE FACT THAT THE PROPHET MICAH HAD ACTUALLY FORETOLD THE EXACT TOWN WHERE JESUS WAS TO BE BORN, THE JEWS FAILED TO RECOGNIZE HIM AS THE CHRIST WHEN HE AROSE IN THE INSIGNIFICANT VILLAGE OF BETHLEHEM. MICAH, ISAIAH, JEREMIAH, DANIEL, ENOCH, EZEKIAL AND OTHER PROPHETS HAVE LIKEWISE TOLD THE EXACT LANDS WHERE THE TWO NEW PROPHETS OF THE MILLENNIAL DISPENSATION WILL ARISE. HAVE WE LATTER-DAY SAINTS, CHRISTIANS AND JEWS LOOKED TO THESE PROPHECIES AND HAVE WE EXAMINED THE MODERN HISTORY OF THESE LANDS TO SEE IF SUCH PROPHECIES MIGHT ALREADY HAVE BEEN FULFILLED?

Lightning From the East:

Isaiah 41:1-2; Matthew 24:25-28 (See also Luke 17:22-24); D. & C. 43:(20-21), 22-23, 29-30; (Reorganized D. & C. 43:(5c-e), 5f-6a, 7b-c) Enoch 56:5 *

Scriptural Prophecy Points Out That the Lord, or Glory of God, Will Come to Israel by Way of the Gate (Forerunner) That Looketh Toward the East:

Op. Cit., Sears, p. 171.

182 . . . *So Great A Cause*

2 Nephi 9:41-43; (Reorganized Edition 2 Nephi 6:79-85); Ezekiel 43:1-7a; Psalm 24:7-10; Revelation 7:2-3

QUESTION ASKED BY JOSEPH SMITH: WHAT ARE WE TO UNDERSTAND BY THE ANGEL ASCENDING FROM THE EAST, REVELATION 7TH CHAPTER AND 2ND VERSE?

The Inspired Answer:

D. & C. 77:9, Utah Edition

B. The First of the Two Holy Prophets Was to Come to Elam (Now Southern Persia)

QUESTION: SINCE THE PROPHETS HAD SAID THAT THE LIGHT OF THE NEW DAY OF GOD WAS TO DAWN TO THE EAST OF ISRAEL, DID ANY OF THEM NAME SPECIFIC LANDS TO WHICH THIS LIGHT WOULD COME?

Jeremiah Named the Land of Elam as the Place Where the Throne of God Would First Be Established in the Latter Days:

Jeremiah 49:38-39

Daniel's Vision of the Latter Days Was in the Province of Elam:

Daniel 8:1-2; 10:13-14

C. A Chief Prince Among the Persians

QUESTION: ARE THERE ALSO PROPHECIES CONCERNING THE PLACE IN WHICH THE SECOND DIVINE MESSENGER WOULD FIRST APPEAR, OR AMONG WHAT PEOPLE HE WOULD BE BORN?

The Prophet Micah, Who Accurately Foretold the Place of Jesus' Birth, Predicted That the Holy One of Israel of the Latter Days Would Come to Israel From the Land of Assyria (Now Northern Persia):

Micah 5:2; 1:3; 2:12; 4:1, 6-7 (5:7-8); 7:12-16, (17-19), 20 (See also Isaiah 9:2-10)

QUESTION: WHAT IS MEANT BY THE REFERENCES IN SCRIPTURE TO HIS BEING A CHIEF PRINCE,

So Great A Cause . . . 183

A KING, AND AS ONE DRESSED IN ROYAL GARMENTS? WAS THE PROMISED ONE TO BE OF ROYAL OR PRINCELY BIRTH?

He Would be a Person of High Rank Among the Persians and a Deliverer of Israel:

Daniel 12:1-3; Jeremiah 23:5-6, (7-8); Isaiah 62:1-3, (10-12); *D. & C.* 133:45-52; (Reorganized *D. & C.* 108:8c-10a) (See also Isaiah 63:1-8)

Like the Great Prince Moses Before Him, He Would Abandon His Inherited Position of Royalty, Becoming a Prisoner and an Exile in Order to Save His People:

D. & C. 133:53; (Reorganized *D. & C.* 108:19b) Isaiah 63:9; Micah 7:12-15,†† Isaiah 52:13-15; 53:1-12 (Also 3 Nephi 20: 43-45; (Reorganized Edition 3 Nephi 9:81-83); 3 Nephi 20:46; 21:7-11, (12-29); [Reorganized Edition 3 Nephi 9:84-85, 93-98; (99-106; 10:1-8)]; John 16:13-15

Out of Prison He Cometh Forth to Reign Spiritually:

Isaiah 49:6-9; Psalms 142:5-7; 76:8-9, 12; 89:18-19, 26-29; Isaiah 14:5; 24-21 (See also Job 34:24-30; Ecclesiastes 4:14; Daniel 7: 13-14; Micah 4:1-3, (4-13); Enoch 10; 56:5 †† (See also Isaiah 9:2-10; *D. & C.* 133:19-25; Reorganized *D. & C.* 108:5d-g)

D. **Israel to Be Redeemed in Babylon (Modern Iraq)**

QUESTION: FOUR OF THE GREAT PROPHETS OF FORMER DISPENSATION—ADAM, ENOCH, NOAH, AND ABRAHAM—ALL FIRST AROSE IN THE LAND ANCIENTLY CALLED SHINAR, LATER BABYLONIA, THEN CHALDEA, AND TODAY IRAQ. THE COLONY OF JARED CAME FROM THIS SAME REGION TO ANCIENT AMERICA, AND THAT OF ABRAHAM FROM THIS SAME LAND TO CANAAN OR ISRAEL. ARE THERE REFERENCES IN SCRIPTURE TO SHOW THAT THE GREAT PROPHET WHO WILL USHER IN THE MILLENNIAL DISPENSATION MIGHT ALSO VISIT THIS HOLY LAND OF THE PROPHETS?

†† These portions of the revelation of Micah and of Enoch are repeated to bring out the prophecies concerning the imprisonment and exile of the Lord, followed

Ezekiel's Visions of the Glory of the Lord Were in the Land of Bayblon:

Ezekiel 1:1, 18; 3:12,23

The Old Testament Promises That the Lord Will Redeem Israel From the Land of Babylon:

Isaiah 48:15, 20; Micah 4:6-7, 10

Zechariah Used the Symbolic Title "Zerubbabel" for the Two Holy Ones Who Would Deliver Israel in the Last Days. The Word "Zerubbabel", When translated, Means—"Begotten in Babylon", "Scattered in Babylon", "Banished in Babylon" or "Stranger in Babylon":

Zechariah 4:8-14++

E. The Significance of Elam, Assyria and Babylonia in the History of Israel

QUESTION: WHAT ARE THE HISTORICAL CONNECTIONS BETWEEN ELAM AND ASSYRIA, NOW CONSTITUTING THE NATION OF PERSIA OR IRAN, AND THE LAND OF BABYLONIA, PRESENTLY CALLED IRAQ, WITH ANCIENT ISRAEL?

The Tribe of Judah Was Promised the Scepter of Authority in Israel Until Another "Shiloh" Should Come:**

by His proclamation to the kings and rulers. The prophecy of Micah shows how He would be sent from His native land, Assyria, and one prison city after another ("fortified cities", "fortress"), finally to arrive near Mount Carmel and the region of Israel anciently known as Bashan and Gilead. The last line shows the length of His public ministry as being comparable to the period of time that the children of Israel were in the wilderness after their exile from Egypt until they were finally permitted to enter the Promised Land, i.e. forty years.

++ The references in verse 9 to Zerubbabel are symbolic of Two Holy Manifestations—the First Manifestation, Abraham, laid the foundation of the house of Israel in Ancient Chaldea or Babylonia—and the second Manifestation, the Promised Messenger, most frequently referred to in the Old Testament as the *"Glory of God"*, was to be a descendant of Abraham Who will *"finish"* or redeem the house of Abraham in Babylon. The references to *"two olive branches," "two golden pipes"* and *"the two anointed ones",* referred to in verses 11 through 14, are to the Twin Manifestations of God Who Should Come in the last days to redeem the whole earth.

** Shiloh was the location of the religious sanctuary of all the tribes of Israel when they first entered the land of Canaan, under the priesthood of Eli. Since Shiloh was located in northern Israel, this blessing seems to foretell a time when a Holy Messenger of God would come to the northern tribes of Israel in the lands of

Genesis 49:10-12; 1 Chronicles 5:1-2

The Descendants of Joseph, Later Divided Into the Two Tribes of Ephraim and Manasseh, Were Given a Blessing Above That of All of the Other Tribes of Israel. The "Shepherd" or "Stone of Israel" Was to Come to This Seed:*+

Genesis 37:5-11; 49:22-26 (See also chapter 42 and 48, especially verses 8-9, 16 and 20 through 22)

Many Years After Entering the Holy Land, the Twelve Tribes of Israel Separated Into Two Kingdoms, Judah and Benjamin Constituting the Southern Kingdom Thereafter Called Judah, and the Other Ten Tribes Constituting the Northern Kingdom Also Called Israel, or Ephraim—After Its Leading Tribe:

1 Kings 12:19-21a, (21b-24)–(See also 2 Chronicles 10 & 11)

In 721 B.C. The Northern Kingdom Fell to the Assyrian Armies and the Leadership of All of the Ten Tribes Were Carried Captive Northward and Planted in Colonies in the Lands of Assyria and Media (Which Occupied the Same Regions as the What Are Now the Northern Portions of Present Day Persia (Iran) and Iraq:

2 Kings 17:(1-3), 4-6, (7-22), 23 (See also Hosea 11:1-7)

In 600 B. C. the Other Two Tribes, Judah and Benjamin, Henceforth Known as Jews, Were Similarly Carried Captive Into Babylonia and Elam (Which Occupied the Same Regions as What Are Now the Southern Portions of Present Day Persia (Iran) and Iraq:

2 Chronicles 36:(1-10), 11-13, (14-16), 17-21 (See also 2 Kings 23:26-28; 25; Jeremiah 21:3-7; 1 Nephi 1:13; Reorganized Edition 1 Nephi 1:12)

Some of the Children of Israel, and Later Some of the Jews, Remained in the Lands of Ephraim and Judah, Intermingling With Other Refugee Peoples Sent Into the Land From Other Parts of the Assyrian and Later Babylonian Empires. This Mixed Racial Group Became What Were Later Referred to As Samaritans in the Bible:

---

their exile. The teachings of this Prophet would bring a new bond of unity to all of the tribes of Israel, just as they shared such unity at the sanctuary of Shiloh of old time. Note the references to the purple garments to be worn by *"Shiloh"* when He comes. These garments are again referred to in later Hebrew prophecy—see Isaiah 63:1-9; *D. & C.* 133:45-52; (Reorganized *D. & C.* 108:8c-10a).

*+ The *"Shepherd"* or *"Stone of Israel"* would appear to be the Same Messenger as *"Shiloh"*.

186 . . . *So Great A Cause*

2 Kings 17:24; 25:11-12

A Small Group of Jews Escaped Into Egypt, While the Two Colonies of Israelites, Lehi and Mulek, Were Led by the Lord to America:

2 Kings 25:25-26; 1 Nephi 1:4; 2:2, 4-5; 7:2, 5; 18:23; Omni 15-16; (Reorganized Edition 1 Nephi 1:3, 26, 28-32; 2:8, 11; 5:212-213; Omni 1:26-27)

F. A Remnant of Israel and of Judah to Be Gathered From the Lands of Their Dispersion, to Be Reunited in the Land of Jerusalem in the Last Days, or at the End of the Age

QUESTION: MANY ANCIENT PROPHETS IN BOTH PALESTINE AND AMERICA FORESAW THE CAPTIVITY AND SCATTERING OF THE HOUSES OF ISRAEL AND OF JUDAH AMONG THE NATIONS. DID THESE PROPHETS LIKEWISE FORETELL THE GATHERING OF THE JEWS IN THE LAST DAYS? IS THERE A PROMISE THAT A REMNANT OF THE TEN TRIBES OF NORTHERN ISRAEL WILL ALSO RETURN FROM ASSYRIA AND MEDIA, OR THE *"LANDS OF THE NORTH"* TO WHICH THEY WERE TAKEN CAPTIVE?

Judah to be Gathered From All Nations. A Remnant of Israel to be Gathered From the "Lands of the North". Assyria, Elam and Shinar (Babylonia or Chaldea) Specifically Named in These Prophecies Concerning the Return and Reunion of the House of Israel:

Isaiah (10:20-23); 11:10-13, 16; (60:1-5); Jeremiah 3:11-12, (13), 14-15, (17), 18; (12:14-15; 16:14-16; 23:3-8; 31:1-11, 20-21; 32: 37-39);Ezekiel 11:16-20; (34:11-13, 16, 22-25, 30-31; 36:37-38); Hosea 11:8-11; (12:6; 14:1-4); Amos (5:14-15, 23-24); 9:8-9, 11-12; Zechariah 10:6-7, (8-9), 10-12; (12:6-7); 2 Nephi (6:14-17; 10:7-9); 25:11, 17; 29:14; (30:7-18); 3 Nephi 16:11, 17-20; (29: 8-9); [Reorganized Edition 2 Nephi (5:36-42; 7:12-16); 11:19-20, 28-29; 12:73-74; (12:85-100); 3 Nephi 7:36, 43-45; (13:61-62)]

QUESTION: DOES MODERN REVELATION CONFIRM THESE ANCIENT PROPHECIES?

The Lord, Jesus Christ, Inspired Joseph Smith With These Revelations:

D. & C. 35:25-26; 38:33; 101:10-19; 84:94-102; (Reorganized D. & C. 34:6a-c; 38:6a-c; 98:4a-e; 83:16d-17c)

Part D

THE WORD OF THE LORD FROM JERUSALEM

Chapter 20

ISRAEL—A LIGHT TO THE NATIONS

A. Two Great Prophets to Be Raised Up to the Children of Israel in the Last Days

QUESTION: ARE THERE REFERENCES IN THE HOLY SCRIPTURES TO TWO PROPHETS TO BE RAISED UP TO THE EXILES OF THE HOUSE OF ISRAEL IN THE LANDS OF THEIR DISPERSION?

Jesus said That God Has "Other Sheep", in Addition to the Jews at Jerusalem and the Nephite-Lamanite Peoples on This Continent, Who Also Must be Gathered in the Last Days, That There Might be Only One Fold and One Shepherd Over All the Earth:

3 Nephi 16:1-5, 11-12; (Reorganized Edition 3 Nephi 7:24-29,36-37)

Joseph Smith Foretold the Return of a Remnant of the Ten Tribes of Israel From the "North Countries" and Prophesied That This Remnant Would Come to the Land of Israel With Their Prophets:

D. & C. 133:26a, 28-35; 77:14-15; (Reorganized D. & C. 108:6a, b-f)

Isaiah and Nephi Foretold The Coming of Three Holy Messengers:
Isaiah 11:1-5, (6-9), 10-12; D. & C. 113:1-6, Utah Edition; 2 Nephi 11:2-3 (See also chapter 30:8-15); (Reorganized Edition 2 Nephi 8:2-6 (12:87-95)

Isaiah and Joseph Smith Spoke Specifically of the Revelation and Power of God Which Would Come Forth to the Scattered Remnants of Israel in the Last Days:

Isaiah 51:17-20; 52:1-2, 6-8 ; (Compare 2 Nephi 8:17-20); D. & C. 113:7-10, Utah Edition; Isaiah 52:6-10

The Covenant People of Abraham Are to be Reunited in Israel— The Word of the Lord is Also to be Gathered in One:

Ezekiel 37:15-22 [See also 1 Nephi 13:38-39, 41-42; 2 Nephi 29:

12-14; (Reorganized Edition 1 Nephi 3:190-191, 194-200; 2 Nephi 12:65-74)]

B. Watch, That Ye May Be Ready

QUESTION: THE PROPHETS AND MESSENGERS OF GOD HAVE ALWAYS BEEN REJECTED BY A MAJORITY OF THE PEOPLE OF THEIR DAY, EVEN THOUGH SUCH PEOPLE MAY CONSIDER THEMSELVES AS THE CHOSEN PEOPLE OF GOD, BLESSED WITH GREATER REVELATION AND INSIGHT INTO THE DIVINE MYSTERIES. WE READ IN THE BOOK OF MORMON THAT SAMUEL, WHO FORETOLD THE COMING OF JESUS CHRIST, WAS REJECTED BY THE NEPHITES, PERHAPS BECAUSE HE WAS A LAMANITE, AND OF A DARK SKIN. EVEN JESUS WAS REJECTED BY A MAJORITY OF THE JEWS, HIS OWN PEOPLE, BECAUSE HE CAME FROM A SMALL VILLAGE, WAS A CARPENTER'S SON, AND DIDN'T COME WITH THE VISIBLE SIGNS THE PEOPLE HAD EXPECTED. JOSEPH SMITH WAS REJECTED AND ACCUSED OF BEING A LIAR BECAUSE HE BROUGHT NEW REVELATION FROM GOD WHEN THE MAJORITY OF THE PEOPLE OF HIS DAY BELIEVED THAT ALL REVELATION HAD CEASED WITH JESUS AND HIS APOSTLES. WILL WE, THE HEIRS OF THIS NEW REVELATION, LIKEWISE REJECT THE GREATER REVELATION WHICH JOSEPH SMITH TOLD US WOULD COME TO ISRAEL AFTER THE RESTORATION OF THE GOSPEL OF JESUS CHRIST IN AMERICA?

The Book of Mormon Warns Us Not to Ignore the Words of the Prophets Which Were Written For Us and For Which Purpose the Gospel Was Restored:

1 Nephi 15:19-20; 2 Nephi 25:7-8; 3 Nephi 23:1-3, 5b, (4-5; 24: 1-4); Mormon 8:21-23a;[Reorganized Edition 1 Nephi 4:30-33; 2 Nephi 11:11-14; 3 Nephi 10:26-28, 32 (29-31; 11:2-7); Mormon 4:26-27]

So Great A Cause . . . 191

The Prophets Have Clearly Foretold That in the Latter Days the Word of the Lord Would be Revealed From Both America and the Holy Land of Israel:

Deuteronomy 4:27, 29-32, 39; 2 Nephi 29:1-14; (Reorganized Edition 2 Nephi 12:42-74) D. & C. 133:10-14, 19-21, 25-26a, 35; (Reorganized D. & C. 108:3c-4b, 5d-e, 5g-6a, f)

An Abundance of Prophecies Have Promised That the Glory of the Lord Would be Revealed in Israel After the Restoration of the Gospel of Jesus Christ in America:

D. & C. 133:37-40a, 45; (Reorganized D. & C. 108:7b-c, 8c) D. & C. 45:28-30, 39, 43-44, 47-49, 56-59; (Reorganized D. & C. 45:4b-d, 6a, d-e, 8a-c, 10b-d); 1 Nephi 21:1, 3, 6-7, 13, 22-23; 22:1-2, 10-12, 24-28; (Reorganized Edition 1 Nephi 6:30-31, 33, 36-37, 43, 52-53; 7:1-4, 21-25, 55-64) (See also Isaiah 49; 2 Nephi 10; Reorganized Edition 2 Nephi 7)

The Greatest Nephite Prophets All Warned Us to Accept the Greater Revelation Which Was to Come of the Father following the Restoration of the Gospel of the Son:

2 Nephi 28:24, 27, 29; 29:8, 12, 14a; Alma 29:8, 17; Mormon 8: 12, 33b-34, (35-41); 9:7-9, (10-11), 15, 27, (28-30); Ether 4:8, 10-14, (15-19); (Reorganized Edition 2 Nephi 12:30, 32, 35, 59-61, 67-70, 73; Alma 15:59; 68-69; Mormon 4:14-15, 44-45, (46-56), 66-68, (69-70), 75-76, 92-93, (94-96); Ether 1:102, 104-110, (111-117)

C. **The Land of Israel is to be Established as a World Capital and as the Center of Worship for All Mankind**

QUESTION: WHAT IS THE DIVINE DESTINY OF THE HOLY LAND OF ISRAEL, AND OF ITS INHABITANTS?

The Land of Jerusalem to be as the Garden of Eden—Living Waters to flow Forth From Israel to Water the Hearts of All Mankind:

Isaiah 35:1-2, 5-7a, 9b-10; 41:17-20; 43:18-19, 20b-21; 51:3; Hosea 14:5-7; Amos 9:13-14 (See also Joel 2:12-27; Ezekiel 34: 26-27, 29-31; 36:28-30, 33-38)

Israel Called to be a Light to the Nations:

Psalm 50:1-6; Zechariah 13:(8-9); 14:16; Joel 2:28-29, 32; 3:16-17; Isaiah 42:1-5a, 6-9; 60:1-5, 12, 19-22; (Also 49:1-3, 6-9, 13;

192 . . . *So Great A Cause*

51:4-9, 11, 15-16; 60:8-18); Isaiah 2:1-5, 10-12; 4:2-4; 8: (13-17) 18; 2 Nephi 30:7-18; (Reorganized Edition 2 Nephi 12:85-99) (Compare Daniel 12:3-4)

The Administrative Authority of God Would be Restored to Israel:

Isaiah 11:10-13; 52:1-2, 7-10; 61:4-6; *D. & C.* 113:5-6, 7-10, Utah Edition; *D. & C.* 110:14-16; 112:15, 34; 85:7a, 8-10, 12, (6-7, 11); (Reorganized *D. & C.* 105:6b, 13b)

The Lord Would Enter Into a New and Everlasting Covenant With the Seed of Abraham:

3 Nephi 16:10-13, 17-20; (Reorganized Edition 3 Nephi 7:34-38, 43-45) Ezekiel 18:(19-23), 30-32; 36:24-28; 37:24-28; Jeremiah 31:31-34, 37-42

The Land of Jerusalem Will Be the Political Capital of a World Federation:

Isaiah 9:2, (3-4), 6-8; Jeremiah 3:17-18; 23:5-6a, (6-8); Daniel 2:27-28, (28-35), 36-45**; 7:13-14; 10:13-14; 12:1

D. **The Valley of Sharon, the Fortified City of Akka, and Mount Carmel are All to Behold the Glory of God, the Great Prophet of the Millennial Dispensation**

QUESTION: THE PROPHET MICAH FORETOLD THAT THE HOLY MANIFESTATION OF THE LATTER DAYS WOULD COME TO ISRAEL FROM PERSIA (ASSYRIA) AND, IN HIS PROPHECY, EVEN DESCRIBED HIS JOURNEY TO THE

** The Babylonian Empire (i.e. the kingdom of Nebuchadnezzar) was followed by the Persian, Greek and Roman Empires. The last of these, the Roman Empire, prevailed over all of the then *"western"* civilized world for many centuries. Its division into two parts still marks the great cleavage between the western and eastern nations of Europe. The breakup of these two Roman Empires into the many nations of Europe, North Africa and the Near East marked the beginning of the intense nationalism which still prevails today. Surely no one can deny that we are now in the time of confusion, referred to by Daniel, at which time he foretold that Michael, or One Like the Son of Man, will come to deliver His covenant people, after which His Kingdom will be set up, at first almost imperceptably but gradually to consume all other kingdoms (governments).

HOLY LAND. DO WE HAVE SIMILAR PROPHECIES TELLING US THE SPECIFIC PLACES WITHIN ISRAEL TO BE VISITED BY THIS HIGH PROPHET OF THE NEW DAY OF GOD?

He Will Come to Israel From Assyria, From Fortified Cities to the River, From Sea to Sea, and From Mountian to Mountain:

Micah 7:7,12

In Israel, the Valleys of Sharon and Achor (Surrounding the Fortress City of Akka), Lebanon, and Mount Carmel (Also Called Mount Zion), Would See His Glory:

Micah 7:13-14; Isaiah 35:1-2; 65:9-10; 2 Nephi 27:28-30; (Reorganized Edition 2 Nephi 11:154-156); Hosea 2:14-15; *D. & C.* 128:19b; (Reorganized *D. & C.* 110:19b); Psalms 48:1-2, 8-11, 14; 102:13-18, 21-22; (See also Psalms 2:6; 50:2; 87:1-3; 110:1-2)

Micah Even Gave the Length of the Lord's Ministry, by Saying that it Would be Equal to the Length of Time the Israelites Sojourned in the Wilderness After Fleeing From Egypt:

Psalm 95:8-11; Micah 7:14-16

The Two Important Dates Implied by Joseph Smith as Those When the People of the East and of the West Might Behold His Person (i.e. 1863 and 1890) Lie Within This Period of Forty Years, Revealed by Micah as the Length of His Ministry:

D. & C. 130:1-2, (9-11), 12-15, Utah Edition %

Brethren, Shall We Not Go On to Partake of the Great Day of the Lord?

D. & C. 128:22a,24a; (Reorganized *D. & C.* 110:22a, 24a)

% See footnotes (} and ** at bottom of page 171, in chapter 16, entitled *"The Time of the Lord's Advent Foretold".*

Chapter 21

THE GATE TO THE KINGDOM AND THE GLORY OF GOD

A. The Distinction Between the Lesser and the Great Prophets or Manifestations of God

> QUESTION: ACCORDING TO THE HOLY SCRIPTURES THERE ARE TWO KINDS OF DIVINE MESSENGERS: ONE OF THESE IS THE GREAT PROPHET OR MANIFESTATION OF THE ATTRIBUTES AND WILL OF GOD. THESE HIGH PROPHETS, SOMETIMES REFERRED TO AS THE WORD OR SON OF GOD, COME AT THE BEGINNING OF EACH NEW DISPENSATION OF THE RELIGION OF GOD, TO RENEW THE REVELATION OF THE LORD AND TO USHER IN A NEW DIVINE SPRINGTIME THROUGH WHICH A REGENERATED CIVILIZATION CAN GROW. THE SECOND KIND OF HOLY MESSENGER IS THE LESSER PROPHET OR SEER, USUALLY SIMPLY REFERRED TO AS PROPHETS, WHO COME AS FORERUNNERS TO THE NEW DAY OF GOD. DO THE SCRIPTURES CLEARLY DISTINGUISH BETWEEN THESE TWO STATIONS OF PROPHETHOOD? WAS JOSEPH SMITH A SEER OR WAS HE THE FOUNDER OF A NEW DISPENSATION OF DIVINE RELIGION?

The Holy Manifestations of God, Who Usher in Each New Dispensation, Derive Their Inspiration Directly From God, Through the Holy Spirit or Holy Ghost:

Moses 6:22-23, 32-34; 8:16, 19, 27; Abraham 3:11-12, 22-23; Moses 1:1-4, 40, 25-26 (See also Exodus 3:11-15)

The Lesser Prophets, or Seers, Derive Their Inspiration From the Great Prophets Within Whose Dispensation They Appear:

Exodus 4:(10-13), 14-17; Numbers 12:1-9

Jesus Christ Was the Manifestation of God Who Ushered in the Christian Dispensation. John the Baptist, in Israel, and Samuel the Lamanite, in America, Were Lesser Prophets Who Came to Herald His Coming and to Call Mankind to Repentance:

John 1:6-9, 15-17, 22-23, (24-27), (33-34); 3:(25-30), 31-36; 5:30-38; (8:42); (10:30, 37-38); Helaman 14:1-2, 9; 3 Nephi 20:10, 23-24; (Reorganized Edition Helaman 5:54-55, 63; 3 Nephi 9:46, 60-62)

John the Baptist and Samuel the Lamanite Came at the End of the Mosaic Dispensation, but After the Birth of the Manifestation Who Was to Usher in the Christian Dispensation, to Prepare Mankind for the New Day of God. Similarly Joseph Smith Came in the Latter Days of the Christian Dispensation to Prepare Mankind for the Dispensation of the Glory of the Father Which Was to Dawn Shortly in the East:

2 Nephi 3:6-8, 15, 24; (Reorganized Edition 2 Nephi 2:10-14, 29-30,46-47;) *D. & C.* 21,1-5; 18:33-36; 27:1; (Reorganized *D. & C.* 19:1a-2b; 16:5e-g; 26:1a)

The Lesser Prophets or Seers Spoke for God Only as They Were Moved Upon by the Holy Spirit, at Other Times They Were as Other Human Beings:

D. & C. 1:24-29; 24:1-2; 35:17-19; 64:5-7; 85:7a, 8; 67;4-9[1]; 93:47-49; 124:1; [2](Reorganized *D. & C.* 1:5a-d; 23:1; 34:4e-5a; 64:2a-b; 67:2[1]; 90:8b-d; 107:1a[2])

The Great Prophet-Founders of Each New Dispensation Manifest the Attributes and Will of God in Their Every Word and Deed:

Moses 7:13, 17-20a, 67, 69; Genesis 7:15; 9:1-2; Moses 8:27; *D. & C.* 132:29, 34-36, Utah Edition; Moses 1:25-26, 31, 39; John 5: 19:20, (22-23), 24-27, 30-31, 36

B. There Will Be Forerunners to the New Day of God Both In the East and In the West

1. This is an excellent test of any writing claiming to be scripture. This same test should be applied against the writings of the two Prophets of the Millennial Dispensation.
2. These revelations were not selected in an attempt to diminish the significance of the role of Joseph Smith in the Divine Plan, but rather to show that his station was that of a lesser prophet or seer, chosen to prepare the way for the Twin Manifestations of the Dispensation of the Fulness of Times, or the Kingdom of God on Earth.

QUESTION: GOD SENT TWO FORERUNNERS TO PREPARE THE WORLD FOR THE ADVENT OF JESUS CHRIST, ONE IN THE EAST AND ONE IN THE WEST. IN THIS NEW DAY, PRIOR TO THE COMING OF THE SON OF MAN IN THE GLORY OF THE FATHER, HE SENT JOSEPH SMITH TO PREPARE THE CHRISTIAN WORLD FOR THE COMING OF THE LORD. ARE THERE REFERENCES IN SCRIPTURE THAT GOD WILL AGAIN SEND A FORERUNNER, OR FORERUNNERS, SIMILAR TO JOHN THE BAPTIST, TO PREPARE THE EASTERN WORLD, AND ESPECIALLY THE OTHER BRANCHES OF THE SEED OF ABRAHAM, FOR THE ADVENT OF HIS HOLY PROPHETS?

God Promised to Send His Angels (Forerunners) to Prepare the Way for the Son of Man:

D. & C. 63:53-54; (Reorganized D. & C. 63:13g-h); Joseph Smith 1:37 (See also Mark 13:27); D. & C. 77:8-9, Utah Edition

God Will Send as Many Witnesses as He Sees Fit, to Establish His Word; He Warns Against Rejecting Any of These Witnesses of His Word:

D. & C. 6:28-31, 34; (Reorganized D. & C. 6:13-14, 16a); 2 Nephi 11:3b; 27:14, (22, 28-30), 33-35; Ether 5:4-5; (Reorganized Edition 2 Nephi 8:5-6; 11:135, (144, 154-156), 158-160; Ether 2:3-4)

C. **The New Messengers of God Will Be Called by New Names Indicative of Their Missions**

QUESTION: IN EACH DISPENSATION THE PROPHETS AND MESSENGERS OF GOD WERE GIVEN A NEW NAME TO SHOW THEIR DIVINE CALLING. FOR EXAMPLE, JOHN, THE FORERUNNER TO JESUS, WAS CALLED *"THE BAPTIST"*, BECAUSE HE BAPTISED WITH WATER AS A SYMBOL OF REPENTANCE AND A SPIRITUAL REBIRTH. JESUS WAS HIMSELF CALLED *"THE CHRIST"*, WHICH MEANS *"THE ANOINTED ONE"*. THE HOLY SCRIPTURES ALSO

So Great A Cause . . . **197**

FORETELL THAT THE LORD OF THE MILLENNIAL DISPENSATION, AS WELL AS HIS FORERUNNER, WILL BE CALLED BY NEW NAMES SUGGESTIVE OF THEIR GREAT MISSIONS. DO THESE BOOKS OF REVELATION GIVE US ANY CLUES AS TO THE NAMES WHEREBY THE NEW MANIFESTATIONS OF GOD SHALL BE CALLED?

In Numerous References the Forerunner to the Son of Man is Called "the Gate" or "the Door" to the Kingdom. Since This Prophet is to Appear in the Land of Elam (Southern Persia) We Might Expect Him to be Called "the Báb", a Title Which Means "the Gate" or "the Door" in That Language:

2 Nephi 9:41-43; (Reorganized Edition 2 Nephi 6:79-85); Ezekiel 43:4; Psalm 24:7-10; Luke 13:23-30; John 10:1-6, 14-15.

The Second Great Prophet is Most Frequently Spoken of in Holy Scripture as "the Glory of God" or "the Glory of the Lord". In the Persian Language This Title Would Appear as "Bahá'u'lláh":

Habakkuk 2:14; Isaiah 35:2b; 40:5; 58:8; 60:1-3; Ezekiel 1:28; 3:13, 23; 43:1-5; Revelation 21:10-11, 23-26.

Other Prophets Spoke of the Time When the Revealed Word of God Would be Given in Its Full Light or Glory:

1 Nephi 22:24-25; Alma 13:24-25; (Reorganized Edition 1 Nephi 7:55-59; Alma 10:23-25); Isaiah 9:6-7; Matthew 16:27; 25:31-32; Mark 8:38; 13:26 (See also Luke 9:26; 21:27); Luke 13:34-35; John 16:12-14; 3 Nephi 26:3-4; (28:7-8);[Reorganized Edition 3 Nephi 11:30-32; (13:18-19)]; 1 Peter 5:1, 4; *D. & C.* 65:5-6; (Reorganized *D. & C.* 65:1d-f) (See also *D. & C.* 88:107-116; Reorganized *D. & C.* 85:33-35)

He Shall be Known by One Name Over the Whole Earth:

Enoch 69:14-15, 26;[e] Zechariah 14:8-9; Habakkuk 2:14; Revelation 19:16

D. The Children of Light or Glory

QUESTION: JESUS CHRIST COMMANDED HIS FOLLOWERS

(e) Sears, Op. Cit. pg. 131.

TO TAKE UPON THEM HIS OWN HOLY NAME. THE WORD *"CHRISTIAN"* MEANS *"FOLLOWERS OF CHRIST"*. THE WORD *"BAHA"* IN PERSIAN MEANS *"LIGHT", "SPLENDOR"* OR *"GLORY"*. ARE THERE REFERENCES IN THE BOOKS OF GOD THAT THE FOLLOWERS OF THE NEW MESSENGER WOULD ALSO BE CALLED AFTER HIS HOLY NAME?

The Light of God:

D. & C. 45:28-29; (Reorganized *D. & C.* 45:4b-c, 10d) Revelation 14:1; 22:3-5

Followers of the Light or Glory of God:

D. & C. 106:4-5; (Reorganized *D. & C.* 103:2) Revelation 3:11-12; 2:17; *D. & C.* 130:9-11, Utah Edition; 88:66-68, 73-75, 126; (Reorganized *D. & C.* 85:17,20, 38c)

Chapter 22

BY THEIR FRUITS YE SHALL KNOW THEM

A. How Shall We Know the Two Great Prophets of the New Day of God

QUESTION: IN THE PRECEDING CHAPTERS WE HAVE EXAMINED NUMEROUS PROPHECIES FROM BOTH ANCIENT AND MODERN SCRIPTURE REFERRING TO THE TIMES AND TO THE PLACES ASSOCIATED WITH THE COMING OF THE TWIN MANIFESTATIONS WHO ARE TO USHER IN THE DISPENSATION OF DIVINE UNITY KNOWN AS THE KINGDOM OF GOD ON EARTH (EVEN SEVERAL REVELATIONS INDICATING THE TITLES BY WHICH THEY SHALL BE KNOWN). IN SPITE OF THE ABUNDANCE OF SUCH REFERENCES WE ALSO KNOW THAT SUCH EVIDENCES ARE STILL ONLY EXTERNAL SIGNS, AND CHRIST WARNED US AGAINST SIMPLY LOOKING FOR VISIBLE SIGNS AND WONDERS. WHAT THEN ARE THE MORE SIGNIFICANT INTERNAL SIGNS WE SHOULD LOOK FOR IN ORDER TO RECOGNIZE THE FORERUNNER WHO WAS TO PREPARE THE WAY, AND AFTER HIM, THE LORD OF THE NEW AGE?

Jesus Said That it is the Inward Truth and Not the Outward Form Which We Must Understand:

Matthew 7:15; John 10:2-4; 6:63 (See Christ's Warning against false prophets in Matthew 24:3-5, 11-13; Joseph Smith 1:21, 22)

The New Messengers of God Would be the Very Spirit of Truth—to lead All Men Everywhere Into All Truth:

John 16:13; 14:26b; 2 Nephi 30:16-18; (Reorganized Edition

12:96-99); *D. & C.* 128:18b; (Reorganized *D. & C.* 110:18e)

We Must Judge Them by the Fruits of Their Lives and Teachings:
Matthew 7:7-8, (13-14), 15-20; Luke 6:43-45; Matthew 12:33-37

All Things Which Are Good Cometh From God:

2 Nephi 28:16, 19-21; Alma 5:36-43; (Reorganized Edition 2 Nephi 12:19-20, 23-26; Alma 3:60-72); James 1:17-20, 22; (2:14-17); Ether 4:8, (9-10), 11-12, (13-16), 17, (18-19); [Reorganized Edition Ether 1:102, (103-104), 105-108, (109-113), 114, (115-117)]; *D. & C.* 11:2, 12-14; (Reorganized *D. & C.* 10:1b-c, 6-7) (See also Moroni 7:3-6, 11-15; 2 Nephi 28:24-31; Reorganized Edition Moroni 7:3-5, 9-13; 2 Nephi 12:30-39)

The Parables of the Twelve Gates to the City of God and of the Twelve Sons (The Twelve Principles of Oneness):

Revelation 21:1-5, 10-14; *D. & C.* 38:24-27; (Reorganized *D. & C.* 38:5d-6a)

The Twelve Fruits of the Tree of Life, Whose Leaves Are for the Healing of the Nations:

Alma 5:33-36; (Reorganized Edition Alma 3:57-60) Revelation 22:1-8a, 12-14

Twelve Principles of Unity to Be Brought by the Great Chief or Spirit of Truth Who Will Arise in the East, An Indian Parable:

There is an interesting parallel between these parabolic references to principles of the coming Kingdom and the ancient Navajo chants concerning the Time of the End. According to these prophetic chants, in the End of the Age the Spirit of the people will live again, and all people will *"melt into one".* These chants go on to say that the Great Spirit will come in the East, in the direction of the rising sun. As He comes He will bring these good things of the spirit and of love, and it will be a most glorious occasion. His coming will be a new Day for mankind in which religion will be renewed and cleansed of the prejudices and misunderstandings that the older religions have accumulated down through the centuries. Annie Kahn, a full-blooded Navajo living in Chinle, Arizona, gives this further elaboration of this ancient prophecy, as related to her by her grandfather and the old medicine men of the tribe:

"The New Faith comes also to the Indians like the sun at dawn. As the sun rises it touches the peaks and buttes first with its light; then

The Chief with the Twelve Feathers

slowly moves down into the canyons. The light is at first visible only to a few who are awake, high up and watching. Some of the Navajos and other Indian peoples are like people down in a deep canyon. They are listening for the Voice of the Great Creator, but they do not know where to look for it yet because the dark shadows blind them. But there are some Indians who are as if they are on the mountain tops and they begin very early to dance and sing with joy when they see the Glory coming.

"The fact that the new Light is said to come like the dawn warns us that, even as the early sunlight rises up through the mists of morning and slowly drives away the dark shadows of the canyons, so the coming of the New Teaching will not be widely visible at first, but will reach in its beginnings only those whose spiritual eyes and ears are open. It is taught, however, in the chants that even the people down in the dark canyons will hear the Voice of the Great Spirit and they will search for Him until they also receive the Light of the New Day. Many of the Navajo people now believe that this glorious light has come, but we must seek it out with understanding hearts, even as lost children seek for their father in the wilderness.

"The chants say that there are two signs of the New Spirit that all the people should look for. The first sign is a nine-pointed star that must come from the East. The number nine is the sign of the highest unity under the sign of the nine-pointed star. Another sign of this coming is that there will be a Great Chief in the East who will wear a head-dress with twelve feathers. The chants say these twelve feathers mean twelve great principles that He will bring to mankind."[1]

B. The Fruits of the Tree of Life

QUESTION: SINCE THE TWO DIVINE TEACHERS OF THE NEW DAY OF GOD WILL BRING TOGETHER

---

1. For a full elaboration of this and other Indian prophecies, concerning the last days and the coming of the Kingdom, see the booklet entitled Four Remarkable Indian Prophecies, as related by Annie Kahn, Olin Karsh and Blu Mundy, and the books, Songs of the New Dawn, by Vinson Brown; Warriors of the Rainbow, subtitled Strange and Prophetic Dreams of the Indian People, by William Willoya and Vinson Brown; Strange Journey, The Vision Life of a Psychic Indian Woman, by Louise Lone Dog; Tapestries in Sand, subtitled The Spirit of Indian Sandpainting, by David Villasenor; The Lord of the Dawn, subtitled Quetzalcoatl, Prophet King of Ancient Mexico, by Tony Shearer (Spotted-tailed Eagle); and Great Upon The Mountain, Crazy Horse of America by Vinson Brown.

So Great A Cause . . . 203

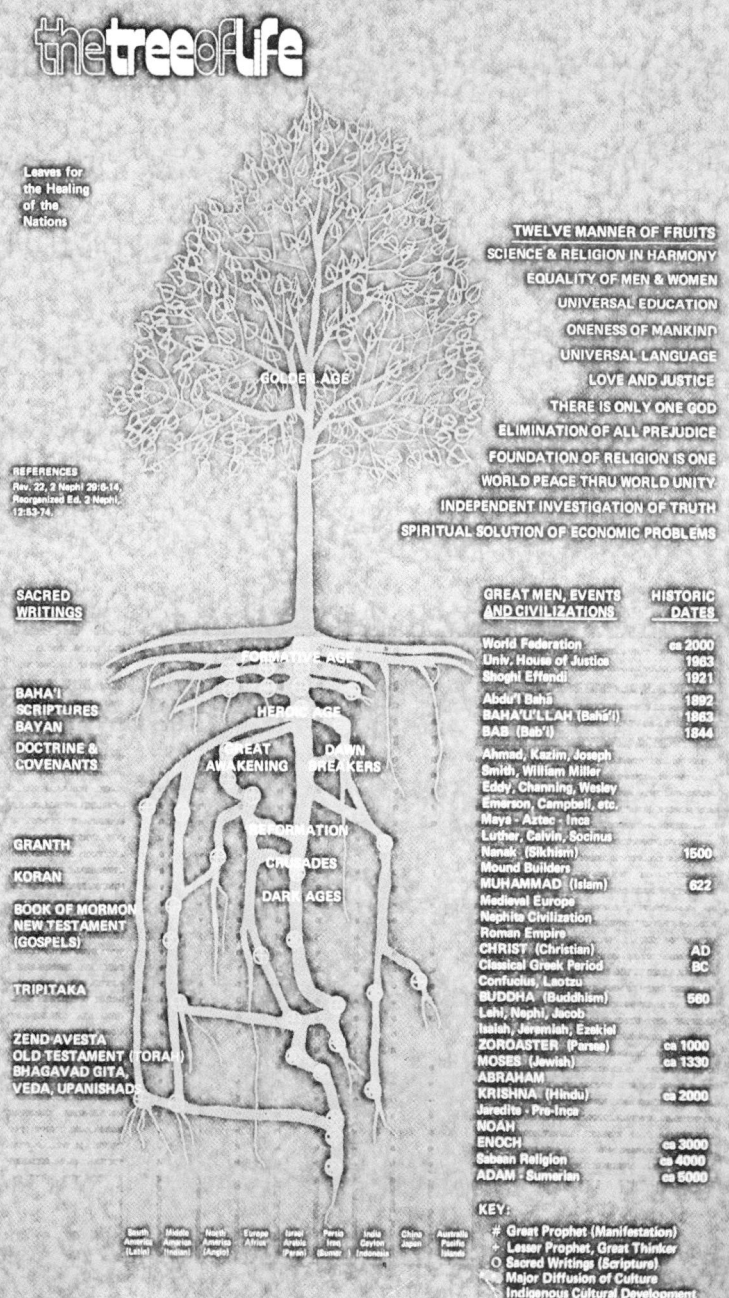

204 . . . *So Great A Cause*

ALL TRUTHS AND WILL FULFILL ALL SCRIPTURE ARE THERE SPECIFIC REFERENCES CONCERNING THE *"FRUITS"* OF THE TREE OF LIFE, AS REFERRED TO BY JOHN, ALMA AND JOSEPH SMITH, AND AS ALLUDED TO IN THE NAVAJO CHANTS, WHICH, WHEN FULLY IMPLEMENTED, WILL BRING ABOUT UNIVERSAL PEACE AND THE UNIFICATION OF MANKIND?

The New Revelation Will Emphasize the Oneness of Mankind and the Equality of the Sexes:

John (10:27-30; 15:1-4, 9-14); 17:(1, 6), 20-23, 26; *D. & C.* 38: 27b; (Reorganized *D. & C.* 38:6a); 2 Nephi 26:23-28, 33; (Reorganized Edition 2 Nephi 11:95-105, 111-115) Mark 16:15; Matthew 28:19-20; Psalm 82:8; Isaiah 66:23; John 10:14-16

All Men Will Live as Brothers, Without Prejudice and Without Discrimination:

Malachi 4:5-6; Zechariah 3:10; Isaiah 66:8b, 19b-20

Democracy Shall Prevail Over the Whole Earth:

Jeremiah 30:21-22; Mosiah 29:16-17, (18-23), 24-26, (27-47); Reorganized Edition Mosiah 13:21-22, (23-32), 33-40, (41-68)

World Government Will be Established, Bringing Justice to All People Through International Law Enforced by a World Executive:

Isaiah 2:1-4; (9:2, 6-8); 11:1-5, 10; 32:1; Psalm 72:1-8, 11-14, 17-19; Daniel 2:44; 7:14; 1 Chronicles 16:33; Jeremiah 33:15; Obadiah 21

Peace and Security Shall Prevail Throughout the Entire Earth:

Isaiah 11:6-9; 52:7-8; 65:25^2; (Compare 2 Nephi 30:8-15; Reorganized Edition 2 Nephi 12:87-95; *D. & C.* 128:19; Reorganized *D. & C.* 110:19); Ezekiel 34:25^2; Hosea 2: 18-20^2; Haggai 2:9^2; Micah 4:3-4^2

A Universal Language Will be Chosen as an Auxiliary to the Mother Tongue to Facilitate Easy Communication Among All People:

Moses 6:6; Genesis 11:1, 6-9; Zephaniah 3:8-9

2. The language of scripture is often confusing to the layman, unfamiliar with the artistry of the prophet's words. The writer of prophecy, like the artist painting a masterpiece, is intent upon portraying the deeper spiritual meaning. His words are timeless and hence must reach beyond the conditions of his own period.

So Great A Cause . . . 205

Mankind Will Turn to a Spiritual Solution for the Economic Problems of the New Age:

D. & C. 38:24-27, 34-36; 42:29-31a, 39; 82:20-21; 105:(1-8), 6, 9-10; 119:1-4; [Reorganized *D. & C.* 38:5c-6a, 8a-c; 42:8a-c, 11b-c; 81:5; 102:(1-3b), 2d, 3c; 106:1]

The Earth Will Yield Its Abundance for All Mankind:

Isaiah 4:2; 30:23-25a; Joel 3:18, 21b; Ezekiel 34:26-27, 30

The Search for Truth Will Not be Fettered by the Traditions and Superstitions of Past Ages:

Psalm 85:8-13; Isaiah 30:20-21; 43:8-9; 35:5; *D. & C.* 58:26-33; 88:118-119; (also 109:7-9); 90:15; (Reorganized *D. & C.* 58:6c-i; 85:36a-b; 87:5b)

There Will be a Spiritual Quickening; Each Person Will Come to Investigate Truth for Himself:

Jeremiah 31:33-34; Ezekial 11:19-20; Joel 2:28-29; *D. & C.* 128:18b; (Reorganized *D. & C.* 110:182); 2 Nephi 28:26, 29-31; (Reorganized Edition 2 Nephi 12:31, 35-39)

Science and Religion Will Walk Hand in Hand for the Advancement of the World of Humanity:

Daniel 12:4; Nahum 2:4; Habakkuk 2:14; *D. & C.* 88: (73-76), 77-80, 86; 101:(22-23), 32-36; 121:26-30; 128:18b; (Reorganized *D. & C.* 85:(20-21a), 21b-e, 24a; 98:(5a), 5g-i; 110:18d-e)[See also John 16:12-14; 2 Nephi 30:15-18; (Reorganized Edition 2 Nephi 12:95-99)]

Physical and Mental Health Will be Continuously Improved and Human Life Prolonged:

Malachi 4:2; Isaiah 65:20-22; *D. & C.* 101:30; 42:43-44; 88:124; 89:4-21;(Reorganized*D. & C.* 98:5f; 42:12c-d; 85:38a-b; 86:1-3)

They cannot be understood in purely literal terms. For example, in showing forth a future age of perfect peace and harmony among men of all races, languages and nations, the prophet uses the symbol of domestic cattle lying down in safety with beasts of prey. The transformation of warlike nations and peoples into lands of peace is portrayed as carnivorous animals *"eating straw like the ox"*. World disarmament is pictured as the transformation of the weapor.s of war into implements of agriculture. A nation is frequently referred to as a house or temple. The land of Israel is sometimes simply spoken of as Jerusalem, after its capitol city. If we thus look to the meaning rather than to the exact words of a scripture we will be in a better position to understand the prophetic message.

Differences of Religious Worship Will be Annulled and All Mankind Will Come to Accept One Lord and One Common Faith: Zechariah 13:2; 14:8-9; Isaiah 31:7; 52:6-10; 56:3a, 5-8; 62:2-3; 3 Nephi 21:16-19; (16:10-13); [Reorganized Edition 3 Nephi 9: 102-105; (7:34-38);] *D. & C.* 10:59-70; 45:49, 53-58;[3] (Reorganized *D. & C.* 3:14c-18; 45:8b-c, 10);[3] 2 Nephi 29:13-14; 30:

Religion Must Be the Cause of Unity In the New Age: 2 Nephi 29:13-14; 30:8-11, 15; *D. & C.* 18:2; (Reorganized *D. & C.* 16:1b); Psalm 22:27-28; Micah 4:1-2; (Reorganized Edition 2 Nephi 12:72-74, 87-91, 95)

---

3. In this prophecy the phrase *"first resurrection"* means a spiritual rebirth or enlightenment, a resurgence or revival, rather than a recreation of the physical body.

Chapter 23

THY KINGDOM COME, THY WILL BE DONE ON EARTH

A. He Will Guide You Unto All Truth. . . And Show You Things to Come

> QUESTION : JESUS TOLD HIS DISCIPLES THAT WHEN THE NEW PROPHET COMES HE WILL BE THE SPIRIT OF TRUTH TO GUIDE MANKIND INTO ALL TRUTH AND SHOW THEM THINGS TO COME. HE WOULD GLORIFY CHRIST BECAUSE HE WOULD ENLARGE UPON THE TRUTHS REVEALED BY HIM. ARE THERE ADDITIONAL SCRIPTURAL REFERENCES TELLING US HOW THESE THINGS SHALL BE BROUGHT ABOUT?

The New Revelation Will be One That Will Emphasize Deeds or Righteous Living Rather Than a Mere Profession of Belief:

3 Nephi 12:3-16; (Reorganized Edition 3 Nephi 5:50-63)(Compare Matthew 5:3-16); Matthew 6:9-10; 7:21-23; John 15:(1-7), 8-17, (18-20)

There Are Three Examples of the Pure Love of God Applied to the Social Order. One is That of the Ancient Civilization of Enoch in Old Testament Times. The Second is That of the Early Christian Community in Palestine. The Third is That of the Early Christian Community in Ancient America. These Three Communities, on a Small Scale, Might be Taken as Indicative of What the Kingdom of God Will be Like When It Comes in Its Fulness:

Moses 7:17-19; Acts 4:31-32, 34-35; 4 Nephi 2-3, 15-18;(Reorganized Edition 4 Nephi 3-4, 17-21)

The New Manifestations of God Will Teach the Oneness of God and of His Prophets:

D. & C. 121:26-28, Utah Edition; Alma 11:26-31; (Reorganized Edition Alma 8:79-84); D. & C. 20:16-19; (Reorganized D. & C. 17:3c-4b)

208 . . . *So Great A Cause*

Matthew 19:17 (also Mark 10:18 and Luke 18:19); 2 Nephi 29: 7-11; Alma 29:5, 8; (Reorganized Edition 2 Nephi 12:64-66; Alma 15:56, 59); *D. & C.* 1:11-14;(Reorganized *D. & C.* 1:3a-c)

They Will Convince Men That Jesus is the Christ and Will Glorify God:

2 Nephi 25:15-18a; 30:7-8; (Reorganized Edition 2 Nephi 11:25-31; 12:85-87); John 6:39-40; Mormon 5:14; Moroni 7:15-19; 10:6; 2 Nephi 33:10-12;(Reorganized Edition Mormon 2:41-42; Moroni 7:14-18; 10:6; 2 Nephi 15:11-13); John 7:14-18; 14:10-12, 15-17; 16:14-15

Additional Scriptures Which Were Promised in the Books of God of Former Dispensations Shall be Revealed in Great Numbers in This, the Dispensation of the Fulness of Times:

2 Nephi 28:29-30; 29:11-13, 14b; 3 Nephi 26:1-4, 6-11; (Reorganized Edition 2 Nephi 12:35-38, 65-72, 73b; 3 Nephi 11:28-32; 12:1-5) *D. & C.* 107:54-57; 128:18b; (Reorganized *D. & C.* 104:28b-29; 110:18e); Revelation 20:12

A Prophet is Able to Understand the Plan of God—Past, Present and Future—and Hence is Able to Foretell Future Events as a Warning to Men to Repent and Turn Unto God:

The Words of Moses in Deuteronomy 18:17-21

B. **The Books of God Are Opened**

> QUESTION: AS WE HAVE SEEN, MUCH OF THE REVELATION IN THE HOLY BOOKS IS GIVEN IN FIGURATIVE OR PARABOLIC FORM. HOW CAN WE BE SURE OF THE MEANING OF SUCH SCRIPTURE? IS THERE A PROMISE THAT THIS MEANING WILL SOMEDAY BE MADE KNOWN TO US?

The Symbolic Meanings of Scripture Will be Unlocked by the Lord of the New Age:

Daniel 12:4; The words of Jesus Christ in Ether 4:16-19; 2 Nephi 30:16-18a;(Reorganized Edition Ether 1:113-117; 2 Nephi 12:96-99)

All Truths Shall be Revealed Unto the Children of Men in That Day:

2 Nephi 25:7-8; 27:6-11, 14-15a, 21-22; (Reorganized Edition 2 Nephi 11:11-14, 125-132, 135-136a, 143-144); Isaiah 29:17-19; 35:1-3, 5; John 16:12-13; Ether 4:10-15; (Reorganized Edition 1:104-112); D. & C. 101:22-23, 32-35; (Reorganized D. & C. 98: 5a, g-h)

C. Some Answered Questions

QUESTION: WHAT IS MEANT BY THE REFERENCES IN SCRIPTURE TO THE "*DAY OF JUDGMENT*"?

The Day of Judgment is Man's Acceptance or Rejection of the Lord of the Kingdom and the Word of God Which is Revealed Through Him:

Moses 7:57; D. & C. 58:14-19; 64:37-40; (Reorganized D. & C. 58:4; 64:7c-8a); 2 Nephi 25:17-18a; 29:10-11; 30:8-10; 29:29, 32; (Reorganized Edition 2 Nephi 11:28-31; 12:64-66, 87-90, 35, 40-41)

QUESTION: WHAT DO THE SCRIPTURES MEAN BY THE REFERENCES TO THE "*END OF THE WORLD*"?

The New Dispensation Will Mark the Ending of the Adamic Cycle or Civilization, Which Began About Four Thousand B.C., and the Beginning of a New Age or Civilization, Which Will Endure Through Many Succeeding Dispensations. This is the Cycle of Unity Which Began in 1844:

Isaish 65:17-19; II Peter 3:13-14; Revelation 21:1-8

The Latter-day Saints Were Told That the Beginning of This New Cycle Was Imminent. They Were Told the Order of Events Leading Up to This New Divine Civilization Beginning With the Mission of Joseph Smith:

D. & C. 29:10-11, 22-25; 38:7-8a; 35:4b, 17-18; 45:24-30; 63: 47-50; 77:15; 133:26a, 35; (Reorganized D. & C. 28:2f-g, 6; 38: 2a-b; 34:2b, 4e-f; 45:3f-4d; 63:13a-d; 108:6a, f)

QUESTION: WHAT IS MEANT BY THE STATEMENTS IN THE HOLY BOOKS THAT SATAN WILL BE BOUND AND THE SON OF MAN SHALL DWELL UPON THE EARTH WITH MAN FOR A THOUSAND YEARS?

These Statements Refer to the "Golden Age" or "Kingdom of God on Earth", Which Will Occur After the Commotions and Judgments of the Lord and the Coming of Unity and Peace to the World. During This "Most Great Peace" and "Most Great Justice" the Power of Evil Over the Hearts of Men Will be Overcome Through the Righteousness of Mankind Over the Whole Earth and as All Men Come to Follow One Lord and Adhere Fully to the Revelations and Will of God as Administered Through a Divinely Inspired Theocracy or Administrative Order:

Moses 7:13, 16b, (17-19), 60-65; D. & C. 43:29-32; 97:15-21; (Reorganized D. & C. 43:7b-e; 94:4a-5c)

When the Kingdom of God is Fully Established Among the Nations Then All Mankind Will Follow the Laws of the Lord:

Amos 6:18-24; John 4:19-21, 23b-24; Luke 17:20-21; D. & C. 38:21-24; 41:3-6; 45:49-50, 54-59; (Reorganized D. & C. 38:5; 41:1b-2c; 45:8b-c, 10)

D. Seek the Guidance of the Holy Spirit in Order to Find the Kingdom of God

QUESTION: FROM THE NUMEROUS REFERENCES ALREADY GIVEN IN THIS BOOK, IT IS CLEARLY EVIDENT THAT THE LORD AND HIS FORERUNNER HAVE BOTH ALREADY COME, AND THAT THE KINGDOM OF GOD IS EVEN NOW ROLLING FORTH TO FILL THE WHOLE EARTH. OUR BELOVED PROPHET, JOSEPH SMITH, WAS, LIKE OURSELVES, BORN IN A TIME OF RELIGIOUS CONFUSION, HOWEVER HE WAS NOT WILLING TO REMAIN IN IGNORANCE, INSTEAD HE SOUGHT ENLIGHTENMENT FROM THE SOURCE OF ALL TRUTH. SHOULD WE NOT TAKE OUR CUE FROM HIM AND THUS GO ON TO DISCOVER THE KINGDOM OF GOD FOR WHICH HE SO WILLINGLY GAVE HIS VERY LIFE?

If Any of You Lack Wisdom, Let Him Ask of God:

Joseph Smith 2:5-15a (Extracts from the History of Joseph Smith)

"Seek Not for Riches but for Wisdom, and Behold, the Mysteries of God Shall be Unfolded Unto You":

D. & C. 6:1-11, 13-20, 26-37; (Reorganized D. & C. 6:1-5c, e, 6-9, 12-16)

Study It Out in Your Mind, Pray, and Have Faith, Believing That You Will Receive:

D. & C. 8:15, 10-11; 9:7-8; 35:10-12, 21; 42:61; (Reorganized D. & C. 8:1-3a, d-f, 9:3a-c; 34:3d-e, 5b; 42:17a)

All Truth is From God; To Him Who Receives the Revelation of God, More Will be Given:

D. & C. 50:17-27, 34-35; (Reorganized D. & C. 50:5, 6d, 7d-e), 2 Nephi 28:29-30; (Reorganized Edition 12:35-38)

E. How Do We Test a Writing Which Claims to Be From God

QUESTION: NEPHI, MORONI AND JOSEPH SMITH EACH CHALLENGED THE READERS OF HIS WRITINGS TO TEST THEM CAREFULLY BUT IN DOING SO TO BE CAREFUL LEST THEY DENY THE REVELATION OF GOD. SURELY THE WORDS OF THESE PROPHETS SHOULD GIVE US SOME KEYS TO UNLOCK THE MYSTERIES OF GOD AND TO DISCERN THE VALIDITY OF THOSE WHO CLAIM TO BE THE NEW PROPHETS OF THE DAY OF GOD IN WHICH WE LIVE, AND FOR WHOM ALL FORMER PROPHETS HAVE PREPARED THE WAY. WILL YOU READ THEIR WRITINGS AND PUT THEM TO THIS TEST?

2 Nephi 33:1-15; Moroni 10:3-8, 19-32; (Reorganized Edition 2 Nephi 15:1-18; Moroni 10:3-9, 14-29); D. & C. 67:4-10, 14; 38: 7-9; 88:66-68, 92; 106:4-5; (Reorganized D. & C. 67:2-3b, 4; 38: 2; 85:17-18, 25c-d; 103:2)

BIBLIOGRAPHY

I. THE HEBREW SCRIPTURES
(The Old Testament of the Christians)

The Names and Order of Books

Genesis	I Samuel	Esther	Jeremiah	Jonah
Exodus	II Samuel	Job	Lamentations	Micah
Leviticus	I Kings	Psalms	Ezekiel	Nahum
Numbers	II Kings	Proverbs	Daniel	Habakkuk
Deuteronomy	I Chronicles	Ecclesiastes	Hosea	Zephaniah
Joshua	II Chronicles	The Song of Solomon	Joel	Haggai
Judges	Ezra		Amos	Zechariah
Ruth	Nehemiah	Isaiah	Obadiah	Malachi

II. THE CHRISTIAN SCRIPTURES
(The New Testament of the Christians)

Matthew	Epistle to the Romans	Philippians	I Timothy	I Peter
Mark		Colossians	II Timothy	II Peter
Luke	I Corinthians	I Thessalonians	Titus	I John
John	II Corinthians		Philemon	II John
Acts of the Apostles	Galatians	II Thessalonians	Hebrews	III John
	Ephesians		The Epistle of James	Jude
				Revelation

III. THE MUSLIM SCRIPTURES
(The Koran of Muhammad)

Divided into 485 Surahs.

IV. ADDITIONAL LATTER-DAY SAINT SCRIPTURES
(The Book of Mormon)

1 Nephi	Enos	The Words of Mormon	Alma	4 Nephi
2 Nephi	Jarom		Helaman	Mormon
Jacob	Omni	Mosiah	3 Nephi	Ether
				Moroni

So Great A Cause. . .213

(The Doctrine and Covenants)

The Utah Edition is divided into 136 Sections plus the Official Declaration, the Missouri Edition into 149 Sections at the time of the publication of this book.

Sections 1, 4 through 9, and 37 through 76, are numbered the same in both editions.

The contents of Sections 22 and 36 in the Missouri Edition are to be found in the Book of Moses, Chapters 1 and 7, published by the Utah Saints as a part of The Pearl of Great Price.

The contents of the following numbered sections in the Utah Edition are not to be found in the Missouri Edition: 2, 13, 77, 85, 87, 108, 109, 111, 1'13, 114, 115, 116, 117, 118, 120, 121, 122, 123, 125, 126, 129, 130, 131, 132, 136 and the Official Declaration. (The Official Declaration of President Wilford Woodruff of the Utah Church abrogated the contents of Section 111 as found in the Missouri Edition, and hence this section was no longer published in the Utah Edition.)

The contents of the following Sections of the Missouri Edition are not in the Utah Edition: 22, 36, 108A, 111, the last paragraph of section 113, and Sections 114 through 149.

The following Sections are found in both Editions but are numbered differently. These are as follows (with the Utah Edition Section listed first and the corresponding Missouri Edition listed after): Sections 3-2, 10-3, 11-10, 12-11, 14-12, 15-13, 16-14, 17-15, 18-16, 19-18, 20-17, 21-19, 22-20, 23-21, 24-23, 25-24, 26-25, 27-26, 28-27, 29-28, 30-29, 31-30, 32-31, 33-32, 34-33, 35-34, 36-35, 78-77, 79-78, 80-79, 81-80, 82-81, 83-82, 84-83, 86-84, 88-85, 87-86, 90-87, 91-88, 92-89, 93-90, 94-91, 95-92, 96-93, 97-94, 98-95, 99-96, 100-97, 101-98, 102-99, 103-100, 104-101, 105-102, 106-103, 107-104, 112-115, 119-106, 125-107, 127-109, 128-110, 133-108, and 135-113.

(The Pearl of Great Price)

The Book of Moses

Chapters 1 and 7 correspond with *D. & C.* sections 22 and 36 in the Missouri Edition. Chapters 2 through 6 correspond with the *Book of Genesis* in the Inspired Revision of the *Bible*, published by the Reorganized Church.

The Book of Abraham

Not published as scripture by the Reorganized Church. This is a translation of the Writings of Abraham while He lived in the land of Egypt.

Joseph Smith I
Corresponds with Matthew, Chapter 23, verse 39 and Chapter 24, in the Inspired Revision of the *Bible*.

Joseph Smith II
These are extracts from the History of the Church, i.e., Joseph Smith's Own Story, of his early visions.

The Articles of Faith
The thirteen original articles as written by Joseph Smith.

V. BAHA'I SACRED WRITINGS
(Mentioned in Section I)

The Scripture Revealed by the Báb
1. *The Bayán*

Books and Tablets Revealed by Bahá'u'lláh
1. *Kitáb-i-Aqdas* (The Book of Laws)
2. *Kitáb-i-Iqán* (The Book of Certitude)
3. *Epistle to the Son of the Wolf*
4. *Proclamations to the Kings*
5. *The Hidden Words*
6. *The Seven Valleys*
7. *The Four Valleys*
8. *Prayers and Meditations*

Inspired Interpretative Writing of Abdu'l-Bahá
1. *Some Answered Questions*

Inspired Interpretative Writing of Shoghi Effendi
1. *World Order of Bahá'u'lláh*
2. *God Passes By (GPB)*

Abridgements of the Principal Writings of Bahá'u'lláh and Abdu'l-Bahá
1. *Glad Tidings of Bahá'u'lláh*
2. *The Bahá'i Revelation*
3. *Gleanings From the Writings of Bahá'u'lláh*
4. *The Reality of Man*
5. *Bahá'i World Faith*

VI. OTHER REFERENCES CITED IN TEXT
Baker, Alonzo L., *Belief and Work of Seventh-day Adventists*, Pacific Publishing Association, Mountain View, California, 1942.

Blomfield, Lady, *The Chosen Highway*, Bahá'i Publishing Trust, London and Wilmette, 1940.

Brown, Vinson, *The Incredible Paradox*, 1960 and *Four Remarkable Indian Prophecies*, Kahn, Karsh, Mundy, 1963, Naturegraph Co., Healdsburg, California.

Esselmont, J.E., *Bahá'u'lláh and the New Era*, Bahá'í Publishing Trust, Wilmette, Illinois, Revised 1950, Third Revised Edition, 1970.

Ferguson, Thomas Stuart, *Cumorah Where?*, Independence, Missouri, 1947, and, *One Fold and One Shepherd*, Olympus Publishing Co., Salt Lake City, Utah, Revised Edition, 1967.

Ferguson, T.S. and Hunter, Milton R., *Ancient America and the Book of Mormon*, Kolob Book Co., Oakland, Calif., Seventh Printing, 1964.

Gladwin, Harold Sterling, *Men Out of Asia*, Whittlesay House, New York, 18, N. Y. 1947.

Hanson, Paul M., *Jesus Christ Among the Ancient Americans*, Independence, Missouri, 1947.

Hunter, Milton R., *Archaeology and the Book of Mormon*, and *Christ in Ancient America*, Deseret Book Co., Salt Lake City, Utah.

Kingsborough, Edward King, *Antiquities of Mexico*, in Nine Volumes, Henry Y. Bohn, London, 1830-1848.

Layton, Lynn C., *An Ideal Book of Mormon Geography*, The Improvement Era, July, 1938.

McCormick, Margery, *Aids to Teaching*, Bahá'í Distribution and Service Department, Wilmette, Illinois, 1963.

Nabíl-i-A'zam, *The Dawn-Breakers*, translated and edited by Shoghi Effendi, Bahá'í Publishing Trust, New York, 1953.

Radin, Paul, *The Story of the American Indian*, Liverright Publishing Corp., New York, 1947.

Ricks, Joel, *Geography of Book of Mormon Lands*, 1940.

Sears, William B., *The Martyr Prophet of a World Faith*, Bahá'í Publishing Committee, Wilmette, Illinois, 1950. *Thief in the Night*, George Ronald, Kidlington, Oxford, England, 1961.

Sweet, William Warren, *The Story of Religion in America*, Harper and Brothers, New York and London, 1939.

Washburn, J.A. and J.N., *An Approach to the Study of Book of Mormon Geography*, Provo, Utah, 1939.

Weinberg, Seymour, *The Lord is One*, National Spiritual Assembly of the Bahá'í's of the United States, 1963.

Widtsoe, John A., *Is Book of Mormon Geography Known?*, The Improvement Era, July, 1950.

Wilde, Orvin G., *Landmarks of Ancient American People*, 1947.

Willoya, William and Vinson Brown, *Warriors of the Rainbow*, Naturegraph Publishers, Healdsburg, California, 1963.

Wissler, Clark, *The American Indian*, Oxford University Press, New York, N.Y. 1938.